THE "YES" LIVES ON
One Hundred Years of Service in the United States

by the Salesian Sisters of Saint John Bosco

by Sister Josephine Carini, FMA, Ph.D.

Salesian Sisters
659 Belmont Avenue
North Haledon, NJ 07508
Toll-free: (877) OUR-NUNS
(877) 687-6867

Website: www.salesiansisters.org

Author
Sister Josephine Carini, FMA

Editor
Dr. Joseph McAleer

Publisher
Éditions du Signe - B.P. 94
F-67038 Strasbourg Cedex 2
France
Tel (33) 03 88 78 91 91
Fax (33) 03 88 78 91 99

Publishing Director
Christian Riehl

Director of Publication
Joëlle Bernhard

Layout
Sylvie Tusinski

Photo credits
Salesian Sisters
John R. Glover

Printed in China
© Éditions du Signe, 2008
ISBN 978-2-7468-2112-5

TABLE OF CONTENTS

Sr. Josephine Carini, always typing, always smiling.

ACKNOWLEDGEMENTS

Sr. Josephine Carini, FMA, Ph.D., the Salesian Sisters' historian, did not live to see the book she wrote published or to celebrate this jubilee. And in a strange sense, this is so typically Sr. Josephine. She taught countless Salesian Sisters the true meaning of giving and giving freely. Her keen intelligence, her rootedness in the Gospel of Jesus, and her deep love for her vocation as a Salesian Sister has made her an icon among all who knew her.

Her expressions of love for each Sister, and the eyes that could read not only your heart, but your soul, flow through the living, though incomplete, manuscript she gave us. Ours was the challenge to honor this manuscript, not because we had to, but out of a deeply-held conviction that Sr. Josephine had captured the mind and the heart, the soul and the pulse of the Sisters in the States. More than perhaps any other Salesian Sister, she personified the "Yes" to God that she expressed so well in the verse on the following pages.

Thank you, Sr. Josephine. Pray for us!

We would like to recognize in a special way those who participated in the completion of this book. First, we thank the two Salesian Provincial Superiors in the United States, Sr. Phyllis Neves in the East and Sr. Sandra Neaves in the West, for their support and prayers. We hope this book will make every Salesian Sister, present and future, proud.

Special thanks go to Dr. Joseph McAleer, the Editor, and to Sr. Mary Mullaly and Veronica Barrios, who added to the manuscript and collected the photographs.

Several Salesian Sisters helped to revise the manuscript, including Sr. Maria Colombo, Sr. Theresa Lee, Sr. Theresa Jones, Sr. Rosalie Di Peri, Sr. Catherine Altamura, Sr. Lucy Balistrieri, St. Mary Anne Zito, Sr. Theresa Kelly, and Sr. Frances Gumino.

We are also indebted to Sr. Mary Rinaldi, Christina McAleer, and the staff of the Salesian Sisters Development Office for their leadership, perseverance, and vision in this major project for the Salesian Sisters' Centennial Celebration.

Christian Riehl and the wonderful team at Editions du Signe were a joy to work with; Merci beaucoup! We also appreciate John R. Glover's beautiful photographs.

Finally, we are grateful to our many friends and benefactors who helped to make this book a reality. We acknowledge their contributions in the Dedication Pages at the close of this volume, pages prepared by Veronica Barrios, Ruth Aniceto, and Karla Villarin.

His Holiness **Pope Benedict XVI**

as a pledge of divine favor bestows the Apostolic Blessing upon

All the Daughters of Mary Help of Christians
and
The entire Salesian Family in the U.S.A.

on the occasion of
the Centenary of the arrival to the United States of America
July 16, 2008

Archbishop Pietro Sambi
Apostolic Nuncio

Washington, D.C.

SECRETARIAT OF STATE

N. 96.109

From the Vatican, 26 July 2008

Dear Sister Phyllis,

The Holy Father has asked me to convey his cordial good wishes and the assurance of his closeness in prayer on the happy occasion of the hundredth anniversary of the first foundation of the Daughters of Mary Help of Christians in the United States of America.

His Holiness prays that this commemoration will be for all of you an occasion of gratitude for the many graces received in the past century and a summons to respond with ever great fervor to the new opportunities and challenges facing the Church at the present time. He is confident that your joyful readiness to follow the Divine Master in the spirit of Saint John Bosco, and in accordance with the evangelical counsels of chastity, poverty and obedience, will bear lasting fruit in apostolic zeal for the spread of the Gospel, the salvation of souls and the growth of God's people in holiness and truth.

Commending the Sisters, their families, benefactors and all associated with the Salesian apostolate in the United States to the protection and prayers of Mary, Mother of the Church, the Holy Father cordially imparts his Apostolic Blessing as a pledge of the grace and peace of Jesus Christ her Son.

With personal good wishes, I remain

Yours sincerely in Christ,

Tarcisio Card. Bertone

Secretary of State

Sister Phyllis Neves, FMA
Provincial Superior
Daughters of Mary Help of Christians
655 Belmont Avenue
Haledon, NJ 07508

DIOCESE OF PATERSON

Diocesan Center
777 Valley Road
Clifton, New Jersey 07013

(973) 777-8818   Fax (973) 777-8976

Office of
THE BISHOP

September 2008

Sister Phyllis Neves, FMA
Salesians – Daughters of
Mary Help of Christians
655 Belmont Avenue
North Haledon, NJ 07508

Dear Sister Phyllis and Sisters,

On behalf of the faithful of this great Diocese of Paterson, I congratulate the Salesian Sisters as you celebrate 100 years of service in America. This is an outstanding milestone.

The history of the Salesian Sisters in America is of particular pride to so many of us. Like many other inspiring moments in the life of our Church, Paterson was the birthplace of your mission. It was in this great City that the Salesian Sisters first dedicated themselves to empowering children both spiritually and academically. The Salesian Sisters did not view these impoverished children as helpless victims of their economic situation. They looked into their eyes and saw hope reflected back. In the poor, they saw Christ and so their mission of service became a way of praising God.

What began in Paterson 100 years ago has expanded across the United States to other inner-cities. As long as there are poor among us, the Salesian Sisters will be their advocates, knowing that Catholic education empowers our youth and strengthens their faith.

For all you have done in the past, and for all you continue to do here in the Paterson Diocese, I thank you from the bottom of my heart. We are blessed to have you in our midst!

Faithfully yours in Christ,

+ Arthur Serratelli

Most Reverend Arthur J. Serratelli, S.T.D., S.S.L., D.D.
Bishop of Paterson

Institute of the Daughters of Mary Help of Christians
Via dell' Ateneo Salesiano, 81
Rome, Italy

September 5, 2008

Dearest Sisters,

In the name of the General Council and the whole Institute, I am happy to be able to write a word of congratulations and best wishes on the occasion of the Centenary Celebration of the Daughters of Mary Help of Christians in the United States.

One hundred years of presence has woven a living history and a fruitful educational commitment in the evangelization and the care of immigrants through schools, youth centers, and parish catechetical training. It is one hundred years of working in collaboration with other members of the Salesian family, and in particular, with out brother Salesians, the Past Pupil Associations, and Cooperators.

The remembrance of these years encourages us to offer our gratitude to the Lord and to all the Daughters of Mary Help of Christians, who in your blessed welcoming land have sown good seeds. Yours is a story marked by the generosity and sacrifice of the pioneer Sisters who made the formation of children and young people the clear objective of their service. Don Bosco's intentions – "to form good Christians and honest citizens" – bore fruit in its time.

I pray that the Salesian life and mission which have shone forth in these one hundred years may continue with the same passion of the early Sisters, and that more pages, filled with faith and dedication marking the years to come, will be written.

May Mary, Mother and Help of Christians, Companion on the Journey, grant you, the Salesian Family and the educating community, the grace to make the experience of God – who is Communion for all His sons and daughters – visible to everyone. May it make you signs and expressions of His all-foreseeing and faithful love. May it help you to discover new educational frontiers in which to encounter the young.

I wish to express my gratitude to the Salesians for their fraternal closeness, to your many benefactors, and to the young people. Thank you, also, to the ecclesiastical and civil authorities who honor us by their presence and support us with their appreciation and help.

Sincerely,

Sr Antonia Colombo

Sr. Antonia Colombo, FMA
Superior General of the Salesian Sisters

A GENEALOGY OF A "YES" TO JESUS CHRIST MADE BY EVERY SALESIAN SISTER

by Sister Josephine Carini, FMA, Ph.D.

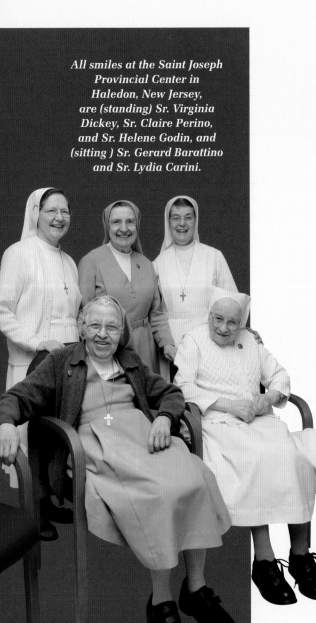

All smiles at the Saint Joseph Provincial Center in Haledon, New Jersey, are (standing) Sr. Virginia Dickey, Sr. Claire Perino, and Sr. Helene Godin, and (sitting) Sr. Gerard Barattino and Sr. Lydia Carini.

In the beginning was the YES.
The YES was with God,
the YES was God.

Through Him, Don Bosco gave life to a YES.
Mary Mazzarello gave life to a feminine YES.

That YES
spoken in turn by now nameless generations,
a YES held in the hands of history,
echoed and reverberated down the decades
    and beckoned new voices
    to refine their responses,
    to give harmony to many voices,
    and to blend as a community
to a YES.

These young YES-es became Sisters,
    then crowds of eager hearts,
    taking time to express
        a vision
        a hope
        a love
Filiae Mariae, daughters of Mary,
helpers with Mary for others,
    students of Don Bosco's educational mission
        pass the YES to…

Followers of Our Lady,
    the helper of Christians
    and non-Christians alike.

Followers of Don Bosco,
    the friend of youth
    the friend of all, women and men alike.

Followers of Mary Mazzarello,
    the wise and determined woman of all time
    pass the YES to…

Lovers of young people
    evangelizers of the poor
    friends of the rejected
    Sisters always present
    women of prayer
        pass the YES to…

Educators who challenge
    teachers who witness
    friends who provide
    Sisters who guide and love and care
        pass the YES to…

Laborers of love
    in the sandals of Christ
    echoes of the Word
    Sisters of prayer and sacrifice
        pass the YES to…

Daughters of Mary
    mirrors of the Beatitudes
    prophets of peace
    Sisters of kindness and grace
        pass the YES to…

Lovers of life
    believers of joy
    flames of charity
    echoes of unity
    pass the YES to…

Pilgrims of hope
    reflections of Mary
    gifts of the self
    Sisters of the spirit
        pass the YES to…

Seeds full blown in faith
    messengers of truth
    rulers of gentleness
    forerunners of Heaven
        pass the YES to…

Generators of love
    unrivaled educators
    committed women
    Sisters and friends
        pass the YES to…

Followers of Jesus
    Mary-like Sisters
    lovers of the young and the young at heart
    guardians, like Joseph, of nature and nature's God.
        Salesian Sisters, all,
        pass the YES.

And the YES echoes on,
    now strong,
    now subdued,
through the everyday to eternity,
from voices that spoke and have gone before
        to the Kingdom…

From voices laboring in the here and now
from voices learning the ways of love, of God, of mystery
from voices that have left to learn
        the form of their own YES.

The YES passes on,
    begun in breathless silence in God's mind and heart,
    and heard in thunderous silence in individuals
    renewed and remembered in celebrated jubilees
    and lived constantly in the here and now.

The sum of generations is unknown
    from Jesus Christ
    to Saint John Bosco
    to Saint Mary Mazzarello
    to the first Salesian Sisters
    to the present
    to the future yet to come.

Yet we know and we believe
    that the YES became flesh
    and lives among us and we see His glory,
    that Mary lives among us still in her own YES
    and the YES is full of grace and truth
    and the YES lives on.

And the YES passes on and on and on…

The Salesian Youth Center/Boys and Girls Club in Tampa, Florida, is a beacon of hope for young people, aided by Sr. Clare Kennelly.

We celebrate a jubilee of women who act uprightly, live in goodness, and walk humbly with the Lord. One hundred years of Salesian Sisters' service to the Lord in the education and formation of the youth of the United States of America spells a celebration of freedom and love!

Sr. Josephine Carini.

The life of each one of the Sisters makes this celebration possible, as a jubilee is really a celebration of persons. Persons who have lived; persons who have loved; persons who have said, "Yes." These persons set a jubilee in motion.

From its humble beginnings on a rocky hillside of an 18th century village in northern Italy named Mornese, to the teeming population of the city of Paterson, New Jersey, the story of the Daughters of Mary Help of Christians, or Salesian Sisters of Saint John Bosco, in the United States is an extraordinary one.

Someone said, "The Lord requires of you... only to do what is right and to have goodness, and to walk humbly with the Lord" (Micah 6:8).

Someone responded, "Let it be."

AND A JUBILEE WAS BORN.

We celebrate a jubilee of persons who came before, who lived in time, and who lived large dreams made in heaven and brought to reality on earth. The dreams became a blessing to many and that led to a celebration of a century of service to youth.

The four immigrant Sisters who boarded a steamship and crossed the Atlantic Ocean to open a Sisters' convent in Paterson to help the children of immigrants receive a Christian education and formation is the stuff of which jubilees (and legends) are made.

This historical narrative features women who were known, but seldom celebrated. It features untold heroism and selfless love of youth. It celebrates women who lived totally immersed in their own culture and time, yet never lost sight of a mission. They adapted, changed, and evolved fully as Americans themselves. This journey sparked a celebration in time on a road less traveled that proved a blessing to many, and that led to a jubilee.

Drawing from a wealth of original documents preserved in the houses of the Sisters, as well as extended oral history, the celebration of accomplishments of the Salesian Sisters in their 100 year history brings to life the heroic women who peopled the Sisters' houses. It also evolves in the celebration of exceptional events that challenged and inspired them.

Certain that this new country was where God led them, they began to gather the youth of the inner cities and formed them into persons who could grow into women and men capable of living and walking in the presence of God, of earning an honest livelihood, and of bringing credit to both their families and to society.

Celebrate this jubilee with us, and celebrate the many Sisters who made it memorable by their lives and by their mission.

When I began this story, I had no preconceived notions. I presumed that it would be an easy task, since I felt comfortable having lived more than 50 years as a Sister among the Sisters. There is a peculiar kind of pleasure looking back and tracking the roundabout paths that led me to the mission entrusted to me.

It was the power of a life, read and reread and reflected upon with ever increasing awe, that had captured my mind and heart. The life of Saint Mary Mazzarello seemed so simple, so apparently insignificant. What mystery could it hold in its depths?

The more I read, the more it triggered my curiosity. That life, observed and lived by women who had come with a single purpose in mind, fueled the spiritual journey, cemented the friendships which led to hours, days, and months of inquiry and exploration, thought, and discussion, that became the book you hold in your hand.

Who could believe that so many stories could come from four women in their twenties and thirties who passed the legacy of Saint John Bosco and Saint Mary Mazzarello to numerous generations of American women? The obvious challenge in writing a history is to know which stories to leave out and which to include. Beyond that, there is the task of characterizing a way of life that, frankly, defies definition.

I learned early in the research that there are things about the Sisters that cannot be put into words. Still less can they be comprehensively published. Yet, I have never stopped trying to find the essence of the Salesian Sisters' lives. I have set out in these pages to narrate the story of women who, in love with Christ, turned to love His children and produced in each one they met a masterpiece of God's creation.

This is not an academic history, footnoted and annotated for scholars, nor is it a "romanced history," nor can it claim to be comprehensive. This book is a history of women, a family memoir, the collective biography of a community of women who over 100 years served in the mission of the education of the youth in the United States of America according to

the ideals given by Saint John Bosco and Saint Mary Mazzarello.

The women are the Daughters of Mary Help of Christians. They are commonly known as Salesian Sisters.

More than once, reading or writing, I have thought of my own early years in the community of Sisters, receiving the wisdom of some of these Sisters, allowing their reminiscences to form a narrative in my willing heart. It is not by memorizing a timeline or a chronological listing of dates and events that I learned the history. I embraced it as a narrative with a beginning, a middle, various crescendos, arias, and silences, with vastness, strengths, missed opportunities, and geographical, economic, and political subplots, recurring themes, conflicts, resolutions, and, above all, meaning and significance.

The Salesian Sisters' history is a graphic reminder of just how much has changed over the course of 100 years. The history is one of change: a change of commitment and mission lived by the Sisters in lives of constant flux. Change is a reason for hope, an invitation to trust, and a great grace of love in various forms. The life lived by Sisters is a mystery, and mysteries are best handled by way of stories.

Change is healthy, necessary, and good. Think of the Sisters who made their vows in Italy and who were certain that they would live stable lives in their homeland. They imagined a simple, straightforward life in a country they knew and loved. Then, envision the day they left all that and set out on the first leg

The Salesian Sisters' coat of arms includes the Congregation's motto, "Da Mihi Animas Cetera Tolle," which means, "Give me souls, take away the rest," the battle cry of Saint John Bosco that he left as a legacy to us.

DA MIHI ANIMAS CETERA TOLLE

of a journey that would take them across an ocean into a crowded city with immense skyscrapers, where everything was magnified by the vastness of the land and sealed by their lack of familiarity with the English language and customs.

This is the legacy of the immigrant Salesian Sisters who founded the Province of Saint Philip the Apostle in the United States of America. The ability to embrace change and not fear it, to look for God's love in every unexplored turn in the road, to read trust and respect in every child's eye is a legacy that changes not only the life of the community, but a personal life as well.

I came to the realization that those 100 years of life in a Salesian community, like the faith in God that inspires and guides it, is ever evolving, expanding, deepening. Paths diverge, history repeats itself, people move, but there is always that "hidden freshness deep down," that mystery of redemption linked to every vestige of creation whose will it is to restore the shattered peace with forgiveness and love.

The Sisters have an enduring impulse to reclaim a wounded world that binds its history and informs its future. This is the story of the Sisters' charism, the unspoken invitation that year-upon-year draws Sisters and visitors alike by its special development of a magnetic call – love of God and love of God's children.

Sr. Josephine Carini, FMA, Ph.D.

Haledon, New Jersey, July 2006

Sr. Josephine Carini

Sr. Josephine Carini passed away on August 11, 2006, age 81, after 63 years of service as a Salesian Sister. Sr. Josephine, like so many Salesian Sisters before her, lived the Beatitudes in the light of the gifts and responsibilities she was given. She had a generous share of talents as well as a lion's share of burdens and responsibilities. She was a gifted teacher and her capacity for leadership – as a Principal, Superior, Education Supervisor, Provincial – showed a selfless service to God and to His people.

A gathering of Salesian Sisters, circa 1948.
The four pioneer Sisters who arrived in New York harbor in 1908 are seated in the front row.

Sr. Fernanda Rossi
Sr. Jeanett Puglisi
Sr. Irene Zaccagnino †'06
Sr. Virginia D'Alessandro
Sr. Antoinette Casertano †'93
Sr. Elvira Lombardini †'74
Sr. Nancy Zingale †'82
Sr. Domenica Minutella †'92
Sr. Mary Rose Barale
Sr. Lucy Camasta †'79
Sr. Angelita Guzman
Sr. Jean Ruscica
Sr. Jerome Parinello †'99
Sr. Patricia Winterscheidt
Sr. Stella Ruiz †'06
Sr. Catherine Sforza †'92
Sr. Adelina Gastaldo †'74
Sr. Cecilia Lanzio †'84
Sr. Angelina Andorno †'53
Sr. Frances Delfino †'67
Sr. Caroline Stazzi †'77

Sr. Ruth Stecker
Sr. Martina Chiaverano †'90
Sr. Theresa Casaro †'74
Sr. Philomena Martorana †'05
Sr. Anita Ferrari †'00
Sr. Mary Sedita †'02
Sr. Mary Palatini †'88
Sr. Ida Ossi †'04
Sr. Helen Mazurek †'76
Sr. Catherine Toronis
Sr. Mary Winterscheidt
Sr. Julia Marzorati †'93
Sr. Mary Spizzirri †'92
Sr. Anna Forte
Sr. Mary Carone
Sr. Rose Oliveri
Sr. Josephine Cardone †'94
Sr. Leonia Pascucci †'84
Sr. Rosina Costanzo †'80
Sr. Mary Ruiz
Sr. Rosalie Di Peri
Sr. Annette Gerace
Sr. Theresa Winterscheidt
Sr. Anna Segalini †'94
Sr. Gisela Bonfiglio
Sr. Antoinette Sferlazza †'03
Sr. Frances Di Santo †'89
Sr. Emilia Di Gennaro †'66
Sr. Gaetana Piccirilli †'92
Sr. Frances Vegetabile †'03
Sr. Rita Bailey
Sr. Mary Di Camillo
Sr. Libroia Calcagno †'91
Sr. Gilda Gentile †'72
Sr. Felicia Tanzella
Sr. Josephine Zito †'85
Sr. Louise Minelli †'01
Sr. Mary Cannizzaro †'77
Sr. Vincent Giaj-Levra †'74
Sr. Providence Favaloro †'95
Sr. Domenica Di Peri
Sr. Mary Zito
Sr. Erminia Moiso †'50
Sr. Angelina Di Santo †'92
Sr. Frances Miculin †'99
Sr. Mary Pollini †'71
Sr. Eugenia Pasquali †'82
Sr. Letizia Sampo †'81
Sr. Caroline Novasconi †'70
Sr. Joanne Passareli †'76
Sr. Margaret Grillone †'55
Sr. Antoinette Beltramo †'74
Sr. Antoinette Agliardi †'65

1 BECOME THE VERY BEST!

The Dream Begins, 1864-1908

"Don't become just seamstresses,"
Saint Mary Mazzarello would tell her eager students.
"Become the very best!" When the clock struck
the hour she would say, "One hour closer to Heaven!"
And again, "Why not make every stitch an act
of love for the Lord!" Occasionally,
she accompanied them home after dark.
"Look at the stars. One day in Heaven
we shall have them under our feet."

The four pioneer Salesian Sisters in 1930, before the statue of Mary Help of Christians: Sr. Angelina Andorno (seated) and (left-right) Sr. Veneranda Zammit, Sr. Antoinette Agliardi, and Sr. Frances Delfino.

From Valdocco to Mornese

It was a warm June night in 1864, and Don Bosco (as the future Saint John Bosco was called) stood on the balcony overlooking the playground at the "Oratory," or youth center, in the Valdocco neighborhood of Turin, Italy. The schoolboys were at their games. Occasionally, some of them would look up at the balcony and wave or shout greetings.

It had been a very busy day for Don Bosco. He was now watching the boys and speaking with Father John Lemoyne, one of his helpers.

"Don Bosco," Father Lemoyne said. "Don't you think something is still missing to complete the work of our Salesian Society?"

"What do you mean, Father?" Don Bosco replied.

"You have done so much for boys, why not something for girls, too? Wouldn't it be wonderful if we had Sisters? They could do for girls what we are doing for boys."

"Don't you suppose Father, I have been thinking of that? I have been dreaming about it." Don Bosco went on to say that he had dreamt he was with the elegant Marquise of Barolo who, out of the clear blue, began to tell him that he should confine his work to boys, since her nuns were taking care of the girls and doing a good job.

"I told her quite simply that a priest's work was to take care of souls, all souls, and that included girls," Don Bosco continued. "And the Marquise retorted, 'Indeed, the Lord came to save all. You don't have to tell me that, Father, I know it.'"

"You might say it's just a dream, but it means that I have been thinking of doing what you propose," Don Bosco concluded. "Please God, we'll get to it soon."

Saint John Bosco (1815-1888) was a remarkable dreamer. His recognized visions number more than 130, and he certainly never recounted all of them to his spiritual sons, the Salesian Priests and Brothers, the congregation he founded in 1859. But one presence marked all of his dreams:

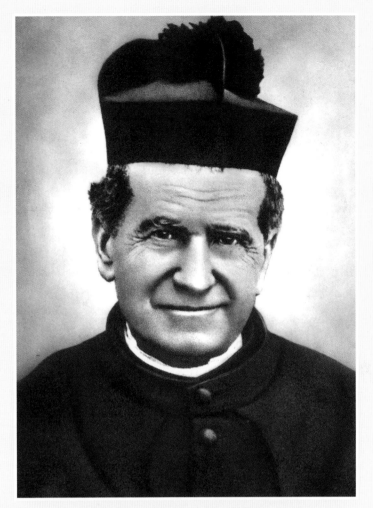

Saint John Bosco, founder of the Salesian Sisters with Saint Mary Mazzarello.

a mysterious Lady who seemed to be his guide and teacher. She laid down for him a clear path to follow in life. Under her guidance, Don Bosco became the modern charismatic leader who was so compelling to boys that they literally fell in line behind him from every corner of Turin and unhesitatingly followed him throughout life. No wonder he has earned the title "Father and Teacher of Youth."

Four months after his conversation with Father Lemoyne, on a bright October day, Don Bosco, with a group of Oratory boys, arrived at the village of Mornese on one of their famed excursions through Piedmont's picturesque Monferrato region. They had persuaded Don Bosco to mount a white horse, and the villagers could hardly believe their eyes when the caravan, accompanied by drums, paraded through the narrow streets all the way to the parish

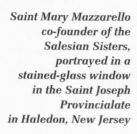

Saint Mary Mazzarello co-founder of the Salesian Sisters, portrayed in a stained-glass window in the Saint Joseph Provincialate in Haledon, New Jersey

church. They were to be overnight guests of the pastor, Father Dominick Pestarino, a Salesian, who had invited them to taste some of the ripe, juicy grapes from the nearby vineyards.

But something more than a pleasure ride had given Don Bosco a motive to visit Mornese. He was anxious to meet a group of young women who, with Father Pestarino's blessing, had formed a club to help in parish work.

"They are my angels," Father Pestarino had told Don Bosco. "They do wonders for the parish, teaching catechism to the young people and conducting a sewing class for the girls. It's just like a tiny oratory. They want to meet you, Father. Who knows what can happen as a result of your visit?"

Mary Domenica Mazzarello was the group's primary mover. She led the way with the energy of a born leader and the unassuming gentleness of a mother. She was enchanted to know that Don Bosco had finally come to Mornese, and directed whatever was needed to make his stay and that of his boys as pleasant as possible.

She, too, was a dreamer. She had also heard a voice, a woman's voice, call her attention to a strange building that appeared on a hill where there were nothing but vineyards. There had been a large crowd of girls playing happily near the building, and the voice had spoken, "I entrust them to you." The dream-vision had faded then, leaving only the familiar vineyards on that hill, and a new-fired love in Mary's mind and heart.

Don Bosco met the group on the following day, after celebrating Mass in the parish church. He encouraged the young women to continue their good work "because the Lord and Our Lady have great things in store for you."

Later that day, after the guests had left Mornese and everything had returned to normal in the village, Mary said to her friends, "I am now more than ever convinced that Don Bosco is a saint."

The tiny Oratory at Mornese under Mary's watchful care was like a cenacle where young girls were indeed being trained for greater things to come. Sewing was not the only reason why mothers of Mornese entrusted their daughters to Mary and her friends. "They are like Sisters," parents used to say. "They know exactly what to do with our girls."

"Don't become just seamstresses," Mary would tell her eager students. "Become the very best!" When the clock struck the hour she would say, "One hour closer to Heaven!" And again, "Why not make every stitch an act of love for the Lord!" Occasionally, she accompanied them home after dark. "Look at the stars. One day in Heaven we shall have them under our feet."

During the months that followed his first visit to Mornese, Don Bosco was in constant touch with Father Pestarino. One day, he returned from Don Bosco with exciting news for the young women.

"Until now you have lived at home," Father Pestarino said. "Don Bosco asked if you would be willing to leave your homes and live together under the same roof." Mary and some of her friends agreed. So the little group and two orphan girls were soon housed in a solid but simple structure that had been built on Father Pestarino's own property.

Mary, the Mother of God herself, further confirmed for Don Bosco the mission that would soon become the Salesian Sisters. He had another dream. The Lady showed him a mob of ragged girls in a desolate plaza. As soon as they caught sight of Don Bosco, they surged toward him, pleading for a youth center for them, too. It was out of the question, Don Bosco protested. Caring for boys already consumed every fragment of his time and energy. It simply could not be done.

Then, the Heavenly Lady intervened. "Take care of them, Don Bosco. They are my children, too."

Well, if the Lady wished him to do it, Don Bosco concluded, then she would show him the way. And she did.

Don Pestarino, the man who introduced Don Bosco to a group of ladies who would later become the first Salesian Sisters. Mary Mazzarello was one of the young ladies.

When the Provincialiate for the new Mary Immaculate Western Province was constructed in San Antonio, Texas, in 1991, stones were brought from Mornese as a symbolic link to Saint Mary Mazzarello.

Not in a dream, but in a dream fulfilled, beyond all expectations.

On August 5, 1872, the Bishop of the diocese received the vows of the new Sisters in Mornese. Don Bosco came from Turin for the historic occasion. He had already informed them that they were to be known as FILIAE MARIAE AUXILIATRICE (FMA), Latin for "Daughters of Mary Help of Christians."

"Your Institute," he told them, "has come into existence because Our Lady willed it. You are to be a living monument of my gratitude to her goodness."

And how that monument would grow! The handful of courageous young women became a legion. From Mornese they swarmed to countries across the world, with a joyous missionary spirit, setting up youth centers, schools, hospitals, leper colonies, camps, spirituality centers, retreats and mission centers. Today, some 14,000 Salesian Sisters – the Daughters of Mary Help of Christians – work with the same spirit and devotion that had marked the life and work of Mary, now Saint Mary Domenica Mazzarello, and her first Sisters in Mornese.

Wherever the Sisters were sent around the world, they brought all that was needed to build a "New Mornese" – a missionary spirit, a smile, and a dream. They added a touch of imagination to their goal of consecrated life, and they brought excitement into the ordinary. They had realistic goals, but they dared to dream of other lands and other young people.

What courage they had! They set out confident and unafraid because Mary, the Lady of the dreams of Saint John Bosco and Saint Mary Mazzarello, was with them. They were women who wanted more in their lives. They had reached for the dream, sight unseen. They had not given up; they had grasped it with open heart and hands.

Don Bosco and Mother Mazzarello gave these young Sisters the momentum to put their dreams into action. They dared to cross oceans and traverse continents. Each of them had a burning desire in her heart. Their blood raced when they remembered the dream, and Mother Mazzarello's simple words: "Do the right thing at the right time in the right way, and for the right reason, only for the love of God." It was what the waves of Sisters who migrated to other mission countries brought with them.

It was what the first four Salesian Sisters who came to the shores of the United States of America in 1908 believed and lived.

From Mornese to the New World

The new century was but eight years old when the first Salesian Sisters came to the United States. They found a country coming into its own in transportation and technology. The Wright brothers fly. The Panama Canal is opened. The Henry Ford Motor Company starts. The New York City subway is up and running.

On the social side, civil rights are coming to the foreground. The U.S. Supreme Court rules that citizens from Puerto Rico cannot be denied entry into America. The National Association for the Advancement of Colored People is founded.

A different world, but the same mission. The first four Sisters made their home in the States, as was their home in Mornese, "the house of the love of God!" The vision and the life of Mornese was now transplanted to American soil.

Mother Catherine Daghero, Mother General of the Institute and successor to Saint Mary Mazzarello, sent the first Salesian Sisters to the U.S.

Vincenza Cianci and Rose Cianci Gasparrini stand before a photo of their great-uncle, Msgr. Felix Cianci, who first welcomed the Salesian Sisters to the U.S. in July 1908.

When did all this begin? The dates are forever marked in the annals of the Salesian Sisters in the United States. On June 24, 1908, the Sisters departed from the port of Genoa, Italy, and on July 16, the Feast of Our Lady of Mount Carmel, these pioneer Sisters set foot in what would become a new Mornese in the New World.

The story, like most Salesian stories, has a humble origin: a poor parish in the industrial town of Paterson, New Jersey, about 22 miles to the west of New York City. Father (later Monsignor) Felix Cianci, a diocesan priest and pastor of Saint Michael Parish, wrote to the Mother General of the Salesian Sisters, Mother Catherine Daghero (who had succeeded Mother Mazzarello as Mother General of the worldwide Institute), asking for help.

The situation was critical. The faith of these immigrants was slowly withering under the pressure of countless difficulties encountered in this new land. The people had little money, little education, and no ability to communicate in English. They were often discriminated against because of their ethnic origins, their family life, and their culture. The few options they had to survive in such circumstances could destroy their Catholic faith.

Father Cianci, good shepherd that he was, had spared himself no sacrifice to help his compatriots. But now, the rising tide of immigrants made collaborators absolutely essential. He needed the help of religious women. He needed Sisters who could learn the language, be willing to sacrifice much, and be overflowing with love for God and for His children.

One sleepless night, while praying before the Eucharistic Lord, Father Cianci thought of the Salesian Sisters of Don Bosco. Father Cianci had known Don Bosco personally and had witnessed the driving love of Don Bosco's religious family. He wrote to Italy, pleading and insisting. He wrote again, refusing to give up until his request was granted. He needed Sisters. He needed them now. He prayed, pleaded, and wrote.

Could he have some Sisters who would devote their energies to the immense needs of the immigrants arriving daily from Italy?

In 1908, his prayers were answered, and the vibrant 100-year history of the Salesian Sisters of Saint John Bosco in the United States began.

On June 24, 1908, Mother Elisa Roncallo, representing Mother Daghero, accompanied four young Sisters to the port of Genoa, Italy, for departure to the new world of America:

- Sr. Angelina Andorno, the leader of the missionary expedition, was 39 years old and had been professed for 15 years.
- Sr. Frances Delfino was 29 years old and had been a Sister for five years.
- Sr. Veneranda Zammit was 26 years old and professed six years when she arrived.
- At 24, Sr. Antoinette Agliardi, the youngest, was motivated to join the Salesian Sisters to take part in the venture to the new world.

All were in love with Christ, and all were determined to make Him known and loved in this new land.

Sr. Antoinette Agliardi (1884-1965)

"Sister was in a coma. We were at her bedside expecting her to draw her last breath from moment to moment. Suddenly, she sat up in bed, her face radiant, her usual inimitable smile on her lips. She nodded her head and extended her arms forward as if accepting an invitation. She then fell back on the pillow in an apparent coma, again. These gestures took place three times. We all remained silent in prayer. Something supernatural was taking place although to us it was invisible. Was it Our Lady coming to reassure and conduct Her faithful daughter to Jesus? We do not know. Early the next morning, July 7, 1965, our beloved Sr. Antoinette peacefully expired, leaving us with beautiful memories of a life totally spent for God and for the salvation of souls."

Sr. Mary Paniga, FMA

Tearfully smiling, they waved farewell from the decks of their steamship, the *Montevideo.* When they docked in New York Harbor nearly three weeks later, all they knew and loved lay 3,000 miles of saltwater and weeks of seasickness behind them. Before them stretched a whole new continent as wide as the ocean they had just crossed.

The four Sisters who landed at Ellis Island on July 10, 1908, had no knowledge of "America the land of the free and the home of the brave." They looked around undaunted, as no one seemed to be at the pier to receive them. Nonetheless, the novelty of unknown buildings and streets, the tremendous number of people who were waiting and disembarking, the strange languages, styles of dress, and various types of luggage did not faze them. They were as strange to others as others were to them.

What does one do in such a circumstance? You pray, and you smile. The Sisters smiled and looked and smiled again. The smile was returned, hesitatingly at first, then more genuinely and sincerely.

Finally, Father Cianci, joined by Father Ernest Coppo, Provincial (superior) of the Salesian Priests and Brothers in the U.S. (who had arrived in this country in 1896), stepped forward from the crowd to welcome the Sisters. They were greeted warmly, but with embarrassment. The Sisters had finally arrived, but they were told that the tiny house that was destined to be the cornerstone of their mission in the

Very Reverend Father Ernest Coppo was the Provincial of the Salesian Fathers that picked up the arriving pioneer Sisters from New York Harbor with Father Felix Cianci. He later became a Bishop.

United States was not ready. Father Coppo arranged for interim lodging with a community of nuns who resided on 14th Street in Manhattan. Here the host Sisters spoke only English. The newly-arrived Sisters spoke only Italian and French. But the Sisters found a thousand creative ways to bridge the language barrier with their hosts who were offering shelter, companionship, and courage. The missionaries were taught a few useful phrases, and also stumbled through a few pages of a primary reader. Notwithstanding the many difficulties, a ready smile always bridged the gap, for they had brought with them the love of Mary and the charism of Don Bosco and Mother Mazzarello.

After one week in the New World, the feast of Our Lady of Mount Carmel, July 16, arrived, and so did Father Cianci. He had a home for the Sisters at 37 Elm Street, an apartment over a stable near Saint Michael Parish in Paterson. The four Sisters began their mission in the name of Our Lady Help of Christians, Don Bosco, and Mother Mazzarello. Fearful, but full of trust in Mary's protection, the four Salesian Sisters gestured their gratitude to their hostesses with warm smiles and handshakes. Then they set out for their new home.

Their first act on reaching Saint Michael in the heart of downtown Paterson was to offer a hymn of thanks to God and to Mary, His mother and theirs. They had passed the first test. The second was already upon them.

The steamship Montevideo transported the pioneer Sisters from Italy to the New World.

The Houses on Elm Street

Our Salesian pioneers faced poverty and privation in Paterson. We rely on the memoirs of Sr. Cecilia Napoli, the third young woman to join the Sisters in 1913, for accounts of these early days.

The first home for the Sisters, at 37 Elm Street, was no grand hotel. It consisted of three bare rooms, no furniture, only half a roof overhead, and a Bethlehem-like stable beneath the living quarters.

Father Cianci, for fear that the Sisters would lose their way, did not allow them any freedom. He provided what little food he thought they needed, but he also provided for their safety — or so he thought. He had the rectory housekeeper lock in the Sisters at night and pocket the key until the next morning!

But the Sisters who had crossed an ocean by themselves were not afraid to be assertive. They asked for their own key and wanted to do their own shopping. The pastor still wished to accompany them. They explained that they had come of their own free will and that there were many

A group of boy orphans, with a painting of Saint John Bosco, in the backyard of the Elm Street home of the Sisters in Paterson.

Italian immigrants in the parish and at the market, so they were able to communicate effectively.

The Sisters realized Father Cianci meant well, but was also totally unaware of their needs. The Sisters convinced the pastor that they knew what to do and where to go. They made friends with the people. Some ladies offered to buy some of the necessary items for the "nuns," as they were called. Some also offered their services. The Sisters gratefully accepted. They went unafraid into the streets and stores, where they were greeted, welcomed, and accepted by adults and children alike.

They also looked for ways to earn some money since the pastor could not provide sufficient funds. Sometimes the Sisters managed to get orders for sewing and embroidery to pay for necessary expenditures. This desperate situation surprised none of the Sisters. They had expected sacrifice, work, and privations. They had foreseen this as part of their offering to the Lord for their mission among the parishioners and their children in this new land.

One day, Father Coppo (who later became Bishop Coppo) came to see the Sisters, and quickly demanded that the Sisters be treated better. They were to have better food and better living conditions and given some form of salary. Things changed with this visit, but not much. The pastor offered a monthly salary of twelve dollars for each teaching Sister! It was little, but better than before.

But the Sisters did more than just teach. The maintenance of the church; the washing, ironing, and mending of altar linens; the weaving of elaborate palms for Holy Week, were all considered donated services. Naturally, it was all done at night, making an 18-hour day the normal state of affairs.

Father Cianci did not know what to do about their living quarters. Again the Sisters took the initiative. They came to an understanding with the pastor and his housekeeper, Donna Rosa. They would manage their own lives, do their own shopping and purchasing, and find a better location for the convent. They would undertake day

jobs to pay the cost as well. This last statement suited the pastor, so he let them (to their great relief) fend for themselves, even if it meant shouldering responsibility for all expenses.

The need for a new home became more urgent, as the four soon became five. Sr. Beatrice Curtis arrived from England. She was 22 years old, generous, active, and – an added bonus – spoke English fluently. She not only served in the schools, but also passed on teaching methods to many generations of Sisters.

Besides the growth in community, the owner of the stable did not renew the lease for the Sisters. The Sisters had to look for more convenient housing. They found a suitable one on Elm Street itself, with more rooms and

Sr. Beatrice Curtis and Sr. Josephine Galassi.

The first classes conducted by the Sisters were held in the basement of Saint Michael Church. Here, Sr. Carmela Cesario leads the lesson.

amenities. The pastor had not a penny to spare, so the courageous Sisters took out the lease (and the mortgage) in their own name. Persons who already knew what the Sisters had done helped to defray the cost. The debt of $3,500 that the Sisters incurred became a concern for the Paterson community. A lady who admired the Sisters advanced the loan without interest. This helped, and little by little, from the stipend and the offerings received, the Sisters were able to defray, not only the daily expenses, but also the entire debt.

Some of the Sisters added to their meager earnings with sewing and embroidery. This occupation – done at night, of course – necessitated an amusing arrangement in the Elm Street workroom. The ceiling was so high that the lonely light bulb hanging from it shed only the dimmest glow on their sewing. The only solution to this dilemma was to raise the floor. The chairs were placed on top of the wide table and there the Sisters sat under the light, sewing while they talked or sang.

The first thought after moving to the new residence was having a chapel in the house. Sr. Frances Delfino, who was the sacristan at Saint Michael's, had met Father Cornelius Phelan from Ocean City, New Jersey. He came to Paterson often to visit his younger sister, Sadie Phelan. She lived near the Sisters and gave them lessons in English and the pedagogical methods.

Sadie confided to her brother that the Sisters really needed a chapel in their new home. He soon arrived with a new altar, a sanctuary lamp, chairs, ciborium, candles — everything needed for this special new guest, Our Lord in the Blessed Sacrament. Kneeling in His Presence, the Sisters drew courage for their mission. The light shining through them drew other kindred souls to their ranks and attracted many vocations. Sadie Phelan, even after Father Cornelius's death, continued to take care of "her brother's chapel."

It is from the early history of the house and from the recorded accounts of Sr. Cecilia that a picture of the first school year emerges. The first classes began on September 28, 1908; they were conducted in the basement of Saint Michael Church on Cross (now Cianci) Street. Classes were separated by wooden partitions; everyone heard whatever one class did or said or recited. Resonance did not make the classroom a convenient place for study or concentration, but everyone philosophically accepted the temporary situation.

Above all, the Sisters were determined to make Jesus known and loved. They taught love for Mary and lived the Salesian charism, or mission. And they smiled, prayed, played, and loved each and every young person.

Lou Costello (of Abbott and Costello fame)
was a native of Paterson, New Jersey,
and a great benefactor of Saint Anthony Parish.

Challenges of Immigration

Less than a year after their arrival in New York Harbor, the Salesian Sisters had established themselves as a beacon of hope and God's love for the families and, especially, the children in their corner of New Jersey. As a sign of their growing presence and importance, especially in educating the young, official documents soon were drawn up, locally and overseas.

In October 1908, the Mother General, Mother Daghero, placed the four American Sisters under the jurisdiction of the Province of Mexico (since 1880, Salesian Sisters had been at work in Central and South America). A few months later, the Mexican Provincial (superior), Mother Brigida Prandi, came to New Jersey to encourage the Sisters and marveled at their hard work.

Another good sign was vocations. In September 1908, Teresa Cianci, niece of Father Cianci, became the first Postulant, receiving her postulant's cape from Father Coppo. Teresa would be the first of many who would "sell all they had, give the money to the poor," and then follow Jesus in a life of chastity, poverty, and obedience at the service of His children. The process of becoming a Salesian Sister takes four years and has several stages of formation, beginning with Candidate (or Aspirant), and rising to Postulant, Novice, and, finally, Sister.

A Certificate of Incorporation with the State of New Jersey was issued on March 19, 1909, and was registered in the state as "The Missionary Society of the Salesian Sisters, Inc." on July 15, 1909. The Sister immigrants were not yet citizens, so Father Coppo signed the document. He also legally changed the name of the Sisters' Institute in order that the Sisters could be listed for tax exemption status. It was a clear sign that the Sisters were here to stay.

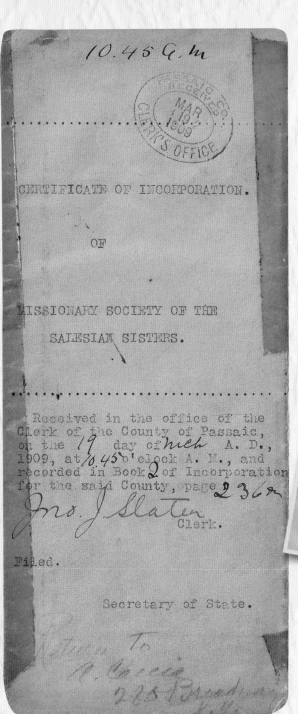

CERTIFICATE OF INCORPORATION.

OF

MISSIONARY SOCIETY OF THE

SALESIAN SISTERS.

Received in the office of the Clerk of the County of Passaic, on the 19 day of *March* A. D., 1909, at 10.45 o'clock A. M., and recorded in Book 2 of Incorporation for the said County, page 236.

Jno. J. Slater
Clerk.

Filed.

Secretary of State.

Incorporation documents for "This Missionary Society of the Salesian Sisters" signed by the pioneer Sisters in 1909.

Saint Michael Church in Paterson.

From these humble beginnings at Saint Michael's, the Sisters continued to build steadily and cheerfully in accord with the Spirit in Whom and for Whom they had been sent. Ever anxious to share the Good News of Christ with others, they began to establish religious education centers and parish schools within and around the Paterson area. Additionally, Italian parishes like Saint Michael's provided space for the statues and feasts of the patrons of the major villages from which their parishioners came.

This attentive expansion in Paterson sought to serve the seemingly endless influx of Italian immigrants. Since 1820, more than five million Italians had emigrated to the United States. Many had found their way to New Jersey, and the 12,989 Italians in the state had increased to 41,865 by 1900. By 1910, that number had almost tripled to 115,444 until, by 1930, first and second generation Italians constituted ten percent of the total state population.

What was causing this explosive growth in the Italian immigrant population? One reason was the unification of Italy, which created overpopulation, economic stagnation, and, thus, intense poverty for those who lived in Sicily and in southern Italy. In search of jobs and money, these southern Italians (all men, many of whom were fathers) were attracted to Paterson by contractors who offered jobs improving city streets. Despite discrimination and low pay, the immigrants soon managed to secure work in the silk mills of Paterson. They also found work in the textile factories of nearby Passaic. Later, as the men acquired some measure of steady income, the other family members immigrated to America.

Father Cianci had already turned his attention to the growing Italian colonies in other parts of the city. In 1909, he requested Bishop John O'Connor of the then Diocese of Newark to entrust the Italians in the Sandy Hill and Peoples Park sections of Paterson to the Salesian Priests and Brothers, who had come to America several years earlier.

Accordingly, Father John Focacci purchased property that had formerly belonged to a Polish church for $5,000. It was located on Beech Street. He then prepared a wooden building as Saint Anthony of Padua Mission Church. Mass was celebrated for the first time on December 8, 1909, the Feast of the Immaculate Conception.

Father Focacci requested the help of the Salesian Sisters. According to Sr. Cecilia's account, he asked for three Sisters to open a facility for after-school care and religion classes. He could offer no monetary recompense, but the children needed the Sisters. They accepted the challenge.

Sr. Angelina Andorno (1869-1953)

"In 1935, Superior Angelina's asthma was alarmingly undermining her health, and Mother Provincial sent her to Watsonville, California, at the doctor's suggestion. The Sisters there never forgot the simplicity and the goodness of their Superior. She would come to the workroom and help us mend clothes. 'After thirty years, I want to see if I can still sew at a machine,' she would say with joy and laughter. During the six months that she was with us, she was a solicitous mother who tried to make our heavy schedule light by her cheerfulness and humor."

Sr. Josephine Pedrazzi, FMA

*Sr. Cecilia Napoli
with students
at Saint Anthony Parish
in Paterson in 1929.*

*Saint Anthony Parish
in Paterson.*

2

THE SEED TAKES ROOT

The 1910's

The Sisters in Nutley, NJ with a first communion class. Sister Giovannina Martinoni and Sr. Amelia Aichino can be seen with the students.

"A reverent silence fell over the students as they listened to the religious instruction. Those otherwise restless little scholars sat attentive and still, totally absorbed in the presentation of their religious heritage. And so the seed took root, slowly spreading and strengthening into healthy, young shoots."

The Mission Grows

The arrival of the Salesian Sisters to the United States was all too soon followed by a decade of strife, including the "war to end all wars," World War I. In an attempt to engage in a battle of words rather than arms, the League of Nations was formed. This group of world leaders met for the first time in New York. Interestingly enough, the United States did not attend the session.

Freedom took on new meaning as garment workers struck, the charter of the Klu Klux Klan was accepted, and Planned Parenthood opened its first clinic. Race riots and peaceful demonstrations reminded the nation that segregation and discrimination prevailed in this land of the free.

Meanwhile, the Sisters opened oratories, orphanages, schools, and catechetical centers, reaching the immigrant family through the immigrant child. These Sisters, the people discovered, were different. They played, prayed, and smiled. They foresaw the future and found it good. Their hope and faith gave courage to young and old alike. Although the people of Paterson had never met Mary Mazzarello, they experienced in the Sisters her spirit, a spirit that urged, "Do freely whatever love requires!"

And they were eager to learn and adapt. At first they were called the Daughters of Mary Help of Christians. They were present in many households in Paterson. But the name was too long and too hard. So they became known as the Salesian Sisters of Saint John Bosco, because they took care of young people as Don Bosco did. The name "Salesian Sisters" didn't seem so menacing in the city streets and in the Italian households.

Mother Enrichetta Sorbone,
Vicar General of the Institute, signed the manifest
in 1913 (second line) when she visited
the Salesian Sisters in New Jersey.

Sr. Theresa Cianci, the first vocation
in the U.S., with her uncle, Msgr. Carlo Cianci,
in Newton, New Jersey.

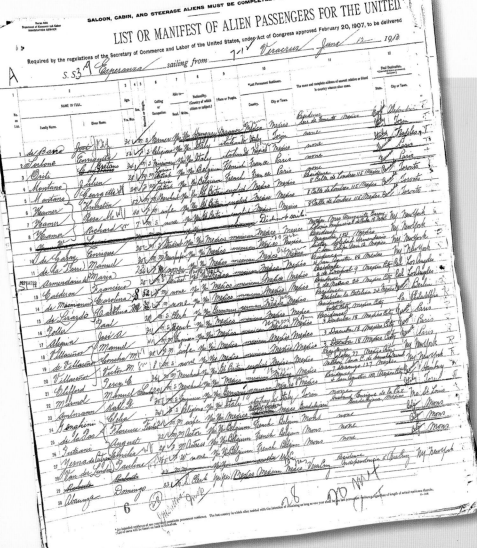

Mother Brigida Prandi, Provincial (superior) of the Mexican Province which oversaw the New Jersey Sisters, understood that the new mission to Saint Anthony of Padua Parish on Beech Street in Paterson was necessary, and that more Sisters were needed. Her response was prompt and faith-filled. Two Novices, Sr. Frances Costanzo and Sr. Cecilia Napoli, set out from Italy on February 26, 1912. At about this time, Sr. Teresa Cianci, the first Postulant, left for Mexico to continue her studies and make her religious profession.

"It was an eventful expedition," Sr. Cecilia wrote with classic understatement in her memoirs. Upon arrival in Paterson, the Sisters planned the move from Saint Michael's to Saint Anthony's. The young boy who had volunteered to help them move provided a makeshift sled for the transportation of their few belongings.

The winter of 1912 has since gone on record for its cold and snowfalls. Sr. Cecilia vouched for this personally: "Our hands were numb; so were the boy's. The streets were empty; the temperature was below zero. At a certain point, our vehicle overturned and spilled our precious cargo on the frozen road."

The benumbed travelers painfully sought to retrieve whatever they could. The 15-minute walk seemed more than an expedition to the Yukon! When the Sisters finally reached their destination, the warm hospitality of the pastor, Father John Focacci, and Brother Rodda compensated for the bitter cold outdoors.

Much to his surprise, the pastor realized that two of the three were mere Novices. Would they be shaken by the demands of the mission? Would they understand their vocation? Their new convent – two houses joined by a small yard – was totally devoid of every comfort. There was no heat, no furniture, no adequate plumbing. Their only "possessions" consisted of a small cooking stove, a rickety table and chairs, and a few beds located in unheated rooms upstairs.

That caused no dismay. Sr. Frances Delfino, like a good "older Sister," helped the other two keep their vision focused on the One in whose Name they had come. Sr. Cecilia recalled that the sacrifices strengthened their vocation. Her joy in relating the most trying episodes, playing down the drama in her usual humorous vein, permits us to glimpse the tremendous faith and love exercised by those noble women, so forgetful of self and so in love with God and God's children. Those privations became the seed of other vocations from Beech Street: Sr. Mary Zito, Sisters Raphael and Mary Spizzirri,

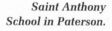

Saint Anthony School in Paterson.

Sisters Amalia and Helen Gatti, Sr. Jeanette Puglisi, and Sr. Lucy Balistrieri.

As before, the good people of Paterson came to the Sisters' aid. "The first helper we met was Mrs. Corina Caprio," Sr. Cecilia wrote. "She bought fuel for a little stove and continued to provide something daily, especially for food and warmth. Peter, her son, continued his mother's custom for many years."

Sr. Cecilia's memoirs describe Beech Street as a living reminder of Saint John Bosco's and Saint Mary Mazzarello's legacy of hard work. The 6:30 a.m. arrival of the children at the convent door necessitated an early rising for the Sisters. Offering the day in meditation and prayer and centering it on the Eucharist was the source of energy for their vigorous lives. This divine union also answered those who questioned, "How is it that you Sisters are always so happy?" An inner joy radiated from them even when at about 3:00 p.m. boys and girls of all ages began to arrive after dismissal from the surrounding public schools. These children would await their hard-working parents in the Sisters' house.

The Sisters taught religion classes, and the Sunday Oratory flourished in Don Bosco's tradition, offering children a safe place to gather to play, learn, and grow in their faith. Soon three new Sisters arrived from England, all fluent in English (thank God!): Sr. Antoinette Pollini, Sr. Maddalena Pezzaglia, and Sr. Agnes Powell.

Sr. Antoinette's musical ability, indispensable to her prayer life, was a welcome addition to the Paterson ministry. She prepared children for choir and taught singing to all.

In 1915, a member of the parish, Raphael Spizzirri, asked to begin her formation, and joined the band of young women who worked with the Sisters.

The Morris House

Before long, it was time for the Sisters to find a new home – again. The lack of sanitary facilities, the long commute from Ward Street in the bitter cold, the growing number of Sisters and Novices, and the need for a permanent school prompted an evaluation. Sr. Teresa Cianci, newly professed, and Sr. Josephine Nebbia, newly arrived from Italy, also joined the Ward Street house. More room was needed.

The Morris House, purchased in 1912.

The Sisters looked around. There on the corner of Ward and Cross Streets stood the majestic Morris House. The manor house had a porch around it, an ample yard with a little garden, and two tall chestnut trees in front. It seemed tailor-made for the children and the Sisters. Sr. Angelina Andorno suggested that they throw a medal of Mary into the needed property, say a fervent Hail Mary, and leave the rest to Our Lady. They did — and the house was put on sale shortly thereafter!

Of course, the debt was once again the Sisters' problem. However, their good work was being discovered and appreciated by the people of the city, who began to look at the Sisters as the best hope for guaranteeing their children's bright future.

The Sisters were still not U.S. citizens, so Father Coppo and Father Cianci co-signed the $1,000 downpayment that the Sisters borrowed from Broadway Trust Co. in New York. The community transferred to the new residence on 41 Ward Street on December 8, 1912, the Feast of the Immaculate Conception.

The Morris House would become much more than a residence for the Salesian Sisters; it would embrace a nursery, orphanage, retreat center and, in time, the Provincial headquarters.

The Morris House hosted two retreats each year so that all the Sisters would have the opportunity to spend a week in prayer, instruction, and spiritual renewal, as required by the Order's Constitutions. The retreat held in August 1915 was memorable because the preacher made "BOSCO" his theme: B for *Bene* (Good); O for *Orazione* (Prayer); S for *Studio e Lavoro* (Study and Work); C for *Caritá* (Charity); and O for *Obbedienza* (Obedience). The Sisters embraced this program as the yearly spiritual task for all.

The Morris House would also become the site of the first Salesian Sisters' House of Formation (for the training of new Sisters) in the United States. In 1912, Frances Costanzo was ready to begin her Novitiate. She was already 27 years old when she informed her father that she would be going to Mexico for her Novitiate.

Sr. Antoinette Pollini,
Directress of Formation and future Provincial.

"Mexico?" her father answered. "Paterson is bad enough. If they can't take care of you there in Paterson, then you can come home."

Evidently, the matter must have been discussed with the superiors in Italy, because Frances began her Novitiate in Paterson. The Holy See approved 41 Ward Street for the formation program of future Sisters, both Postulants and Novices, in an official document dated January 13, 1913. And none too soon. Within a week, five young ladies, all in their twenties, asked to begin their formation as Postulants. They were Joanne Passarelli and Carmela Avigliano from Paterson; Rose Costanzo from Brooklyn; and Erminia Caruso and Santina Bensi from New York City. The formation program was entrusted to Sr. Antoinette Pollini, who was given the responsibility of the program with the title of Directress of Formation. Her piety alone was a compelling example to all.

In 1918, the Sisters were asked to take care of another pressing need. The Spanish influenza was affecting many persons, and often single parent households with children remained. A few girls, bereft of mothers, needed the care and guidance that a working father could not give. A small part of the Morris House was partitioned for them so that this need could be met. This multi-purpose house had found yet another calling – an orphanage.

Real Estate Boon

Amid all their activities and responsibilities, the Salesian Sisters continued to make the children's education their priority. The number of schoolchildren at Saint Michael's had increased so they could no longer remain in the crowded church basement.

The Lee Mansion in Paterson, NJ
served as the first official school building in 1915.

The Lee Mansion, directly across Ward Street from the new convent, was put on sale. The owner sold the building and the property to Saint Michael's. There was true rejoicing throughout the parish and especially among the school population. With its spacious rooms and long corridors, the Lee Mansion was an answer to prayers. This remained the official school building until a new edifice was built in 1948. Everything was falling into place, and everyone thanked God and the Sisters who had turned things around by their life and their faith.

The first graduation at Saint Michael School took place on June 24, 1918. Peter De Domenico received the first award for proficiency in his work, and Adelina Peretti won the second award for the year's work. Parents were pleased that the children were being given a good education and would succeed at building a better future for their families. The Sisters, praised for being able to do so much with so little, were happy to see that the dream was becoming a reality in the lives of the children and their families.

Despite these auspicious beginnings, some real estate issues needed attention. First, the building next to the Morris House, the so-called Lockwood House, had windows on every floor that faced the playground and the Sisters' convent. There was no privacy. Second, Dr. Sabatino, a pediatrician who saw patients throughout the day and evening, lived on the first floor. He belonged to the Masonic Lodge and the members often had their meetings on the balcony. Third, a "spiritist" inhabited the top floor. She muttered, sang, and often spoke of the various "spirits" who were walking in the playground with the children!

Mother Enrichetta Sorbone, Vicar General of the Salesian Sisters, was visiting the community with her secretary, Sr. Clelia Genghini. A disciple and close friend of Mother Mazzarello, Mother Enrichetta possessed a soul steeped in faith and the virtues established at Mornese. She saw that space was at a premium in the convent and that something had to be done about the neighbors. She did not think these tenants helped to establish an appropriate environment for the Novitiate or benefited the education of the children.

Observing the surroundings, Mother Enrichetta turned to one of the Novices, Frances Costanzo. She gave her a medal of Mary Help of Christians and said, "Please, with all your faith and all your might, throw this medal across the fence." Sr. Frances did so at once, praying as she threw the medal.

The result? In no time, the Lockwood property was put up for sale! Friends notified the Sisters at once. The transaction was done expediently and to everyone's satisfaction.

The Lockwood House had two complete residences. The Sisters used the first house for boarders, with space for a cafeteria for the schoolchildren and after-school homework and activities. The second floor would be reserved for the Sisters' residence and the orphans' dormitory. The smaller house on the property was used for the family who served as caretakers for the church and school.

A class of Saint Michael School in the Lee Mansion in the 1940s.

Sister Frances Delfino worked at Saint Michael School, Atlantic City. She would walk the famous boardwalk there to meet and invite the children to attend Saint Michael's.

It seemed that everything had come together to everyone's satisfaction. The debt, as always, became the Sisters' responsibility, but faith, hard work, and sacrifice helped to liquidate this financial obligation in time.

News of the Salesian Sisters and their tireless work among the poor and the young was spreading beyond the Paterson city limits. In 1911, a request for assistance came from a far-off place: Atlantic City.

The seaside resort is 130 miles south of Paterson – a relatively quick journey today, but 100 years ago they might as well have traveled to Siberia!

The pastor of Saint Michael Parish in Atlantic City, Father John Quaremba, was a friend of Father Cianci's who loved Don Bosco and wanted to imitate him in his love for the spread of the Kingdom. Since 1904, this zealous pastor and compatriot had labored untiringly to construct not only a church but a school. However, he desperately needed teachers, and so he set his sights on the Salesian Sisters of Saint John Bosco. Saint Michael's parishioners were largely Italian immigrants, and he wanted a school so that the children would be assisted in learning and living the faith.

Saint Michael Parish and School in Atlantic City, New Jersey.

Father Quaremba got his wish. Finally, his persistent petition was granted and the jubilant priest set out immediately for Paterson, personally escorting four Sisters selected for the mission to their new home: Sr. Teresa Gaiottino, Sr. Beatrice Curtis, Sr. Maddalena Pezzaglia, and Sr. Margaret Grillone. Arriving in Atlantic City on January 14, 1913, they were met by crowds of cheering parishioners who brightened the bleak winter sky and the steel-gray ocean. They lined the streets from the railroad station to the new school. It was a welcome sight indeed. Their enthusiasm quickly dispelled any misgivings among the new arrivals, encouraging them to face the work ahead.

They certainly did not find the seaside gambling resort that is known today. In the earlier period of its development, Atlantic City had attracted a sizeable number of Italian immigrants seeking a new beginning in the New World. All too often, in their search for material prosperity, these newcomers fell victim to the spiritual and moral dangers surrounding them. That was why Father Quaremba wanted a school staffed by teachers he trusted for his future parishioners. That was why he wanted the Salesian Sisters.

The Sisters faced a huge challenge. The exterior of the school building was impressive, but the poverty within those newly-erected walls was a stark contrast. While thoughtful parishioners, themselves poor and financially unable to give help, visited nearby markets to beg for food

for "their" Sisters, the latter, accustomed to privations of every kind, focused their attention on readying the school and meeting the parish youth. Within a week, they began religious instruction, followed soon after by daily rehearsals to prepare a musical drama for the inauguration of the new school.

The great day arrived quickly. On February 2, 1913, Saint Michael School was officially opened with great pageantry. A small parade sporting American and Italian flags led the eager children through the streets of the community to the church for a solemn Eucharistic celebration. Ice cream followed for all, while registrations of the children took place. Ninety-nine children were registered that day. Considering that it was the middle of the school year, all were satisfied.

This was only the beginning. The cry of Don Bosco, "Give me souls, take away the rest," continued to motivate the Sisters in their mission.

Sr. Margherita Grillone
(1879-1955)

"While a new Chapel and Novitiate were being built in North Haledon, the Blessed Sacrament was reserved in the little alcove of old Saint Joseph Parlor. As one entered the improvised Chapel, the sanctuary could be seen through the window. One evening, Sr. Margaret came in exhausted from a long day at the university. As she entered, she placed her tired head on the windowsill and whispered audibly, 'Jesus, I am Yours. Help me!' I happened to be near but made a hasty retreat at that moment when our dear Mother Mistress received the strength to carry on her many and difficult tasks."

Sr. Providence Favoloro, FMA

Sr. Rosalba Garcia in Atlantic City, New Jersey
on the Feast of Saint John Bosco, 1981.

Sr. Magdalen Pezzaglia with girls at
Saint Anthony School

A reunion of Salesian Sisters on the 75th anniversary of Saint Michael School in Atlantic City in 1984.

Evening Italian classes began on February 19, followed by the re-organization of various associations and church groups, and the initiation of the youth center. In addition, the Sisters visited families and took care of liturgical celebrations. Sr. Ercolina Perinciolo, the organist, added to each festivity by the preparation of not only an adult choir, but a children's choir, too.

Eventually, the school became too small for the numerous activities. Another venture – a multi-purpose center, with a gymnasium and additional classrooms – was undertaken. The "Dante Alighieri Community Center," completed in 1926, satisfied the growing needs of both school and parish.

To this day, even with the coming of the casinos, the Saint Michael complex stands as an imposing memorial of the love, dedication, and service of the dreams set in motion by the early Sisters. Although the school did not survive the change of environment in Atlantic City (the exodus of families with children coincided with the construction of the casinos), the living examples of this dream are visible. The first vocation from Atlantic City was Sr. Rose Bucci, professed as a Sister in 1927. Others followed: Sisters Marie and Regina Dunn, Sr. Virginia D'Alessandro, Sr. Theresa Kelly, Sr. Loretta De Domenicis, Sr. Joanne Holloman, and Sr. Lou Ann Fantauzza. These Sisters and their many wonderful collaborators and friends continue the dream with dedication, keeping alive the love for Our Lady brought by the pioneer Sisters.

Today, even with the surrounding casinos, Mary is honored each year with a tradition brought by the early Italian settlers. On August 15, in the "blessing of the sea," a statue of Mary is carried in procession to the ocean, accompanied by prayers and hymns.

From Nutley to Niagara Falls

By the end of the 1910's, the original complement of four Salesian Sisters had grown into an impressive community. As if in answer to their sacrifices, the Sisters received help from new candidates and from the missionaries who arrived from Italy and England to help the band of apostles already in mission. Sr. Erminia Falco, Sr. Caroline Novasconi, Sr. Caroline Stazzi, Sr. Anna Landoni, Sr. Erminia Moisio, and Sr. Winifred Elley had no idea of the tremendous mission that awaited them among the youth of this vast continent. But they were young, fired with love for God and America's youth, and eager to live the dream.

In 1916, the Sisters undertook the education of the children at Riverside in Paterson. They walked to and from school each day, teaching wherever they could. Classes were held sometimes in church, sometimes in private homes, sometimes in the church basement. Not even the Spanish influenza of 1918 stopped them.

Sr. Erminia Falco (1888-1965)

"One summer, instead of making the retreat after summer studies, I was hospitalized for surgery. After the retreat, Sr. Erminia came to visit me. As she entered the room, she exclaimed, 'Thank God, you are in the hospital!' I was taken aback by the unusual remark. Then Sister explained that when she didn't see me at the retreat, she thought I had left the Congregation (I was a Junior Professed). Frequently, during the retreat, she prayed for me. Actually, she barely knew me. Her concern for my vocation was what I consider her zeal for souls."

Sr. Cesira Pierotti, FMA

News of the Salesian Sisters and their concern for immigrant families spread to various Italian communities in the region. The Sisters walked the streets as Jesus did in order to bring the Good News to the families of Lodi, Clifton, Nutley, and Mahwah, all towns in New Jersey. In Totowa, classes were held above a dry cleaning shop. Always, the Sisters were present, smiling, speaking, and bringing a message of hope and faith. While some of these missions increased and flourished, others were short-lived. In each place, the soil was prepared, the seed planted and tended, and some seedlings were left for God to give the increase.

Saint Joseph School in Niagara Falls, New York, was one such mission further afield, staffed by the Salesian Sisters from 1914 until 1918. When they arrived, the three Sisters, led by the intrepid pioneer, Sr. Angelina Andorno, found the new school still under construction. What were they to do?

With over 200 children enrolled, there was only one possible solution: the convent. True to their Salesian spirit of creative concern for the children, they set to work immediately. They converted the rooms, including bedrooms and even the spacious attic, into temporary classrooms. Children from kindergarten through grade eight filled the makeshift schoolhouse, using chairs for desks, as they knelt on the floor to write.

The chronicler of the time writes, "While this cluttered environment provided ample opportunity for the more talkative young people to pursue their conversational gifts, a reverent silence fell over the students as they listened to the religious instruction. Those otherwise restless little scholars sat attentive and still, totally absorbed in the presentation of their religious heritage. And so the seed took root, slowly spreading and strengthening into healthy, young shoots."

St. Michael's playground in 1946 with Sr. Caroline Stazzi, Sr. Jerome Parinello, and Sr. Florence Bona.

First Holy Communion at Saint Anthony's in 1936. At left is Sr. Helen Gatti, at right are Sr. Angelina Di Santo and Sr. Catherine Sforza.

Within three months, the pastor, Father Frederick Sbrocca, announced that the school was ready. The students, though happy to relocate to their brand new classrooms, would always retain nostalgia for those early months in their primitive educational facilities.

The Salesian sowers remained for only four years, just long enough to reap the beginnings of a rich harvest. The pastor thanked the Sisters, but told them that he had other Sisters who spoke English more fluently.

Several years after the Sisters left Niagara Falls, the seed blossomed when vocations knocked at the door of the Sisters' house in Paterson. The tangible signs of God's

blessings on the many hidden sacrifices of his daughters were rewarded. Sisters Antoinette and Josephine Zito, and Sr. Mary Di Camillo became educators for other young people for many years. Sr. Cesira Pierotti and Sr. Elizabeth Russo would find their way from the northern New York diocese to the Salesian Sisters' Novitiate in their own time.

In the New Jersey area, a mission was temporarily established in Mahwah until the pastor could find Polish-speaking Sisters. The Sisters of Saint Felix eventually took over the mission, but the generous donation of the Salesian Sisters bore fruit in Sr. Veronica Milyo's vocation some years later.

3 ADVENTURES OF THE DAY

The 1920's

Orphans in front
of the White House
in the early 1920s.

"The best time for the children was when they were dropped off
on Main Street. The police often had to stop the traffic so that
they could cross the street, or return to the bus for their books.
Every day the children discovered a new toy in the store windows,
and they forgot about school until Sr. Mary Pollini reminded them.
The same took place when school was over.
Sr. Mary was a good sport, and often provided a good laugh
for all as she recounted the adventures of the day."

Increasing vocations were a blessing to the community in New Jersey. Joining Sr. Rose Ottavia,
Mother Antoinette Pollini (seated), and Sr. Antoinette Grozino in the 1920s were (left-right) Julia Marzorati, Lucy Cesario,
Mary Louise Cerraf, Felicia Simonetti, Lena Capozzi, Mary Ligregni, Rose Torisi, Teresa Erriga,
and Mary Rusciano. Mary Rusciano was the first resident from Mary Help of Christians who went on to become a Salesian Sister.

Needs of the Novitiate

The "Roaring Twenties," as this decade is remembered, brought its blessings and its challenges. World War I officially ended. The first woman governor in U.S. history took office. Prohibition was raging, the Scopes Monkey Trial would challenge a belief system, and women's right to vote gave the country a sense of adventure, conquest, and self-determination. This ended all too soon with the crash of the stock market in 1929. Poverty and destitution became the order of the day.

Poverty was already no stranger to the Salesian Sisters. With empty hands and full hearts, they lived Don Bosco's mandate "to suffer heat, cold, hunger, thirst, fatigue, and contempt" and sacrifice everything to save young people!

And soon there were many young women seeking to become Salesian Sisters. The Novitiate was not neglected, despite the constant arrivals and departures for the new missions. Sr. Antoinette Pollini had been named the first Directress of Novices. She seemed to be always at prayer and always ready for anyone who wished to speak with her.

Her spirit of piety was an inspiration to all, but especially to the Novices. They all hoped to pray like their directress.

Each new year saw some candidates admitted to the Novitiate as others made their first profession of vows and joined the wonderful adventure in the education of American youth. Growth also meant overcrowding at the Provincial House at 41 Ward Street, a reality that could not be denied and could no longer be ignored. Children, Postulants, Novices, and Sisters presented a vibrant witness of Gospel living, but the physical space was no longer adequate for their number. A new home was needed, and soon.

Mother Brigida Prandi, Provincial at the time, searched for a suitable place. Her first thought was to provide a place for the orphans' education and for the future expansion of the Province. The Provincial House would remain at 41 Ward Street and house the necessary personnel to govern the Province as well as the Sisters who served at Saint Michael School. The place to be purchased would need enough space to house the orphans and to provide for their education, as well as offer living quarters for the formation program of both Postulants and Novices.

In the end, the Sisters did not have to look very far.

A New Home in Haledon

A spacious, adequate, and promising estate was for sale. The Muhs Estate in Haledon (now North Haledon) seemed to be a perfect answer for the needs of the expanding community. However, the family of the deceased owner was unwilling to sell to a bunch of Sisters who were always surrounded by a group of rowdy kids! The fear was that the children would destroy the trees that had been imported to grace the sloping acreage. Besides, Haledon seemed to be the end of the world. The streets of the town were not even paved. There was no public transportation. The orphans needed to go to school. The family had so many concerns. And where was the money?

Mother Brigida persisted, certain that God Himself had directed the Sisters to this spacious site. There were three homes on the property. The largest house belonged to the Muhs family, and the other two residences were those of two married daughters (the Harris House and the Sowerbutt House). Finally, in order to settle the family's opposition towards the children, the lawyer, Robert McDermott, a friend of the Sisters, cleverly decided to purchase the estate for himself and then sell it to the Sisters in 1921.

The discharge of the mortgage and the residency in the borough became a reality when the Sisters signed the documents for the 16.33 acres. The debt incurred was not part of the dream, but surely the Lord and Mary herself would provide. Auspiciously, Mr. Perini, a friend of the Sisters, used his automobile to bring the first resident to the new property, the statue of Mary Help of Christians, the best guarantor that the debt would be liquidated!

On November 21, 1921, the day dedicated to Mary's Presentation in the Temple, the Sisters and girls finally took possession of the property, and the sounds of prayer, singing, and laughter could be heard in the country air. Again it was the Sisters who had purchased, furnished, and settled the land and house.

The main house, located at the top of the driveway and painted white, was immediately dubbed "The White House." This was the name known to generations of Sisters and girls who lived there and loved the house, the fountain that fronted it, and the pond that served as drainage for the

The Muhs Estate in Haledon in 1921, affectionately called "The White House" by the Salesian Sisters.

The Harris House, as it stands today in North Haledon, was the first school for orphans.

estate. At the top of the hill was the Harris House, still standing today in its almost original form (it is now called the Marian Residence and is used for family and guests). It became the first school building on the property. At the turn of the driveway was the Sowerbutt House, first used as the chapel and Sacred Heart Novitiate, and later as Salesian College, which relocated to Newton when it merged with Don Bosco College in 1973.

A White House for the Orphans

The Sisters who accompanied the girls were Sr. Antoinette Agliardi, Sr. Rosina Costanzo, Sr. Mary Pollini, and Sr. Mary Simonetti. They immediately set up a small altar in the parlor of the White House. Father John Focacci, pastor of Saint Anthony's, had lent it to them, and he came to celebrate Mass the next morning. Father Felix Cianci chose the name given to the new residence: Saint Michael Orphanage. Since he was the pastor who had called the Sisters to Saint Michael Parish in Paterson, and since the young girls who were housed there lived as boarders, the name seemed appropriate.

Forty-two orphans, all girls, moved into the White House with the four Sisters. Most of the girls who were listed as orphans and were given hospitality had at least one parent. However, since the parent had to work, the residency was truly a need for these young girls.

But the new property had no school. What could be done?

It was decided that the girls would finish the school year at Saint Michael's. Cars were out of the question. So, it was a hike every day or a bus ride on some days.

This 1922 photo, taken on the front porch of Saint Michael Orphanage in the White House, shows the orphans and the first four Sisters who accompanied them to the Muhs Estate: Sr. Mary Simonetti, Sr. Antoinette Agliardi, Sr. Mary Pollini, and Sr. Rosina Costanzo.

Class of 1921 of Saint Michael School in Paterson, New Jersey, with Sr. Caroline Novasconi, Father Carlo Cianci, and Sr. Mary Pash.

Saint Michael School, Paterson, New Jersey

"I received my First Holy Communion while attending Saint Michael School. There were ten children in my family. There was no money for a beautiful dress or veil. Leave it to the Salesian Sisters. They took me into the convent, then made me try on different dresses until they were satisfied that this dress was the prettiest on me. I have never forgotten the kindness and caring they gave a little girl so she could feel beautiful on this wonderful day."

Bernice Titmas

Sr. Cecilia Napoli's recorded account gives some idea of the "joys" of transporting 42 children daily from North Haledon to Paterson in 1921-22:

"Sr. Mary Pollini patiently lined up the children every school morning for a trip to Saint Michael. Who can rush young people? They have all the time in the world. It was so during the memorable winter of 1921 and the spring of 1922. The roads were not paved, frozen through, no houses around — a frozen desert! The leather bags, books, gloves, umbrellas, handkerchiefs, and all kinds of supplies and belongings were scattered along the way. The driver often stopped the bus to wait for the collection of lost articles. Most often the bus was empty until it reached the city limits, so the children had the grandest time.

"The best time for the children was when they were dropped off on Main Street. The police often had to stop the traffic so that they could cross the street, or return to the bus for their books. Every day the children discovered a new toy in the store windows, and they forgot about school until Sr. Mary Pollini reminded them. The same

took place when school was over. Sr. Mary was a good sport, and often provided a good laugh for all as she recounted the adventures of the day."

On June 4, 1922, the Haledon community was finally inaugurated and received the name of Mary Help of Christians. This not only gave it legal status in the Congregation, but it also confirmed the autonomy of the foundation in the name of Mary. Sr. Angelina Andorno was appointed Superior of the new community, and Sr. Margaret Grillone served as Directress of the Novices.

Westward Ho!

The pioneering days were finally over. It seemed that everyone had room and possibilities for growth and expansion. The Province now began to experience stability with a house for the Provincial and her staff and for the Sisters who taught at Saint Michael's. Haledon provided for the formation program of the Postulants and Novices. The students had their own home.

Though not yet completely settled, the Sisters' situation had improved. The mission had begun in earnest. Children were being educated. Parents and friends were helped. God's work was flourishing, and Mary Help of Christians had come into this new land of hers to stay.

We have seen how these pioneers were indeed women of promise. With full trust in Jesus and Mary Help of Christians, and the total donation of their energies, these Sisters were able to see their dream grow and flourish.

In 1921, Mother Brigida decided it was time to take another bold step. With three houses, nine Sisters, with perpetual vows, and five temporary professed Sisters, she decided it was time to expand the mission, 3,000 miles to the West. She sent three Sisters to Watsonville, California, to help the Salesian Fathers who had a minor seminary there. Sr. Frances Delfino, Sr. Anna Capra, and Sr. Mary Puppione were to take care of the laundry and kitchen of the Salesian minor seminary and thus help in the formation of future Salesian priests. This difficult decision further isolated some of the Sisters. Undaunted, they felt that it was their mission, and that Mary was with them on the journey.

Sr. Mary Campi serving students in Watsonville, California.

One of the earliest communities in Watsonville, California,
in the 1920s included (standing) Sr. Mary Puppione,
Sr. Emma Buffoli, and Sr. Pierna Martinello;
(seated) Sr. Mary Campi, Sr. Frances Delfino, and Sr. Theresa Gaiottino.

Closer to home, Saint Anthony Parish was able to open a parish school on Madison Street in Paterson in 1921. Sr. Mary Riposi, Sr. Caroline Stazzi, and Sr. Joanne Passarelli went to the new school to receive the children. There were 203 students registered in grades K-8. School ended at 3:15 p.m., but the Sisters did not return to Ward Street until about 6:00 p.m. because of after-school activities and homework. Here, too, the Sisters took care of the children who waited for their parents to finish their working day.

It became evident that the house on Madison Street was insufficient for the growing school population. Father Focacci donated funds received from his Silver Jubilee of ordination to purchase the former Public School No. 11 on nearby Summer Street from the city. After renovations, the building was opened in September 1925 as the new school. Nursery school and after-school care continued in the Madison Street location, with the Sisters residing on the second floor. June 1926 saw the first graduation of 16 young women and men.

A New Provincial

Mother Gemma Muttis was appointed Provincial (superior) in 1923. She had observed first hand the growth and development of the new Province. The personnel had increased to the point where it was necessary to chart a firm course for the Province into the future. It was also time to update the Province formation program. Mother Gemma was especially concerned about the professional preparation of the enthusiastic Sisters who were called to continue the educational mission of Don Bosco to the young.

Sisters from the Mexican Province enjoying their time together in New Jersey.

As soon as she could, Mother Gemma formed the first Provincial Council with two councilors, Sr. Antoinette Pollini and Sr. Angelina Andorno; a secretary, Sr. Caroline Novasconi; and a treasurer, Sr. Veneranda Zammit, a pioneer who remained in this important position until her death.

One of the Provincial Council's first acts was to relocate the Novitiate. The Postulants and Novices were transferred to the Sowerbutt House in North Haledon, which became the Sacred Heart Novitiate in 1925. Here too, God's Providence directed the new foundation. Religious persecution had broken out in Mexico. The Novices of that country and some from the South American countries were accepted with the candidates of the United States for their formation and until they could return to their own Provinces.

The Novices now had a regular community and schedule of their own as well as the personnel and classes necessary for their formation in the consecrated religious life. They also had their own little chapel. The Sisters and girls remained in the White House, and school was held daily at Harris House. Little by little, the Sisters were regularizing their lives, their mission, and their formation.

Students and Sisters gather in North Haledon, New Jersey, in the 1920's.
In the top row are Sr. Caroline Stazzi, Sr. Margaret Grillone,
Sr. Josephine Galassi, and Sr. Madeline Pezzaglia.
In the first row are Sr. Antoinette Pollini, Mother Gemma Muttis,
and Sr. Veneranda Zammit.

Sr. Mary Reposi and Sr. Anna Capra in
Watsonville, California, working with a group of
women to maintain the clothes of the young men
in the seminary there.

In July 1928 Mother Gemma left for Italy to participate in the General Chapter, held every six years, when Salesian Sisters gather from throughout the world to assess their spiritual and ministerial journeys and make projections for the future. Sr. Caroline Novasconi was the delegate from the Province. Before she left, Mother Gemma had the foresight to initiate the professional preparation of the Sisters, to see the first Sisters acquire the needed qualifications and degrees to become certified teachers in the school systems. She also set the formation program on a sound path with its own residence and directress. Furthermore, she had encouraged the foundation of two new schools in New York City. During her service of leadership, the number of young women asking for admission into the life of the Sisters increased from three candidates in 1915 to 28 in 1928.

Mother Gemma had not only given inspiration but had also continued the preparation of the dream so that the dream would become a reality. The first difficult steps had been taken. The dream was ready for the wearing.

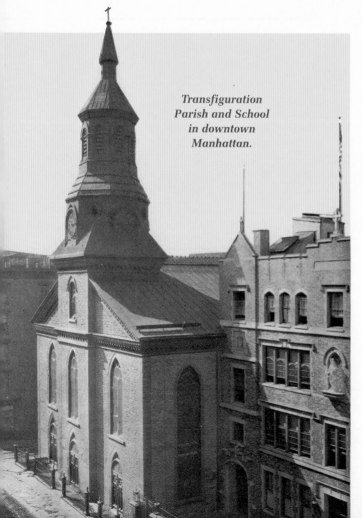

Transfiguration Parish and School in downtown Manhattan.

Jimmy Durante, a member of Transfiguration Parish and a friend to the Sisters.

On to New York City

At the beginning of the 20th century, one of the Italian immigrants who scrubbed basement floors was the future Mother Frances Cabrini, America's first saint. During this time, the Salesian priests and brothers were invited to take over the future saint's parish, Transfiguration Parish in New York City. They were quick to recognize the importance of the family unit in Italian society.

Salesian leadership put great emphasis on the moral development and strengthening of the family. The priest's role was an educational and supportive one, teaching the young in the ways of the faith, presiding over major celebrations, baptisms, marriages, as well as burying the dead with dignity. Their mission was personal and supportive, building strong relations with the Italian families.

The Salesian priests asked the Sisters to help them with the children's education. The Sisters arrived in 1924 and gave a fresh opportunity, especially to the young. If some of the richness of the Old World would be lost, much could be gained from the New. The Sisters opened English and citizenship classes in response to laws that restricted citizenship to English-speaking people. A high-rise on Park Street served as a convent for the Sisters, and the ground floor was used as a meeting room for youth activities.

The Bowery was nearby. It was a tourist attraction with its nickelodeons and beer halls. Chinatown began to emerge as a major tourist center in Manhattan. One of the young singing waiters at the Chatham Club was Irving Berlin. Mr. Durante, a barber on Mott Street, was disappointed because his son, Jimmy, did not know classical music, although he could bang out on the piano all the latest tunes with ease. Jimmy Durante remained one of Transfiguration's oldest and dearest friends, having never forgotten the neighborhood where he was born, grew up, and literally "sang for his supper" with a young Eddie Cantor in the local bars.

Pictured here are some of the students from Transfiguration Parish in the 1920's. Sr. Martina Chiaverano is seen among the children.

The Salesians were not long in addressing the needs of the sizeable Chinese community in the parish. The Bishop of Canton, an area of China from which most of Chinatown's residents had come, sent Father Montanar to begin a Chinese Mission in the parish. He opened the Mission on Park Street, celebrated the Eucharist daily, and gave instruction. This Mission formed a sympathetic link with the Chinese community that developed through the years to make it an integral part of the parish. In fact, Transfiguration became the largest Chinese-Catholic community in the United States.

When World War I was over and "Giovanni" came marching home again, he found a neighborhood entering a decade of prosperity. The second-generation Italians became a major force in the trade union movement and a strong voice for the working classes. The Sisters continued to serve the community of working-class families, made up of conservative, frugal, and industrious people who hardly noticed the excitements of the Jazz Age. Father John Voghera took advantage of the improved economy to renovate the church, replace the wooden floor with tile, and install new pews. The basement was remodeled to serve as an auditorium and gymnasium, and, in 1922, ground was broken for a new school. The Sisters rejoiced in the increased capacity.

The Sisters served Transfiguration Parish for 21 years from 1924-1945. Several vocations resulted as permanent witnesses to the work of the Sisters there: Sr. Katherine Di Biasi, Sr. Frances Inciardi, Sisters Angelina and Frances Di Santo, Sr. Mary Brucato, Sr. Gaetana Piccirilli, Sr. Leonia Pascucci, Sr. Santina Bensi, Sr. Frances Principale, and Sisters Lydia and Josephine Carini.

Salesian Sisters (and real-life sisters) Sr. Antoinette and Sr. Philomena Martorana.

Two Schools for Mary Help of Christians

The Institute of the Daughters of Mary Help of Christians founded its first community-owned educational establishment in North Haledon. In the beginning of the 1924-1925 school year, Harris House became Mary Help of Christians School, with 76 residents and five day students. They were a picture of earnestness as they dutifully climbed the steps to go "up Harris," as the classrooms came to be called.

Sr. Mary Pash, who had come from England with the proper qualifications, was the first principal. Her mind and heart centered on the good of each student. She committed the program to educational excellence as she delved into the needs of the girls entrusted to the Sisters.

On September 8, 1926, the Sisters began another new school dedicated to Mary Help of Christians in New York City's Lower East Side. The Mission Helpers of the Sacred Heart were already in the parish. Now the Salesian Sisters took care of the catechetical and sacramental preparation of the children. They also operated a kindergarten and a day care center, and had after-school activities in their convent building at 12th Street, which was directly across the street from the parish church.

The school opened with an enrollment of 183 students in grades 1-4. The parents were on hand that first day, happy that their children would be educated in a Catholic environment. They went to their jobs with confidence that their children would be safe, well cared for, and given opportunities they had never had.

Sr. Mary Pash, principal of Mary Help of Christians School, with one of the first graduating classes.

At Saint Joseph School in Niagara Falls, New York, students were instructed by Sr. Frances Inciardi and Sr. Frances Miculin.

The Sisters were encouraged and helped by Miss Elizabeth Broderick, a retired principal from city public schools. She gave invaluable help to the teachers concerning New York City standards and regulations. Every year a new grade was added until the elementary school graduated the first class on January 26, 1931. Uninterrupted classes and graduations followed. When the Sisters moved the school to the new location on 12th Street, they also took over the religious education program, the kindergarten, and the after-school care.

The Sisters had the children and the classes. However, they did not have living quarters in the parish. They packed their belongings and boarded the subway daily to their convent in Transfiguration Parish.

A New Building

Meanwhile, on the North Haledon property, space became an issue once more. The White House could no longer serve as residence for both the Sisters and the students. The Provincial Council, having heard the opinion of the Sisters, asked for permission to build an edifice that might ease the crunch. The Council was asked to submit plans and to study the financial situation very carefully. This done, and permission granted, construction of a new building began on May 24, 1929.

It would have two floors. The bottom floor could be used for many purposes, and the top floor would be the dormitory and the washrooms for the resident students. The basement was large enough for a dining room for the girls. The original plan was adequate for the needs of the time.

Appropriately, the new edifice was named "Don Bosco Hall" because, on June 2, 1929, Don Bosco became Blessed John Bosco. Father Joseph Binetti, in charge of the Salesian novices in Newton, presided at the solemn dedication and procession. An altar was placed at the main entrance of the White House, and the image of Don Bosco

was carried in triumph to its new residence. Even the local newspaper carried an article of the event. Father Richard Pittini, Provincial Superior of the Salesian Priests, gave the homily for the occasion. Everyone felt that they had touched the future, and that nothing could top the experience.

There was no prophetic voice among them to foretell what would truly happen. The transformation and adaptations made to Don Bosco Hall due to Province growth is one of the tales that still amazes both past students who visit, and the Sisters who lived through its many evolutions.

Sr. Beatrice Curtis (1886-1973)

"To be on time for Chapel, Sr. Beatrice would rise at 5:00 a.m. When she was on time she would joyfully (and audibly, because she was deaf) whisper, 'Jesus, thank You! I made it!' Whenever she was late, she would apologize, 'I'm sorry, Sweet Jesus, I'm late!'' Since she could not hear, she was grateful when anyone wrote out for her the subject of our conversations, summaries of conferences, or sermons. She repeated over and over again that everyone was too good to her. 'God bless you! God love you! Our Sweet Mother Mary smile upon you!' was her refrain for any service she received."

Sr. Josephine Carini, FMA

4 TO THE SOUTH AND WEST
The 1930'S

Sr. Barbara Pisacane (top) and Sr. Jerome Parinello lead the orange picking at Rinaldi Family Farm in Florida.

*"Twenty-five years have passed.
The mustard seed has grown and developed,
slowly but steadily, blessed by the showers of heaven,
helped by the cooperation of the good,
supported by many known sacrifices,
and still more by many hidden ones,
noted only by the One who inspired them.
Let us congratulate our pioneers!
With them let us blend our voices
in a solemn 'Magnificat' of acknowledgement
of the work of God."*

"Come and See"

The 1930's found the Salesian Sisters in a period of growth in many ways. Their spirit of joy was contagious, attracting young women to the community and young people to the mission. Their lives echoed that of Mary Mazzarello who said, "Be always cheerful. Happiness is a sign of a heart that loves the Lord!"

In May 1931, the first procession that carried the statue of Our Lady Help of Christians wound through the spacious and beautiful grounds in North Haledon, New Jersey. The Sisters were happy that they owned a place where Mary could be honored adequately for all that had been accomplished. The custom continued well into the 1960's when it was incorporated into the Salesian Family Celebration held in Newton. The Sisters, with the students, celebrated Marian days and weeks in various parishes and schools to keep the special devotion to Our Lady alive and well. The Sisters seldom forgot that Don Bosco wanted them to be a living monument of thanks to Mary for all that she was doing to bring people to Jesus.

The Sisters who taught religion classes in Mahwah, Lodi, Clifton, and other cities invited the young ladies who were members of the Children of Mary Sodality to spend some time in North Haledon for prayer, relaxation, and conversation to get to know one another. These gatherings proved very satisfactory, since the young ladies felt that this time was exclusively for them.

This gave rise to some discussion among the Sisters. The introduction of the process towards the beatification of the first Mother General, Mary Mazzarello, had been moving forward. The Sisters had already begun the renovation of the boathouse on the island of the existing pond. The property was certainly large enough, was beautiful, and would lend itself as a place of rest and leisure, as well as prayer. The Provincial Council listened and decided to combine the thoughts that had surfaced. They considered the construction of two wooden cabins to allow young

The first four Sisters to go to Easton, Pennsylvania, in 1938 were Sisters Anna Segalini, Raphael Spizzirri, Frances Miculin, and Angelina Puppione.

Camp Mary Mazzarello attracted many vocations. Future Sisters Rena Ossi, Mary Palatini, Providence Favaloro, and Domenica Minutella enjoyed a boat ride with a friend.

One of the cabins built in 1930 when Camp Mary Mazzarello opened in North Haledon, New Jersey.

The dining room cabin at Camp Mary Mazzarello.

women to enjoy a week or weekends. The construction would be named Camp Mary Mazzarello, in recognition of the 50th anniversary of the birth of Mary Mazzarello; to celebrate the 25th anniversary of the arrival of the Sisters in the U.S.; and to develop a place for young ladies during summer weekends for personal and group prayer and to learn about the mission of the Sisters.

The idea began to take shape on April 3, 1932. Excavations began up on the hill. The construction of the two wooden cabins took less time than anticipated. Inauguration of the cabins was scheduled for July 8, 1932. Camp was ready and the Sisters invited young ladies to "come and see." The upper cabin had a center washroom complete with showers, and the remainder of the cabin on both sides divided into three large sections, each containing about ten beds. The lower cabin had a dining room, rooms for meetings, and places for games and conversations.

Father Richard Pittini celebrated the first Eucharist, blessed the cabins, and congratulated all on a timely and innovative undertaking. In fact, several vocations resulted from these days of leisure and prayer. Sr. Mary Palatini,

Sisters Ida and Rena Ossi, Sr. Rose Oliveri, Sr. Mildred Zanetti, Sr. Providence Favaloro, Sr. Lydia Carini, and Sr. Veronica Milyo are some of the young women who became Sisters as a result of the camp experience.

Twenty-five Years in America

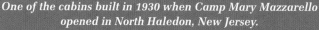

The Province leadership, aware of Mary's help and the response of the many persons, especially parents who were grateful for the education and formation given to their children, decided to make their thanks public by celebrating the silver jubilee of the Sisters' arrival in the United States of America. They were very aware that the chapel in the Novitiate was much too small for the growing community of Sisters, girls, Novices, and Postulants who resided in North Haledon.

As a special act of thanksgiving for all that had been accomplished in twenty-five years, the Sisters decided to open the summer Camp Mary Mazzarello not only to the young ladies, but to children as well. This dream, consolidated in its many forms throughout the Province,

was an inspired one. The many services provided by the camps in various locations in the Province brought the dream of helping children and parents far beyond the silver jubilee of the arrival of the Sisters to the United States.

The celebrations of the silver jubilee of the coming of the Sisters continued throughout the year in every school, catechetical center, community, and mission where the Sisters were stationed. Silver bells sounded at the completion of the year of jubilee to the great satisfaction of the many who had lived through some of the beginnings.

For the four pioneer Sisters, it was an affirmation of their faith, their love, their devotion to Mary, and their faithfulness to the educational mission of Don Bosco and Mary Mazzarello. For those who had joined them, it was a challenge to continue in faith and hope towards a future that beckoned with love in service of God and youth.

The Province had seen difficult times, but the expansion was phenomenal. The preparation of the Sisters for their mission had been successful. The formation of the Sisters had been constant with both spiritual and Salesian

The first graduating class of Mary Help of Christians School, New York City, in 1931. The future Sr. Philomena Martorana is in the second row, third from right.

dimensions, and their professional preparation as educators was progressing gradually for each Sister. There were now 11 Salesian communities, and more were in progress. Everywhere, the joy of serving the Lord in his children was evident.

The words of Mother Antoinette Pollini, the new Provincial, best summarize the occasion:

> "Twenty-five years have passed. The mustard seed has grown and developed, slowly but steadily, blessed by the showers of heaven, helped by the cooperation of the good, supported by many known sacrifices, and still more by many hidden ones, noted only by the One who inspired them. Let us congratulate our pioneers! With them let us blend our voices in a solemn 'Magnificat' of acknowledgement of the work of God… May God bless us and accept our pledge to save many souls, through an ever better understanding and application of their infallible method."

A New Chapel

The silver jubilee inspired the Provincial and her council to, once again, study the situation in the Province and the finances. The Council decided on an addition to the existing Novitiate in order to provide a chapel to meet the needs of the expanding community in North Haledon. The construction of the building would be adjacent to the parlor of the Novitiate proper.

Getting the permission to build this latest dream of the Sisters was not that easy. From Italy, the leadership of the Institute asked questions. Were the Sisters too optimistic? Were they taking serious risks? Were they aware of the cost?

At the Sacred Heart Novitiate in 1932,
Sr. Veronica Milyo visits with her nieces and family.

Sr. Margaret Grillone, then Provincial Secretary, wrote to the General Council of the particulars for the proposed construction. She presented the need to build an addition to the Novitiate for a chapel to seat about 400 on the first floor with a dormitory above the chapel for the Novices. She specifically stated some facts that would facilitate the construction: the Province had $6,000 in the bank; no house had debts; Sisters turned over to the Province almost their total stipends; and the construction of the chapel/dormitory had been reduced to minimum

requirements. Mother Pollini, a woman of faith and prayer, promised her daily reminder to the Lord. The approval was given, and the work begun.

All Sisters, friends, and their current and past students joined the Postulants and Novices who resided in North Haledon for the blessing of the new chapel on February 26, 1933. It was one of the highlights of the jubilee year! A jubilee booklet had been prepared for the occasion and distributed to all. It contained letters of commendation from the Holy See, Bishops, Salesians, and civil authorities congratulating the Sisters for the tremendous mission accomplished in 25 years.

The highlight of the day occurred in the early afternoon when a statue of the Sacred Heart was unveiled in front of the Novitiate while a congratulatory cable from Pope Pius XI was read. Soon after, on August 29, the Novices passed through the door into the new Chapel of the Sacred Heart to begin their time of preparation for their consecration as professed Sisters.

Sr. Antoinette Pollini (seated) was the first Director of Novices. She is pictured here in the early 1930s with Novices and Sisters: (left-right) Mary Brucato, Sr. Rose Ottavia, Mary Cannizaro, Rose Torrisi, Lucy Camasta, Gaetana Piccirilli, Theresa Errigo, Mary Ligregni, Sr. Emilia De Gennaro, Mary Sedita, Mary Riscagno, and Lena Capozzi.

An Invitation from Florida

Mother Pollini, a woman of prayer, responded to the invitation to begin the mission of the Salesian Sisters in Florida. Not the perfume of orange groves nor the graceful dance of lofty palms, but SOULS drew the Sisters to the sands of Florida's Gulf Coast.

The summons came from Father Richard Pittini, who pleaded for Sisters to work among the Italian and Hispanic immigrants at the Salesian parish of Saint Joseph's in Tampa. Some 1,100 miles lay between Tampa and the Provincial Center in New Jersey! In Depression-era travel terms, that meant three days by boat, then seven hours by train. But Messengers of the Word have always gauged distance by other standards... and so, on September 8, 1930, Sr. Cecilia Lanzio and her companions, Sr. Raphael Spizzirri and Sr. Ottavia Rossi, took up residence in the Sunshine State.

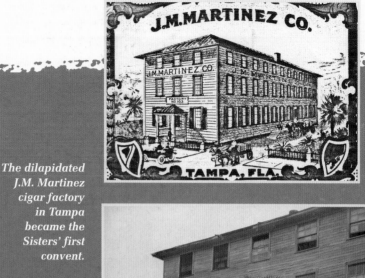

The dilapidated J.M. Martinez cigar factory in Tampa became the Sisters' first convent.

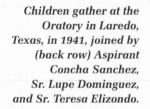

Children gather at the Oratory in Laredo, Texas, in 1941, joined by (back row) Aspirant Concha Sanchez, Sr. Lupe Dominguez, and Sr. Teresa Elizondo.

As a means of getting acquainted, the Sisters immediately began house-to-house visits and soon gathered several adults and dozens of children for religious instruction and recreational activities. Sr. Helen Mazurek became famous for her work with adults who needed to learn the truths of the faith in preparation for marriage. She offered detailed instructions for the celebration of the Sacrament of Matrimony, complete with a wedding cake and a lavish party!

The first lodging for the Sisters was an abandoned, former cigar factory on the corner of Spruce and Somerset Avenues. It was this "cigar factory convent" that also served as a parish social center where plays, skits, and parish entertainments were first held. The Sisters entertained the children with games and simple instruction during the day, and visited the families in the evenings. The cigar factory also offered hospitality to families on weekends, with meetings, games, and instructions.

The Sisters endured many hardships in that building. At times it seemed like an open house for homeless insects and rodents of the neighborhood! And they often had open umbrellas over their heads as they went to bed on rainy nights. It is said that the Bishop once came to celebrate Mass and it rained so hard that he got wet when he was at the altar! Needless to say, he was soon in favor of a new convent. He commented, "Jesus was born in a stable, but He didn't live there for 20 years!"

In 1934, there were 150 children in school and, of these, 100 were in the kindergarten and first grade. The others were scattered throughout the remaining grades. The school building was purchased from the Sisters of the Holy Names for $4,000.

The little seed, planted in the soil of Tampa, took a long time to grow, and even though it seemed it might wither away, the tenacity of the pastors, Sisters, and good parishioners, who watered it with prayer, patience, and faith, succeeded in making Saint Joseph Parish and School one of the finest and one of the lasting educational institutions in Tampa.

Ybor City

It was religious education that had first brought the Salesian Sisters into contact with another, highly receptive group of Catholics in a Tampa neighborhood called Ybor City. Most Holy Names Parish, in fact, was one of the catechetical centers serviced from Saint Joseph Convent. In 1933, "as a sign of gratitude to Our Heavenly Mother during the silver jubilee of the Province," a house was opened in

Children at play in Ybor City, Tampa.

61

The sewing club for public and parochial school girls at Saint Joseph Parish in Tampa.

the parish. Sr. Antoinette Agliardi, Sr. Christine Silenzio, and Sr. Gaetana Sferlazza formed the first community.

The Sisters immediately assumed the direction of a sewing club. By October, a number of young girls had joined the parish Rosary group. Sunday gatherings for games and religion lessons were organized; and a kindergarten was opened, with each of the eight pupils paying just 25 cents tuition per month. But the negligible tuition and consequent poverty were no match for the administration's resourcefulness. Sisters, lay teachers, parents, and parish ministers became adept at finding other sources of revenue in order to finance the various activities.

The spiritual results of the Sisters' mission speak more eloquently. With baptisms of adults and children, the celebration of numerous marriages, and the conversion of a good number of Protestants to the faith – Most Holy Names Parish became the focal point of Ybor City.

Later, a school opened in 1937 with the first grade and the addition of a grade each year. Sr. Christine Silenzio said

that one of the parishioners came to her with tears in his eyes as she played the organ during the school's opening Eucharistic celebration. "It is years that I have waited for this day," he said. "Thank you for coming to play like an angel." She, too, had tears in her eyes when she recounted the incident.

Texas Calls

December 13, 1934, marks the beginning of the Salesian works in Texas with Sr. Josefina Garcia and Sr. Dolores Hurtado, who took up residence on Santa Rosa Street in San Antonio. Eventually they found their way to North Laredo Street in the Parish of the Immaculate Conception, at the request of the pastor, Father Romero. Here, they had classes for kindergarten, painting, and piano, among other things.

It must be remembered that the Sisters who were in Texas had fled or had been exiled from the religious

Saint Joseph students participated in the festive "Lollypop Lane Parade" in Tampa in the 1930s.

persecution in Mexico. They did not know the English language, were not yet qualified to teach in the United States, and had to find the means to sustain themselves, while they lived out their vows and their beloved Salesian mission for youth in a new land.

The citizens of Laredo on the U.S. bank of the Rio Grande generously offered their homes to many clergy and religious who were expelled, exiled, or had fled Mexico. At one time, there were 14 bishops and archbishops living in Laredo!

As the Sisters' presence became known and as their mission became a true service to the youth of Texas, the quarters in which they were housed proved to be more and more inadequate. Changes were many and frequent: to Monterrey Street, West Commerce Street across from Sacred Heart Church, Southolm Street, and then to 904 Arbor Place. In the neighborhood of Saint Agnes Church, the Sisters taught religion classes.

At the request of the pastor of Saint Alphonsus Parish, an oratory was started there. Later, the Sisters opened a morning kindergarten and taught sewing, homemaking, catechism, and sacramental preparation. At the same time the Sisters also began their apostolate at the Church of the Sacred Heart. The pastor of San Fernando Cathedral asked for the services of the Sisters, and a catechetical school began that summer. Meanwhile, Mr. and Mrs. Chapa asked the Sisters to begin an oratory on their property. The Sisters came willingly, providing games and religious instruction for all the children.

Mother Caroline Novasconi (1890-1970)

"I had just made my profession in 1959 when Mother Caroline was here on her unofficial visit. The Sisters were given an opportunity of a few minutes of her precious time. I was last on line and, since the car was waiting for Mother, the Secretary told me not to go in. As we gathered to say our goodbyes, dear Mother Caroline spotted me and said, 'I didn't see you, did I?' I answered, 'No, Mother, but that's alright. You have to leave.' Taking me by the hand and leading me into the office, she said, 'The car can wait.' We talked as if she had no other commitment in the world. Who can ever forget such *bontá*, the goodness from the heart that Our Lady gave as a legacy to Don Bosco?"

Sr. Theresa Kelly, FMA

1934

Nineteen Thirty-Four was a watershed year for the Salesian Sisters, filled with joys and sorrows.

A solemn Eucharist opened the day's festivities in North Haledon on April 1, 1934, to celebrate the canonization of Saint John Bosco. Father Joseph Costanzo gave the homily for the occasion. The festivities ended in the late afternoon with Benediction of the Blessed Sacrament in thanksgiving for the recognition of the virtues of the Salesian Congregation's founder and "Father of Youth." On June 19, the communities and students of surrounding areas joined in the celebration of the same event at Saint Patrick Cathedral in New York City.

Four months later, the joyful sounds of celebration became more hushed as Sr. Veneranda Zammit, one of the pioneer Sisters, went to her home in Heaven. Her death on

October 14, 1934, came as a reminder that there is no lasting dwelling place on this earth. The funeral Mass was celebrated at Saint Michael Parish on October 17, and the internment was the first in the cemetery at the top of the hill in North Haledon. Her passing was received with mixed feelings, but with the certainty that Sr. Veneranda would be rewarded for her mission in the United States. With this celebration, the life of the Sisters in the U.S. had taken on a permanent and final seal.

In this same year, the appointment of Mother Caroline Novasconi as Provincial was greeted enthusiastically. Sr. Caroline had been in the Province from its beginning and was dearly loved by most of the Sisters, missionaries, and native vocations alike. The Sisters felt that they had a leader whom they trusted and admired. They felt her appointment was a gift from God Himself! To the tumultuous congratulations, Mother Caroline answered, "But you Sisters are too good. Let us pray together that nothing will go wrong."

The Shrine to Saint John Bosco at the priests' rectory on Beech Street was blessed in the 1930s by Father Dominic Cecere (center), in the presence of (left-right) Sr. Cecilia Napoli, Sr. Mary Palatini, Sr. Elvira Lombardini, Sr. Beatrice Curtis, and Sr. Magdalene Pezzaglia.

Kindergarten children playing at Saint Michael School in Paterson, New Jersey, in 1930. The church towers are seen in the background.

Mother Caroline continued her service as superior of the Provincial House, while she listened to and provided for the needs of any Sister who came to her. Her constant care for the youth in any house and situation became legendary. Her leadership made each Sister aware that she was a member of a large family. The young people felt that they, too, formed part of the family of the Sisters. The past pupils looked to the new Provincial for guidance and affirmation.

The House on Hidalgo Street

Fanning out from San Antonio, the Salesian Sisters expanded their mission in Texas. Sr. Margarita Moreno and Sr. Guadalupe Segura went in search of a suitable location in Laredo. Originally taken in by various pious families in the city, they soon found quarters downtown at 1514 Hidalgo Street on March 9, 1935. Sr. Mercedes (Mercy) Romo and Sr. Bonifacia (Bonny) Galindo, followed a few days later by Sr. Anita Marinez, became very important in

the developing border town and in the establishment of the Salesian way of life and love on the unpaved streets of Laredo, which were expanding as more and more Mexican citizens found a refuge.

Margaret Novoa, a future Sister but then a young lady who lived in the vicinity wrote, "The house on Hidalgo Street was indeed poor, to say the least. It consisted of three or four small rooms. One served as a chapel containing an altar and four chairs. The second room was the kindergarten. A third room was used for classes in sewing, painting and embroidery, while the fourth was the Sisters' living quarters."

Eight days after the Sisters moved into the Hidalgo residence, they began an oratory and had sixty girls the first day. Eventually the number grew to more than 160. By March 18, two Sisters began the catechetical apostolate in Our Lady of Guadalupe Church at the request of the pastor. Soon, the Sisters opened a kindergarten. In April 1935, the Sisters gave their assistance to the sacramental program for the youth of Holy Redeemer Parish.

While the apostolate was flourishing at Hidalgo Street, the Sisters undertook still another journey. Sr. Margaret Moreno, Sr. Anita Marinez, and Sr. Mercedes Romo traveled to the town of San Ignacio to begin sowing the Word of God. Since travel was by no means easy, they remained there for eight days, then proceeded to Zapata, another small town for their mission of evangelization.

As this missionary expansion was taking place, more young people found their way to the Sisters' house. New facilities were needed. The chronicler writes, "Not being able to continue in the house of Hidalgo Street, we moved to Houston Street." This was the understatement of the year! The lack of space, the financial conditions, the need for security and stability, the courage to move yet again, and many other factors were never expressed.

Sr. Margaret Novoa, the first Texan vocation, related some of the hardships:

"Sister Superior explained to us that our house was too small, and that since our number was growing daily, it had become necessary to find a larger house. Sisters and girls set out on this search armed with medals of Mary Help of Christians. In no time at all, they spotted a suitable house. It was a medical clinic operated by Dr. Isaac Newton Frost at the corner of Houston Street. The medals were accompanied by fervent Hail Marys by Sisters and girls."

The prayers were heard after three Sunday visits. Dr. Frost decided to move to Brownsville. The house belonged to the Volpe family who generously agreed to rent it to the Sisters. Laredo had lost a clinic, but had gained a family of religious dedicated to the formation and education of youth. This became the first Mary Help of Christians School in Laredo. The move to 1717 Houston Street took place on the Feast of the Holy Rosary, October 7, 1935.

In January of the following year, Father Valentin Rodriguez asked and obtained the Sisters' aid in the evangelization of his parish, the infamous "Rincon del Diablo." The Sisters quickly changed the name to "Rincon

Children playing outside the Cigar Factory which housed the Sisters' convent in Tampa, Florida.

The Class of 1932 at Saint Joseph School in Tampa included a future vocation, Sr. Wilma Sanchez (left).

Don Bosco" as the young people gathered in the name of Don Bosco to worship God and to learn about His Mother. Outstanding was the "Don Bosco Circle" that Sr. Bonny Galindo opened during the Lenten season of 1935. The purpose of this group was to provide religious instruction for the working girls of the area.

Two Villas

In January 1936, a good friend of the Sisters, Alicia Gonzalez Neve, who lived in Tampa, deeded her home and property to the Sisters to be used for educational opportunities for children. The property on Columbus Drive was named "Villa Madonna della Neve," Our Lady of the Snow, both to honor Our Lady in Heaven and the generous widow with a mother's heart. A day school began in September with a few students.

Mrs. Neve would remain in her house as a guest of the Sisters until her death, receiving a modest, monthly honorarium for her living expenses. She remained a great

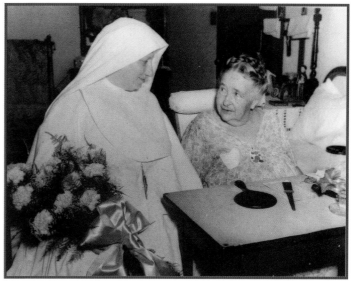

Mother Caroline with Mrs. Alicia Gonzalez Neve.

and generous friend, volunteering to drive to New Jersey and back several times to transport the Sisters.

At the same time the Sisters received the Neve estate, Mother Caroline and Sr. Antoinette Beltramo, the Province's financial administrator, became aware that the property adjacent to Mary Help of Christians Academy in North Haledon had been put on the market. The property

consisted of a restaurant/pub and a nightclub that had played loud music into the early hours of the morning. After the necessary plans and the study of the financial possibilities were evaluated, the Sisters decided to purchase the property. Father John Quaremba, the pastor of Saint Michael's in Atlantic City, lent the Sisters $25,000 without charging interest. This helped in the purchase.

Sr. Antoinette served as the administrator for the property and the house. She erected an outdoor shrine to the Immaculate Conception complete with Saint Bernadette, where even neighborhood children at times came to recite the Rosary with the Sisters. It was a novel situation. It helped the young people to see the Sisters, and it gave the Sisters an opportunity to interact with the local children. The name Villa Don Bosco was given to the property to honor Don Bosco's elevation to the rank of Saint in 1934.

The Neve estate, which was rechristened Villa Madonna della Neve, Our Lady of the Snows.

Seventh- and eighth-grade students at Saint Michael School in Atlantic City, New Jersey, in 1934.

Mexico and Pennsylvania

During the summer of 1938, Mother Caroline was delegated by the Institute as an Extraordinary Visitor to the Salesian Sisters in Mexico. The political situation of the world was precarious, and the Sisters in Mexico still had untold difficulties because of continued religious persecution. Mother Caroline was asked to visit these Sisters in order to have personal experience when she reported on the actual situation of the Sisters.

At Mother Caroline's suggestion, some Sisters and postulants from Mexico arrived in 1939, and served as a reminder to everyone that not every country was willing to allow freedom of religion. The candidates for formation would join those of the U.S. Province until the situation changed in Mexico. This plan continued for many years to the mutual benefit of both Provinces, and served as a model of inter-Province collaboration.

On December 27, 1939, one Sister and one postulant from Colombia came to reside in North Haledon in order to study the English language. They remained for approximately two years before they returned to Colombia, or decided to join the U.S. Province. This service as a center for study of the English language for some of the Provinces in the Institute continued for many years.

Before she left for Mexico, Mother Caroline appointed Sr. Joanne Passarrelli with two Sisters to begin a new mission at Our Lady of Mount Carmel Parish in Roseto, Pennsylvania. The pastor, Father Joseph Ducci, had asked the Sisters for the foundation of a school in this peaceful community. The adults had successfully established themselves as hard working manufacturers of blouses, so much so that a number of them owned the businesses and gave jobs to members of the community.

The Sisters began their mission by visiting the families and making friends with the children. They began a kindergarten and, in two years, the number registered were 45. The Sisters continued the family visits and began religious instruction classes. The pastor, meanwhile, constructed a school building. In 1943, the first grade began, and the elementary school added one grade per year.

Another foundation for social work was also begun in Easton, Pennsylvania. Sr. Frances Miculin, with four other Sisters, answered the request of Father Francis Barbato. He was concerned about the Christian living of his parishioners. So the Sisters began a census of the parishioners, keeping a record of the sacramental needs of each family. Meanwhile, they also began religion classes, especially for the children. The visits to the families proved very rewarding: 65 marriages were regularized; 85 adolescents were baptized; 15 adults embraced Catholicism; 34 adults received the Sacraments of the Eucharist and Confirmation. Each year, the parish saw a growth and a revival of parish life in direct proportion to the parish visitation of the Sisters.

Sr. Margarita Moreno (1879-1974)

"Her first years were spent in Puebla, Morelia, and Guadalajara, Mexico. In 1921, she was made Superior in Puebla and then sent to Linares in the same capacity. When the revolution broke out and the Sisters were required to close the house, she went to Peru in South America. Here again, Sr. Margarita was to meet with direct persecution. When the soldiers came to take possession of the house of San Angel Tenavitha, she and the Sisters consumed the consecrated hosts, thus saving the Blessed Sacrament from being desecrated. They were threatened with jail but were saved by some good ladies from the Catholic Action Center."

Anonymous

A Bolt of Lightning!

The decade ended with a bolt of lightning – that is, a special grace from the Lord! The point of view depended on what side of the Atlantic Ocean the Sister resided.

Mother Caroline had returned from Mexico after several months spent on her fact-finding mission. Everyone rejoiced and listened attentively as the visitor gave the Sisters some idea of the suffering of the Sisters stationed to the south. The Sisters readily understood. Nonetheless, Mother Caroline's goodness and her compassionate narration of the plight of others only made it more difficult when a telegram received.

The telegram asked that Mother Caroline put Province affairs in order and leave to join the central government in Turin, Italy. She had been appointed one of the General Councilors for the Institute!

On October 28, 1939, Mother Caroline left her missionary land behind, sorrowful Sisters who felt her loss, and many past pupils who had learned from her both human and religious values. She returned to her native Italy, she, a much richer person for having been a missionary, and the Province's Sisters, a legacy of love, commitment, and unending friendship.

Sr. Antoinette Mazzia enjoys a fun time with children at Saint Mary's Oratory in Easton, Pennsylvania.

5

WAR AND PEACE

The 1940's

"*Having lived in the austere poverty of India, Mother Tullia considered the 'few' comforts we then enjoyed, superfluous. Therefore, she constantly spoke of mortification, backing her conferences and instructions by her own spirit of self-denial. She never demanded of her Sisters what she had not, or was not, practicing.*"

The First Holy Communion classes process through the streets of Reading, Pennsylvania.

New Saint, New Provincial

As the world plunged into war and mechanized slaughter, the descent into barbarism once more revealed the frailty of civilization. But the war had a galvanizing effect on America, vividly manifested in its thriving popular culture. The Salesian Sisters were again cut off from the center of their Institute during a world war. Communication was a reality only within the circle of their mission and life. Maturity came rapidly as they had to make momentous decisions, with no guidance except that of the Spirit and love.

Early in the war, on May 7, 1941, the United States was detached from the Province of Mexico and officially designated an independent Province under the title of Saint Philip the Apostle (probably because it was the Salesian Priests' Province name). The many unrecorded sacrifices and struggles had matured into a new offering to the Lord: a Province of Sisters with the desire to glorify His name and share in the saving mission of the Church.

The appointment of the new Provincial, Mother Tullia De Berardinis, in 1940 coincided with the celebration of the beatification of Mother Mary Mazzarello in Saint John the Baptist Cathedral in Paterson. Bishop Thomas McLaughlin presided, and the young people of the nearby schools participated in the singing. It was a triumph and a fitting tribute not only to their humble co-foundress, but also a recognition of the authentic value of the education given to youth.

At the end of January 1940, Mother Tullia arrived from Italy. Since she had been stationed in India and knew English, this was a decided advantage for the Province. Small of stature, alert, and totally dedicated to the Salesian mission, she began her service immediately. It took her time to come to know the new culture and the Catholic educational system, but she understood and stressed the continuation of the formation and preparation of the Sisters that had been begun effectively by her predecessors.

Soon the United States entered World War II, and Italy joined Germany against the Allies. The Sisters continued to pray and to work for peace, each in her own way. They had learned from the experience of the first war, and substituted prayer for unobtainable advice when decisions had to be made.

From Mexico, these Salesian Sisters were the forerunners of the Western Province: Sr. Julia Garcia, Sr. Margarita Moreno, Sr. Anita Marinez, and Sr. Mercedes Romo.

Procession in honor of Blessed Mary Mazzarello in North Haledon.

A special Mass was celebrated in Don Bosco Hall to honor the beatification of Mother Mary Mazzarello.

A High School

Consideration had already been given to the question of the education of the girls who resided in North Haledon and who frequented Mary Help of Christians School. It was now necessary to take some course of action. The idea had surfaced as early as 1935, because some girls were completing the 8th grade curriculum. Then what would happen? Graduation from the 8th grade did not qualify the girls for anything. Education had to extend beyond elementary school.

Sr. Mary Palatini and Sr. Margaret Grillone were the ones who made contacts, studied layout and faculty issues, and submitted recommendations. It was generally agreed that a high school building would be necessary. The location chosen for the new construction was directly across from the side door of the "White House."

It took a long time to receive the necessary permission to build because of the difficulties in communication. Architect Joseph Bellomo drew the sketches for construction and wrote the specifications for a three-story high school building. With permission having been obtained from the Bishop of Paterson, Thomas McLaughlin, the Frank

Sr. Ruth Stecker, Sr. Domenica Di Peri and Lucy Nardella in 1994, on the fiftieth anniversary of their graduation from Mary Help of Christians Academy. They're in the photo below – can you spot them?

The first graduating class of Mary Help of Christians Academy in North Haledon, New Jersey, in 1944.

Gallagher Construction Co. began the foundation and completed the construction.

By 1940, Mary Help of Christians Academy was ready and waiting. So were the students. Sr. Mary Palatini, the first Principal, began with the students of the ninth grade, and each year saw the addition of other students. From the commercial program, the school added the general program and finally, the academic program in order to complete the cycle and give the necessary choices to the students. Sr. Mary followed each student, and set the secondary education on the right track.

Don Bosco Hall was used as the gym and classes were held in the new Auxilium Hall (1941). Under the diligent preparation of Sr. Mary, Mary Help received accreditation from the State of New Jersey in 1944. Three decades later,

Sr. Mary Anne Zito chaired the Middle States Evaluation for accreditation in 1977.

The Sisters had met the challenge. They had felt that they had done something to prepare the girls for their future and a post-war nation.

Expansion in Texas and Pennsylvania

As we have seen, the dream that had begun in New Jersey did not stop there. It spread to neighboring states where it grew just as well as it did in its original foundations. Even during the war years, the mission of Don Bosco continued.

In Laredo, Texas, in 1943, Novices gather with Sr. Stella Ruiz, Sr. Anita Marinez, and Sr. Ida Chagin.

In answer to His call, Sr. Guadalupe Segura, with Sr. Julia Garcia and Sr. Mary De Filippi, opened a new mission in the valley at Raymondville, Texas, in January 1941. Saint Anthony Parish hosted the newcomers, and Father Clement Ayala gave his welcome. As always, the Sisters began their apostolate among the young. This soon evolved into the care of the school, religious education in the parish, and the evening gathering for adults and teenagers.

The young adults were particularly impressed with the Salesian joy and the vitality of the Sisters. Even though the school had to be closed 24 years later in 1965, a group of past pupils from Raymondville remain active in the church today, and come to see "their Sisters" on special occasions. Sr. Angelita Guzman joined the Sisters from Raymondville.

In 1942, Father Vincent Gallione, pastor in Ellwood City, Pennsylvania, asked for the Sisters' help. Four Sisters responded to the need of the new mission. The Sisters began among the parishioners, visiting families and giving catechesis either in groups or to individuals.

The Sisters did their very best. However, the pastor was not satisfied. He announced that he wanted a school begun with all grades. Of course, this meant teachers with degrees and appropriate pay – an impossible task! With regret the Sisters left the parish in June 1944. The Lord blessed the Sisters' work, nevertheless, with the vocation of Sr. Alice Fusco.

Meanwhile, five Sisters departed for Reading, Pennsylvania on August 15, 1942. The education of the children from kindergarten through Grade 8 was complemented with the preparation for the parish liturgy each Sunday. It was a small parish but with enough challenges for the five Sisters who worked with simplicity and love. Though the student body was never large, the children's ability to learn Gregorian Chant and to use this in the Sunday liturgy gave a new vitality to the Eucharistic celebration.

The parish was very happy with the Sisters' work. The summers were spent in teaching the faith daily to adults

Lined up for a procession are First Holy Communion children in Ellwood City, Pennsylvania.

and children. Activities for younger children coincided with Sunday visits to homes, to make friends of parishioners. After about 25 years, the parish lost so many parishioners that the pastor retired, and the diocese decided that neither school nor parish served any need in that section of the city. Goodbyes were difficult, but the friendships and prayers remained intact.

On January 2, 1943, Father Barbato asked the Sisters for help with another part of his parish. In Easton, a group of parishioners did not attend the parish, but had formed a kind of club to substitute for the lack of parish activities. He asked the Sisters to visit the families and offer some kind of religious service as part of their preparation to rejoin the parish.

Little by little, the Sisters were able to rekindle in many families the faith they had lost. The daily visits, the after-school presence with the children, the constant friendship and caring paid off. Precisely on the spot where the club met, the parishioners built a small chapel in which they worshipped and to which Father Barbato came weekly for instruction and the celebration of the Eucharist. Members of the Altar Society, the people who took care of the chapel, were the first to regularize their marriages and celebrate them properly as a sacrament. More than 200 families not only received the Sacrament of Matrimony, but also had children baptized and began to live Christian lives.

By 1966, both sections of the parish united in joyful celebration, and the Sisters formed one community in service to the parish of Saint Anthony in Easton. It was a wonderful accomplishment and good for all the people.

Changes in Haledon

Another change took place on September 12, 1943. The Novitiate was transferred to Villa Don Bosco on the adjacent Haledon property that had been purchased by the Sisters. It had a home with spacious rooms and beautiful gardens.

The three women who were guests at the Villa, and the four Sisters, Sr. Pierina Martinetto, Sr. Mary Paniga, Sr. Mary Pash, and Sr. Frances Werwas, transferred to the ex-novitiate building in North Haledon. This became known as Saint Joseph's, and would serve as an infirmary for the retired and ill Sisters for some years to come. Until the Novitiate was able to provide its own chapel and chaplain, the community worshipped in North Haledon.

Sr. Mary Paniga.

Sisters and students in front of their first house in Raymondville, Texas, 1953.

Sisters and students pay their respects
at the first Salesian Sisters' cemetery in Haledon.

Sr. Adelina Gastaldo was the directress of the Novices, Sr. Mary Canizzaro, the assistant, and Mother Antoinette Pollini, the former Provincial, was the superior and chef. The self-contained community for the Novitiate provided another step for better and continuous guidance and accompaniment during the two crucial years of the Novitiate.

In June 1944, the first graduation from Mary Help of Christians Academy took place. Sr. Mary Palatini, as first Principal, had seen the seven students through the four years of preparation. They were: Margaret L. Boos, Stella M. De La Rosa, Domenica R. Di Peri, Lena M. Galliano, Lucy R. Nardella, Ruth J. Stecker, and Frances C. Sweeney. It had

been a long and difficult path, but the students were prepared for their next step in life.

Truly, this milestone graduation was a nod from the Spirit that all goes well for those who love God and His children. In fact, Domenica Di Peri and Ruth Stecker asked to begin their preparation for the life of the Sisters! The first four Sisters to be housed in North Haledon now had counterparts in the high school graduates who would make their own mark as honest citizens and good Christians.

On September 15, 1945, after continued effort and correspondence, the official document that allowed the permanent location of the cemetery on the property at North Haledon was given by the State of New Jersey (thanks to the assistance of a relative of Sr. Veneranda Zammit). A public announcement was published in the *Paterson Evening News* on September 15, 1945 (but the consecration of the cemetery did not take place until 1948). It was a perfect location, allowing for visits, for remembrances, and for the telling of a history of those women who had made the narrative possible.

Mother Antoinette Pollini (1884-1960)

"An amusing incident occurred on the day of Sr. Erminia Moiso's funeral. As we were getting into the car to go from Saint Michael Church in Atlantic City to North Haledon for the burial, Mother noticed that I had no shawl. She immediately gave me hers. Some of the parishioners noticed it. In three weeks, every Sister in the community received a warm shawl as a Christmas gift since Mother Antoinette had to give hers away to Sister."

Sr. Philomena Martorana, FMA

The Salesian Sisters' cemetery as it appears today,
atop the hill in North Haledon.

New Beginnings in New York

The house and school of Holy Rosary in Port Chester, New York had a different beginning. The pastor of Holy Rosary Parish, the Salesian Father Aloysius Triffari, had acquired and remodeled a public school. Holy Rosary School began with 185 students enrolled from kindergarten through fourth grade. The large and spacious classrooms were built on the top of one of the hills.

Sr. Letizia Sampo and five Sisters began the mission among the young. They were: Sr. Mary Carone, Sr. Theresa Cianci, Sr. Mary Di Camillo, Sr. Marie Dunn, and Sr. Jane Sanchez. Their first residence consisted of two of the large classrooms in the school building. Francis Cardinal Spellman of New York came to bless the new building and its educative mission on the first Sunday of October, 1945. The decorations were beautiful sketches on every blackboard and special "God sees me" signs over every crucifix. An immense crowd gathered for the blessing with best wishes for every success.

The Sisters resided in the school until 1966 when every classroom had to used for the students. The parish constructed a convent to provide a home for the Sisters so that the students could be accommodated in the school. The chapel of the convent served also for the parishioners during the week. The school with its manifold activities lasted under the administration of the Salesian Sisters until 1992. Then, because of changes in the population trend, as well as the economic situation, some of the classrooms were used for social work and for parish activities.

Father Aloysius Trifari (right), Pastor of Holy Rosary Parish in Port Chester, invited the Salesian Sisters to open a school in 1945. Pictured with the first students are Sr. Theresa Cianci, Sr. Mary Carone, and Sr. Wilma Sanchez.

The eighth-grade class of Holy Rosary School, Port Chester, New York, in 1945,
makes good use of the library with Sr. Cecilia Lanzio, Principal, and their teacher, Sr. Winifred Elley.

The Sisters moved to the nearby convent in Corpus Christi Parish in Port Chester and commuted daily for a few years. In 2008, Holy Rosary School merged with Corpus Christi School (opened in 1959), under the leadership of the Salesian Sisters.

The work of the Sisters remains as a witness to the initial beginnings. Holy Rosary Parish continues as a beacon and a tribute to the Salesian priests who still minister to the Catholic population of the village itself.

Holy Rosary School, Port Chester, NY

"Many memories of the Salesian Sisters, especially Sr. Virginia D'Alessandro, my own classroom teacher, leap to my mind as I remember those wonderful years in elementary school. One thing which is very clear is the reverence of the Sisters at Mass. Our parish church was located about three blocks from our school. The Sisters' living quarters were located in the school building. They walked as a group to morning Mass and always sat together in the front pews. I remember the reverent way they walked back to their seats after receiving Holy Communion. There was almost a glow around them.

"At the time we had nine Sisters in our school. They taught us many things, some things simply by their wonderful example."

Ed Legutko, State College, Pennsylvania

Farewell, Mother Tullia

Mother Tullia came to the Province with a long history of missionary work, especially in India. Having lived in the austere poverty of India, Mother Tullia considered the "few" comforts the Sisters then enjoyed, superfluous. Therefore, she constantly spoke of mortification, backing her conferences and instructions by her own spirit of self-denial. She never demanded of her Sisters what she had not, or was not, practicing.

She loved the congregation so much that each of the visits to the individual communities became a search for vocations. However, her missionary life had taken a heavy toll. She was never well, but in 1945 she became seriously ill. An infection contracted in India progressively worsened until the doctor recommended that she be relieved of her responsibilities and that she return to her native Italy. When war conditions finally permitted Mother Tullia to return to Italy, she left behind memories of a very unassuming Sister imbued with the spirit of mortification and poverty, a religious who drew the Sisters to Christ more by her example than by her words.

It became necessary to appoint a Provincial again. The appointment fell once more on a person who had dreamed

Mother Tullia

of a missionary vocation, had prepared the dream of the original foundation, and had been a part of the dream in its earliest years.

Mother Antoinette Pollini had been happily carrying on her work as superior of the Novitiate, and had never anticipated serving as Provincial another term. If anything, Mother Antoinette had progressed to the point where God's will was the sole measure of her response, no matter what her own personal preferences might be. Most of the Sisters knew her well, and they thanked God for such an auspicious choice in leadership. Mother Antoinette would be God's instrument for beginning the Salesian Sisters' missions in both California and Canada.

Mother Antoinette began her second term as Provincial at about the same time that the Allied victory was declared on both fronts of action in Europe and Japan. The casualties had mounted during the war. Women had taken many of the jobs that had previously been the domain of men alone. There was dancing in the streets to mark the end of the war. Returning veterans were given the option of working or going to college on the G.I. Bill. Many of those who returned married and began families. Prosperity and signs of hope that there would be no more wars gave

In 1941 in Ybor City, Florida, the Most Holy Names School community included Sr. Mary Brucato, Sr. Christina Silencio, Sr. Magdaline Pezzaglia, Sr. Rose Bucci and Sr. Vincent Giaj Levra.

impetus to an increased sense of security and well-being.

The General Chapter meeting of the worldwide Salesian Sisters saw the mission in the context of history, and set a new direction to the mission in each country, giving more autonomy to the provinces to make the necessary choices. The experience of two World Wars that had cut off some provinces from the Center of the Institute was both enlightening and sobering for many of the issues that arose.

There was great rejoicing when Mother Caroline Novasconi, the former Provincial, was designated as an Extraordinary Visitor to the Province in 1949. June saw the flowering of nature when the special visitor was welcomed with great affection. A thanksgiving hymn to the good Lord for His tender love towards His daughters was on everyone's lips. The Sisters welcomed the visitor with joy and anticipation. The Sisters who knew her had spoken to the Sisters who did not, and enthusiasm grew with the expectation of great things to come.

After her visits to the various Sisters and the communities, Mother Caroline ended her visit with a general meeting in North Haledon for all the Sisters who could attend. She spoke with affection and with maternal concern for the Sisters. She told the assembled Sisters that they should have better meals. She recommended that a complete breakfast be served according to the custom of the nation, that some time for relaxation be set aside for the Sisters each day so that the recreation would be a time for easing the burden of the day's constant activity. She further recommended that English be used in community, and that English hymns should be generally used. She recommended that the summer camps be used for the formation and growth of the young people as good Christians and wholesome citizens. She stressed that resident students in North Haledon should be accepted only from the fifth grade and/or older in order to give the students the necessary education, allowing the younger students to remain in their own families, in an environment that was necessary for normal growth. She stressed the adequate spiritual and professional preparation of the younger Sisters before assigning them to the older students.

One last topic that Mother Caroline addressed was permission for Novices to make veils for First Communicants and some sacred vestments for particular occasions for the O'Toole Company in New York. This would help financially with the Novitiate's expenses, both for the candidates of the United States and Mexico.

The Sisters took to heart the recommendations and felt that a new era had begun in the history of the Province.

Sr. Frances Principale with four sisters who were resident students in North Haledon in 1943.

6

DISTANCE MEANS LITTLE TO GOD
The 1950's

"Cardinal James McIntyre of Los Angeles visited Saint Margaret Mary School. He admired the well-constructed facility and congratulated the parishioners on the functional and effective structure and especially, on the education given by the Salesian Sisters. He walked through the classes, and kept saying, 'Incredible… Good… Functional… Continue.' He left pleased and impressed by the tremendous work done in such a short time. He wished the best to each teacher, student, and family, satisfied that the Salesian Sisters were finally working in the Archdiocese of Los Angeles."

Oh, Canada! Relaxing by the Bay of Chafleur in New Brunswick are Sr. Suzanne Motte, Sr. Catherine Novo, and Sr. Gabrielle Lagace.

Journeying West, Again

While the nation was torn apart by issues of race and discrimination, it was thrust into a war on the Korean Peninsula. Through it all, Explorer I, the first American satellite, was launched. The hydrogen bomb was made. Racial segregation was banned in school. Rosa Parks refused to sit in the back of a bus, causing Dr. Martin Luther King, Jr., to lead the successful boycott of the Montgomery bus system.

All of these events did little to change the focus of the Salesian Sisters. There was only one criterion upon which a person's value was based: "It is enough that you are young for me to love you." And so, the Sisters did.

The United States Province was also confronted with some difficult decisions. Mother Antoinette Pollini and her Provincial Council had to take into account that the postwar years demanded different and difficult choices regarding the direction for the future. The year 1950 witnessed an expansion of the Province that few had foreseen or imagined. The historical advice of "Go West, Young Man," took on its feminine dimension as the Sisters literally took off for the West, to Lomita, California (near Los Angeles), and to San Francisco.

Both missions were many miles away, and while there was rejoicing, there were also tears. The Sisters knew from the experience with the Sisters who had been assigned to Watsonville, California that it would be some time before there would be a reunion of East and West. Nevertheless, congratulations, goodbyes, prayers, and best wishes prevailed, "till we meet again."

The Salesian priests were already working in the parish of Saints Peter and Paul in San Francisco. It was located in the North Beach section of the city, a section that had been settled largely by Italian immigrants. They had built a spacious and beautiful parish church, still today called the "Italian Cathedral." The marble, the statues, and

The girls of the Canadian oratory in 1954.

Sr. Frances Gumino with second-graders at Halloween in 1958.

the stained glass that decorate the church remain as a testimony to the faith of the original immigrants and the priests who inspired them. The parents, however, knew that the children needed to learn the language, the culture, and the ways of the new land, so they also constructed the school as part of the church. The school was reached by climbing more than 100 steps, as if one were on the way to Heaven!

The Presentation Sisters had helped establish the school and had collaborated with the Salesian priests from the beginning. For several years they had asked the Salesians if they could find other Sisters for the school. They were interested in beginning a private school of their own as soon as possible.

Both the Salesian Provincial of the West and the pastor, Father Joseph Costanzo, had repeatedly asked for the Salesian Sisters. Sr. Anita Ferrari, the first vocation from the parish, was already a professed Sister. This fact lent even more urgency to the request.

Sr. Letizia Sampo and six Sisters headed for San Francisco on August 19, 1950. The Sisters chosen for this new foundation were Sr. Anita Ferrari, Sr. Florence Bona, Sr. Elvira Lombardini, Sr. Veronica Milyo, Sr. Wilma Sanchez, and Sr. Irene Zaccagnino. About 465 students were enrolled, so two Salesian priests helped in some classes for a while until the Sisters were able to hire the necessary teachers to complete the staffing.

School finally opened on September 5, 1950. The playground and parking lot were literally lined with parents eager to get a glimpse of the Sisters of Don Bosco. Father Costanzo had introduced the Sisters at the Eucharist celebrated on various Sundays, but this first day of school proved very satisfying to many parents.

The Province's Golden Jubilee was celebrated with Msgr. Cianci, Sr. Antoinette Agliardi, Bishop McNulty, Sr. Frances Delfino, and Mother Josephine Galassi.

A picnic welcome for Mother Caroline Novasconi in Easton, Pennsylvania.

The work was somewhat difficult because the area was slowly being transformed into a commercial center. The Italians gradually relocated to the suburbs, since with their new homes, they were also able to have some land for gardens and trees. Chinese and Japanese immigrants bought most of the houses left vacant. The relocation of the Italian families posed a problem for the parish, but the conviction that evangelization was as important as keeping the faith has allowed the mission to be alive and well to this day.

Farther south in the Golden State, on August 13, 1950, Sisters headed for Saint Margaret Mary School and Parish in Lomita: Sr. Lydia Carini as Principal, Sr. Josephine Cardone, Sr. Claire Perino, Sr. Louise Vallese, and Sr. Mary Winterscheidt. Mother Antoinette, the Provincial, accompanied them. The pastor, Father John Vincent Hegarty, and parishioners welcomed the Sisters to the parish and school.

A construction workers' strike had delayed the completion of the school, but this did not discourage the Sisters. The children were registered from first through sixth grades. One grade found shelter in the parish church itself. One grade settled in a garage. Several began regular classes in private homes. One class settled in an empty room of another house. The parishioners provided these spaces without any expectation of compensation and at their own personal inconvenience. The Sisters, of course, took no notice of the sacrifice on their part. The construction of the school proper was finally completed and the moving took place during Christmas vacation.

Cardinal James McIntyre visited the school on the Feast of the Epiphany. He admired the well-constructed facility and congratulated the parishioners on the functional and effective structure and especially on the education

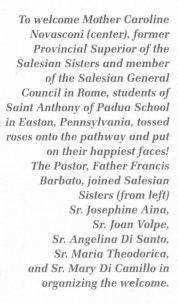

To welcome Mother Caroline Novasconi (center), former Provincial Superior of the Salesian Sisters and member of the Salesian General Council in Rome, students of Saint Anthony of Padua School in Easton, Pennsylvania, tossed roses onto the pathway and put on their happiest faces! The Pastor, Father Francis Barbato, joined Salesian Sisters (from left) Sr. Josephine Aina, Sr. Joan Volpe, Sr. Angelina Di Santo, Sr. Maria Theodorica, and Sr. Mary Di Camillo in organizing the welcome.

given by the Sisters. He walked through the classes, and kept saying, "Incredible... Good... Functional... Continue..." He left impressed by the tremendous work done in such a short time. He wished the best to each teacher, student, and family, pleased that the Salesian Sisters were finally serving in the Archdiocese of Los Angeles.

The school progressed and became a landmark for the parish. Three priests and at least ten Sisters were part of the results of the education given, including Sr. Patricia King, Sr. Marie Gannon, Sr. Guadalupe Arroyo, Sr. Barbara Campbell, and Sr. Beatrice Valot.

One feature can be cited that still made a connection between East and West and shows how little distance means to God. One day, the Provincial Office in North Haledon received a call from Saint Margaret Mary Parish to ask which Sister principal was named "Frances," since it was not on record. One of the stained glass windows of the Church had been dedicated to the memory of "Sr. Frances Principale." To whom did it refer?

The answer was easy. "Principale" was the surname of Sr. Frances, one of the Sisters from New York City who had died at the age of 22 in North Haledon. Her family had moved to the parish of Saint Margaret Mary and had opted to remember their deceased daughter through the memorial window. The family saw this as a loving way to have her remembered and to guarantee that prayers would be said on both the East and West coasts in her memory.

New Calls from Texas

In the 1950's, a new call came from the Diocese of Austin, Texas. Saint John Church in San Marcos was the only Catholic Church in this university town. In the shadow of the campus of Southwest Texas State University, the alma mater of President Lyndon B. Johnson, the Sisters began their work in school and in religious education classes for the youth of the area. Because of the need and the people's inevitable difficulties with language and culture, the mission soon spread to the *barrios*. The transition was smoothed over by the Sisters who knew how to make the best of both cultures, the university students with their particular questions and needs, and the Hispanics who made up the bulk of the permanent residents. It was from here that Sr. Margaret Natal joined the Sisters. Other places asked for the Sisters, and they expanded as far as they could.

In 1951, Father John Morkovsky, the Superintendent of Catholic Schools who was later to become the Bishop of Houston, Texas, visited Saint John Bosco School on West Travis in San Antonio. While he was impressed with such a large enrollment, he found the school building to be inadequate, and urged the Sisters to move to more suitable quarters. Sr. Anita Marinez, the Superior, encouraged by Father Peter Caballer, C.M.F., Pastor of San Fernando Cathedral, asked Archbishop Robert E. Lucey if the Salesian Sisters could serve at San Fernando Cathedral School which needed an administrator and teaching staff. While Archbishop Lucey did not grant the request at that time, he

Aspirants Teresita Delgado and Rosalba Garcia enjoyed a picnic in Laredo, Texas, in 1953. They were best friends from San Antonio.

reconsidered, and in 1954, granted permission to the Sisters. This allowed the Sisters time to seek out an adequate site and the financing for the venture of moving Saint John Bosco School. The major criterion for the Sisters was that the future site also be in a low-income part of the city, as was West Travis.

The growth of the church and of the educational establishments in Texas was caught up in the rapid development of the United States as a whole. The talk of accreditation, of verifiable competence of teachers (with degrees), and of effective administrative procedures were realities to be faced. Once again, it was the first Sisters, aided by the enthusiastic and creative leadership of Sr. Consuelo Spezia and Sr. Aida Chagin, who recognized the need to prepare the personnel. Blessed with vision and creativity, they helped organize the formation program. Arrangements were made for the new candidates to be formed in the Province of the United States, to take care of the language requirements, the teaching degrees, and certification.

The statue of Saint Mary Mazzarello is installed at Mother Mazzarello Hall in North Haledon, New Jersey, in the 1950s.

The statue as it looks today.

Honoring the Newest Saint

Taking into account that more space in North Haledon was (again!) a necessity, because of the increase in both the number of students and of initial formation candidates, the Provincial Council decided that the construction of an addition to the school was imperative. This addition to Auxilium Hall, which would be called Mazzarello Hall, opened in September 1950.

Bishop Thomas Boland of Newark blessed the new three-story building. It had a large dormitory with showers and rest rooms for the resident students on the third floor. This floor directly connected to the White House; the second floor had a functional kitchenette and cafeteria plus a study hall and a library for the students. The ground floor consisted of a large recreation area with rooms for yearbook

production and maintenance, as well as room for varied games and activities.

Less than one year later, an unforgettable day occurred on June 24, 1951. Mother Mary Domenica Mazzarello, the co-founder of the Salesian Sisters, was declared a Saint! It was a triumph for her who was so humble that she was compared to a hidden, fragrant violet. Sixteen Sisters and three alumnae departed for Rome on June 20. There they participated in the celebrations. They returned on August 16, filled with awe and experiences that they willingly retold. Energized by their vivid narratives, the celebrations in the Province became a triumph for Mother Mazzarello. At the same time, the event created a school of study, research, and spiritual growth for the Sisters.

The celebration of the canonization of Saint Mazzarello at Saint Patrick's Cathedral in New York City proved to be the highlight of 1951. Eighteen buses left Paterson for New York. The chronicler added that even nature cooperated because clear weather with just enough sunshine joined in the day's celebrations!

The students of the schools and youth centers throughout the Province celebrated the joyful event on September 17 at Saint John Cathedral in Paterson. Sisters, parents, teachers, and friends joined in the solemn Eucharistic celebration. Afterwards, all enjoyed a gala dinner in North Haledon.

This joyous event at the beginning of the school year marked the continuation of celebrations in each one of the schools, parishes, and centers. Past pupils, parents, friends, and well-wishers joined in specific celebrations throughout the Province. Some places began a Mother Mazzarello Club for the older students so that they could study the life of the new saint and learn of the contributions she gave to the Salesian spirit of Saint John Bosco.

Canada Calls

We can smell the sweet flowers of success, but if we want to pick them, we have to get up. We have ideas, but if we're going to use them creatively, we don't wait for life to hand them to us on a silver platter. Sisters and young women acted on the dream, once again!

The celebrations of the canonization of Mother Mazzarello were still resonating with joy when the Saint Philip the Apostle Province of the Salesian Sisters went international. In 1953, their dreams for youth slipped almost unnoticed across the border into Canada.

Sr. Joanne Passarelli (1899-1976)

"Sr. Joanne loved each novice dearly. She was always on the lookout for little things that would make us happy. Sometimes, she would approach me and ask my honest opinion about the food. She wanted to be assured that we Novices were not being subjected to unnecessary sacrifices."

Sr. Mary Mullaly, FMA

Aspirants enjoy a New Jersey snowfall in February 1958.

Sr. Joanne Passarelli, Sr. Catherine Novo, Sr. Suzanne Motte, and Sr. Gabrielle Cottet, plus Sr. Antoinette Beltramo, the financial administrator of the U.S. Province, entered Canada and settled in one of its northeastern provinces: New Brunswick, near the Bay of Chaleur in the village of Pointe Verte. These Sisters joined the original dreamers who had crossed the Atlantic from Italy and arrived in New York.

They began their mission in a small house across the street from the parish church and adjacent to a new school under construction. On the other side of the house, the Atlantic Ocean ended in the Bay of Chaleur.

The community was something of a microcosm: Sr. Joanne Passarelli was American, Sr. Gabrielle Cottet was Swiss; Sr. Suzanne Motte came from France, and Sr. Catherine Novo from Italy. To further complicate the cultural and linguistics issues, the Sisters had to teach in English since the government schools gave all the exams in that language, while the everyday language spoken in the families and the parish was French.

Pointe Verte had a very active pastor, Father Francis Casey, and his parish of Saint Vincent de Paul was situated in a small village of fishermen and loggers. Some farming was done in the short growing season. The children frequented a small rural school adjacent to the convent. In fact, two classes were conducted in the convent itself. The house of the Sisters had a chapel, a kitchen, a dining room, and four bedrooms. The small hall that housed the two classrooms completed the edifice.

The pastor knew the Salesian Priests. He had long asked for the presence of the Sisters in the parish to help especially with the youth, who had nowhere to go and nothing to do during the long, harsh winter months. He hoped that the Sisters would improve the life of his parishioners, especially in religious instruction and the complete education of the person.

The children of the parish had long ago outgrown the two little existing schoolrooms. The new, larger school for

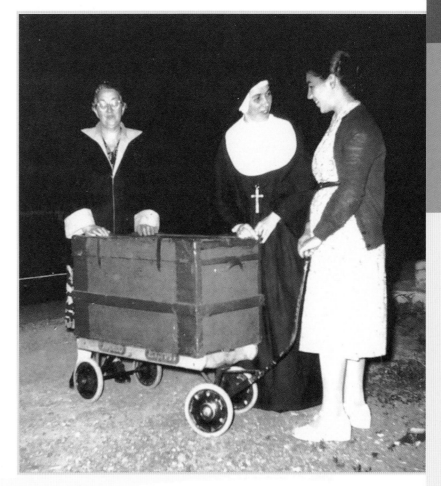

In Canada, Sr. Suzanne Motte welcomes a new vocation, Claudette Parent, with her mother and a trunk of belongings.

the district, though requested by the pastor, was financed by the government and was still under construction. This gave the Sisters some time to orient themselves, get the necessary licenses to teach, and meet the people, especially the children.

On October 1, 1953, the official date for the opening of the school year, the Sisters entered the school for the first time. The first week of school was an event in itself. The whole village was buzzing with excitement and everyone took turns to meet the Sisters and to receive the assurance that they were really there to stay. The 78 students were placed under the protection of Saint John Bosco and Saint Mary Mazzarello.

The Sisters themselves had prepared a novel event for the end of the first week. They invited the children to join them on Sunday afternoon at the Oratory. In Don Bosco's

tradition, the Oratory was a blend of youthful exuberance and consisted of games, prayer, music, refreshments, and friendship. For Don Bosco and Mother Mazzarello, the Oratory was a form of captivating the young and, through all sorts of activities, forming them into honest citizens and good, moral, wholesome human beings.

Young and not-so-young were intrigued by the idea. Who had ever seen Sisters who could out-play, out-run, and out-yell all the young people? The Sisters were also extremely good at making prayer creative and enticing, and they smiled at everyone. Yet, they noticed the child who was lonely, the girl who didn't know the game, the adult who needed a friend or a confidante. The Oratory was such a success that it took place every Sunday and every holiday.

On November 3, a new pastor, Father Henri Leveque, arrived. He proved to be a friend to the Sisters. In his farewell speech, Father Casey publicly announced, "I can now retire in peace, since I have brought the Salesian Sisters to Pointe Verte."

At the end of the first year, Sr. Joanne Passarelli asked for a change of assignment. She could not tolerate the rigors of the cold winter that seemed never to end (a popular song expressed this concept: "My land is not land; it's snow"). Sr. Rose Oliveri succeeded her. This move was providential for both the community and the school. Sr. Rose, as the first principal of the regional high school, was able to implement and stabilize the regular scholastic programs demanded by the state, while at the same time she also implemented the initial formation program for the candidates. Under her guidance, a viable educational community flourished in the area.

On April 3, 1954, the death of Sr. Angelina Andorno came as a reminder of one's mortality. She was 84 years old and had been professed for 60 years. As leader of the missionary Sisters who had arrived in 1908, she was simple in her lifestyle, made few demands on others, and coped with the new customs, the new formation of the Sisters, and, especially, with the new language and the accreditations necessary in the new schools. She loved the Sisters, and tried to give them whatever help she could. She encouraged and enjoyed any gathering of the Sisters in the Provincial House. She suffered from heart trouble during the later years, yet she never expected any special care or attention.

Simple, prayerful, and always loving, she expected little from others, but did all she could to ensure that the spirit of Don Bosco and Mary Mazzarello remained alive among the Sisters and the young people.

Mother Theresa Casaro, Provincial (center) prepares new Postulants, Sr. Ann Hottot (right), and Sr. Alphonsine Roy, a future Provincial in Canada.

A New School in New Jersey

In 1954, the Sisters undertook the opening and administration of Saint Anthony School in Elizabeth, New Jersey. The Salesians had a thriving parish for the immigrant Italian families, and it was time to take care of the education of the children. The kindergarten and first grade class opened in September 1954 with 74 students. The enrollment increased as a new facility opened. This enabled students to be enrolled in all grades. Sr. Joanne Passarelli was the first Superior and Principal.

By 1958, a new edifice, with all the amenities that the development of the parish and school required, was completed. The new building was blessed in 1958 and is still one of the great achievements of the parish. Not too many years later, the Sisters' convent was also constructed, and this helped in the total mission of education for the parish itself. The Oratory, popularly known as the Salesian Girls' Club, immediately attracted the young girls, and the camp began that summer. Religious instruction for the public school children was added during the school year. The educational mission continued with Sr. Marie Dunn as Principal and flourished for many years.

Also in 1954, Bishop James McNulty of Paterson asked for at least two Spanish-speaking Sisters who would be willing to dedicate themselves to the assistance and spiritual welfare of the many Puerto Ricans flocking into the Paterson and Passaic areas. Sr. Stella Ruiz and Sr. Jane Sanchez responded to this need, entirely new to the Province. These two missionaries, in imitation of Our Lady, and with the "Magnificat" in their hearts, began to establish contacts, encouraging people to attend the Sunday liturgies, setting up visits to the families in order to provide religious instruction, and to facilitate contact with the social services needed for the newcomers. Soon Sr. Mary Arciga and Sr. Theresa Murillo joined them in this mission.

The first community to serve at Saint Anthony Parish in Elizabeth, New Jersey, in 1954 included Sr. Theodora Carabin, Sr. Joanne Passarelli, and Sr. Mary Carone.

The Bishop gave them a station wagon for travel throughout the Diocese. This helped tremendously, and the mission soon showed the wisdom of the Bishop in his care for the new arrivals. The visits to the families and the constancy of the Sisters saw 74 Baptisms of adults and the Sacrament of Matrimony celebrated in 114 households by the end of a year. This made a tremendous impact on the people themselves as well as on the growth of the Paterson Diocese. The Sisters continued to live in the Provincial House until a center for the spiritual direction of the Hispanic mission was established, first in Paterson, then in Passaic and the surrounding areas.

Sr. Grace Ruiz joined the Hispanic apostolate at Our Lady of Fatima Parish in Passaic, New Jersey.

California and Texas Flower

During the springtime of 1955, the extraordinary visit of the Very Reverend Renato Ziggiotti, the Rector Major of the worldwide Salesian Congregation, gave a special timbre to the Province of the Sisters. It was the first time that a visit by Don Bosco's successor to the U.S. took place. Many of the Sisters from the various houses gathered in North Haledon to greet the visitor and to participate in a special liturgy. He exclaimed, "We men have merely buildings. You Sisters have a wonderful park. With the academic culture, you also unite nature's oxygen and beauty." He greeted everyone, Sisters and students, and then celebrated Mass for the intentions of all. It was a welcome and unexpected visit, as if Don Bosco himself had deigned to come so that all could be affirmed in the education of youth.

Mother Josephine Galassi and Sr. Nancy Zingale with a young charge in North Haledon.

Another and completely unexpected need arose in the Province during 1955. In the environs of Los Angeles, the education in Lomita was flourishing, and the Salesian parish of Dominic Savio in Bellflower asked for the Sisters to administer and staff the school. From Paterson, Sr. Marie Dunn, Sr. Mary Rusciano, and Sr. Lucy Balistrieri joined Sr. Elvira Lombardini from San Francisco.

Here, too, the school flourished and vocations blossomed. From its inception, the spiritual life of the students had priority, and the response of the girls was as unhesitant and open as the landscape. School officially opened on September 11, 1956, with 279 students. By 1960, the number had increased to over 600.

A small, one-family house provided a temporary residence for the Sisters. Since the house had no chapel and the church was not yet erected, the Sisters celebrated the Eucharist with the neighboring Saint John Bosco School for boys. Good times alternated with difficult times at the beginning, but the signs of progress attested to God's unfailing help and the generosity of the Sisters.

Many of the girls followed in the footsteps of the Sisters. Stella Tafoya, Sally Brown, Grace Ruiz, Mary Mullaly, Elaine Reeves, Jean Erickson, Kathleen Curd, Juanita Chavez, Phyllis Neves, and Patricia Roche are among the names of Sisters who have become familiar in the annals of the Province.

In San Antonio, Texas, a site was finally found "out in the country" for the relocation of Saint John Bosco School. With the help of Petrita Wallingford, the aunt of Sr. Esther Lopez, the protective counseling of Gayetano Lucchese, a Salesian Cooperator and benefactor, and Allen Menger who authorized the construction loan, the building began to take shape. The property, duly deeded and signed, saw the building of a modern school in the district. Though the trees and brush were still to be cleared, the presence of the school brought water and utilities into the district, while the Sisters' presence did a great deal for the establishment of a stable community.

Sr. Jane Sanchez became the first Sister to obtain a driver's license! She's driving the first Province car as Sr. Stella Ruiz happily looks on.

The groundbreaking of the "new" Saint John Bosco School on 36th Street and West Commerce took place on March 21, 1956, with Rector Major Ziggiotti, Mother Ersilia Crugnola, Provincial of the Mexican Province, and various other officials in attendance. The blessing of the new school took place on September 1, 1957.

The Sisters were also blessed in their neighbors. The Williamses, the Fraeymans, the Langfelds, and others helped in numerous ways. Mr. Williams, an attorney, lived on the property across the street from the Sisters. He stated that he had known the people before the Sisters came, and could vouch for the change in attitude and behavior of the families and their children since the Sisters' arrival. He wanted to be included in the work of the Sisters and deeded his property across the street, from 36th Street to the creek, for the educational work of the Sisters at Saint John Bosco School. Later on, the property was used as the site for the new Western Provincial quarters, opened in 1993.

The school drew a population and homes began to be built. A neighborhood became a reality on the west side of San Antonio. Mr. and Mrs. Williams kept a refrigerator and a freezer on their front porch with the sign, "Take what you need." Many of the poor did just that. The people were willing to work, and the presence of a school did more than any other single factor to give a sense of purpose and dignity to the residents of the area.

Sr. Margarita Moreno was instrumental not only in finding the location at West Commerce Street, but also the organization and early development of Saint John Bosco School at the present site. Sr. Aida Chagin, whose intrepid leadership gave a tremendous boost to the Sisters' mission in Texas, expanded upon the original plans for the school.

Mother Theresa Casaro (1913-1974)

"It was Mother Theresa who taught me how to apply Don Bosco's 'Preventive System' in a practical way. I shall never forget the love with which she followed the needs of the resident students. After her 'Good-nights,' she'd have a long line of girls waiting to see her about a problem, etc. One night, after waiting half an hour for her to finish, and realizing how tired she must have been, I told the last girls to see her the next morning. Mother was very displeased with me. 'How can you let the girls go to bed with something disturbing them?' she asked me. She was motherliness personified."

Sr. Rosalie Di Peri, FMA

Golden Jubilee

The Salesian Minor Seminary for the training of new priests, located in Ipswich, Massachusetts, had asked for help from the Sisters. In November 1957, three Sisters, Sr. Antoinette Agliardi, Sr. Anna Capra, and Sr. Anna Ragogna took up residence in a little rustic cottage on the lovely wooded property of Sacred Heart Juniorate.

For nearly twenty years, the Sisters poured their energies, prayer, and sacrifice into year-round domestic services for the Salesians, seminarians, weekend retreats, and summer camps. Sr. Antoinette, one of the pioneers, set the style of silent, joyful service. Paying no attention to the burden of her advancing years, she devoted herself to the

Sisters' community and served with the marvelous serenity and orderliness that had characterized her. Often she would slip down to the kitchen before meals to help carry pots and pans, returning words of thanks with the unfailing smile of one who carries a hidden Treasure in her heart.

Sisters such as she were also treasures of the Province as it celebrated its Golden Jubilee on July 18, 1958, reviewing the blessings and difficulties of fifty years of life. The celebration of the solemn Eucharist at Saint Michael's with Bishop McNulty lent the appropriate air of solemnity. However, since summer camps and classes were in full swing, and Mother Josephine Galassi was about to leave to take part in the General Chapter in Italy, plans for additional festivities were delayed until her return in the fall of that year. These were the projections of the Province leadership. But God had other plans.

In August, Mother Josephine and the delegate, Sr. Caroline Stazzi, sailed for Italy. As was customary, Mother Josephine left everything in order. During the General Chapter, she did not feel well, but attributed her condition to the change of food, climate, and work. When she fell ill during the return voyage in the fall of 1958, the ship's doctor diagnosed it as a simple case of seasickness.

The Provincial arrived at Ward Street to be greeted by an exultant throng of Sisters and young people with song and flowers. A short while later, pleading tiredness, she retired. It was during the night that her condition became critical. The priest and doctor both came to her bedside, and she was rushed to Saint Joseph's Hospital.

It was too late. Mother Josephine was pronounced dead of pneumonia in the early morning. What a shock everyone had! Her bags were still unpacked in her room. No one could believe it. Even in the Provincial House, her death seemed an impossible event. Today, her memory still lingers among the Sisters tinged with joy and sorrow as the Sisters remember her jovial goodness, her ready wit, and her unexpected and untimely death.

Gathered on July 16, 1958, to honor the 50th anniversary of the arrival of the first Sisters are Sr. Rena Ossi, Sr. Louise Passero, Mother Josephine Galassi, Sr. Frances Delfino, Sr. Mildred Zanetti, and Sr. Alice Fusco.

A successor for Mother Josephine was not announced until January 1959. The Sisters accepted Mother Theresa Casaro as the eighth Provincial with joy and sisterly enthusiasm. She finished the year as Principal of Mary Help of Christians School in New York City, passed the summer in North Haledon, and moved into the Provincial House at the end of September.

Her gentleness and piety had been proverbial ever since her arrival from Italy as a missionary in 1947. "Her intelligence and her determination helped her learn the English language in a short time. Her conferences and 'good nights' provided spiritual nourishment, achieving the positive through being positive," recalls a future Provincial, Sr. Judith Suprys.

In Ipswich, Massachusetts, Sr. Michelle Corrado (and bicycle!), Sr. Mary Baroni, and Sr. Frances Mitacchione.

Sr. Rose McShane directs the Sisters' choir in 1959.

Newton

Mother Theresa arranged that the postponed Province Golden Jubilee celebration coincide with the blessing of the new Sacred Heart Novitiate in Newton, New Jersey. The solemn function took place on April 11, 1959, a thanksgiving celebration for fifty years of grace and spiritual development, and a petition for the years that lay ahead. The petition drew blessings beyond the expectations of the most optimistic individuals.

One month later, on May 14, 1959, the Novices moved from Haledon to their new home. The cinderblock construction, encircled by spurs of blue mountains, was full of light and airy space. The chapel was not only the best room in the house, but it was a testimony to the new liturgical innovations. The Novices moved from Haledon, and Novitiate life settled into its formative routines of prayer, study, and work. A sense of family and peacefulness, true to the Salesian spirit, imbued the place.

That same summer, the spiritual retreats for the Novices as well as for the Sisters were organized in the Novitiate. The Postulants and Novices began their retreat on July 27 and were joined by the Sisters on the 29th. The week of intense prayer and instruction culminated on August 5, Feast of Our Lady of the Snows. As at Mornese in 1872, the day witnessed several impressive functions: the reception of the Postulants into the Novitiate; the first profession of the second year Novices; the renewal of vows by temporary professed Sisters; and the solemn final profession of Sisters.

For the Sisters who had already passed these milestones in their religious formation, the events were an impetus to a recommitment of life and love in the service of God through the education of youth. From this first retreat through the following years, the retreats held in Newton also allowed the summer activities in North Haledon to continue to the end of July. Sacred Heart Novitiate, in its new location, provided a welcome and truly secluded place for the Novices.

Corpus Christi Parish

On September 2, 1959, the Sisters responded positively to the request of Father Peter Rinaldi, pastor of Corpus Christi Parish in Port Chester, New York, for a new school. Father Rinaldi was the uncle of the future Sr. Mary Rinaldi and nephew of Blessed Philip Rinaldi, third successor of Saint John Bosco of the Salesian priests and Brothers. Sr. Ida Ossi, Sr. Frances Gumino, Sr. Theodore Carabin, and Sr. Concetta Ragusa arrived to begin the educational venture amid best wishes and special welcomes.

Two hundred students from kindergarten through fourth grade registered and began their classes on September 14. On the Sunday after Easter, 1960, Cardinal Francis Spellman came to the parish for the blessing of the school, convent, and the athletic center. The band played, the students sang, and the parishioners clapped and enjoyed the event. The Pastor felt that he had done something positive for his parishioners and for the Church.

Mother Theresa Casaro leading the procession into Don Bosco Hall. This is an example of a religious clothing ceremony in the 1950's.

The addition of a class each year until the eighth grade soon completed the elementary education program. A vital catechetical program for the high school students of Port Chester High School every Thursday afternoon rounded out the parish program. The preparation for the Sacraments proved to be the crowning achievement of the religious education given in the parish.

Corpus Christi students are still part of the mission of the Sisters, and the generations of past students

Sr. Jane Sanchez with children in Passaic, New Jersey, in 1954.

attest to the vibrancy of the service that the Sisters have given to the parish of Corpus Christi from that first response to the invitation of Father Rinaldi.

More Canada

At the Parish of Saint Augustine in Lagacéville, Canada, the first community began on September 3, 1959. It consisted of Sr. Victoria Graziani, Sr. Gabriele Cottet, Sr. Jacqueline Roy, and Sr. Amelia Callegarin. Sr. Antoinette Beltramo, the financial officer for the Province, remained until all legal and religious aspects of the new foundation were completed.

One of the real difficulties the Sisters faced was that the children were in nine small schools spread throughout the area. The education of the area's children was in disarray, and many of them had not completed the necessary requirements.

The Sisters began their work with the children from the sixth through twelfth grades with the help of Mrs. Edmund LeBoutillier. The departmental setup of the classes allowed Sr. Victoria to teach English to all the classes, and the other Sisters taught in French. It is interesting to note that the stipend for the Sisters amounted to $633.33 monthly, and this was the budget on which the Sisters calculated their living expenses.

In 1955, the Salesian Rector, Father Renato Zigiotti, S.D.B. (seated) visited Holy Rosary School in Port Chester, New York. Welcoming him were (left-right) Sr. Amalia Gatti, Sr. Patricia Winterscheidt, Sr. Elisa Madriz, Sr. Amalia Aichino, Sr. Antoinette Casertano, Sr. Virginia D'Alessandro, Sr. Mary Rose Barale, Sr. Stella Tafoya, and Sr. Anna Forte.

7 CHANGE AND RENEWAL

The 1960's

"Holy Father, Pope Paul VI, we are the Daughters of Mary Help of Christians, the Salesian Sisters of Saint John Bosco from the United States. We live far, yes, but we are always close to the Vicar of Christ."

Mother Theresa Casaro visits with the aspirants in Aptos, California, in 1962.

Aspirants in the West

Racial confrontation, the Cuban missile crisis, and Vietnam catalyzed a decade of unrest, and the counterculture was its expression. Politicized college campuses, mass marches – it seemed as if a whole generation had taken to the streets. Charismatic leaders who effected powerful change and held promise for an even greater nation were assassinated in soul-sickening succession: John F. Kennedy, Dr. Martin Luther King, Jr., and Robert F. Kennedy.

The Catholic Church began to change amid some confusion and opposition. The consecrated life of priests and religious was questioned. Vatican II mandated changes in music and liturgical celebrations, and religious life. Frustration, questions, and rebellion became a way of life. Above all, confusion reigned.

The Civil Rights Act became the first step in bringing equality to all people. Dr. Martin Luther King Jr. gave his famous speech, "I Have a Dream," in which he said, "I have a dream that one day a person is judged by the character of his soul and not by the color of his skin."

And the Salesian Sisters? They, too, were interested in souls and lived Don Bosco's motto: "Give me souls, take away the rest!"

The first Candidates from the West had already settled in for the initial years of formation in the community of Saints Peter and Paul in San Francisco; it seemed inopportune to have Candidates travel 3,000 miles in order to begin their formation in religious life. In 1960, the Province purchased property in Aptos, California. To meet the needs of the Candidates, a high school was begun under the name of Mary Help of Christians. Proper accreditation was important to the Candidates beginning their formation in the Western part of the Province.

San Fernando Cathedral School Drum
and Bugle Corps in San Antonio, Texas, in 1964.

Saints Peter and Paul School had a marked and dramatic effect on the population of this important Western city. Many of the students in the early years were from families of first and second-generation Italian immigrants, and were, therefore hardworking and loyal to the Catholic faith. Father Joseph Costanzo and the priests of the parish were partners with the parents in taking care of the young. In fact, the Boys' Club was a focal point for the young men of San Francisco. Five young men became priests, and the Sisters also had girls who asked for admission to the formation program.

Sr. Anita Ferrari was already a Sister when the Sisters began their mission in the parish and school. Sr. Fernanda Rossi, Sr. Filomena Conti, Sr. Kathleen Gibson, Sr. Rosann Ruiz, Sr. Celine Lomeli, Sr. Rachel Crotti, and Sr. Lucy Yuen are some of the vocations that came from the parish.

Mary Help of Christians Academy

"For my two sisters and me, our arrival in the U.S. from Cuba in the Sixties was mostly a smooth transition from the Salesian school we attended in Cuba. Mary Help of Christians Academy continued to build on the solid academic foundation we had brought with us. At a time when the uncertainty of seeing our family again was very painful, the loving care provided by many of the Sisters was very comforting.

"Sisters such as Sr. Fernanda Rossi, Sr. Josephine Carini, Sr. Marcia Kelly, Sr. Rose Zorzi, Sr. Rose McShane, Sr. Mary Zito, Sr. Fanny Florez, Sr. Julia Mazorati, and others made Mary Help truly a home away from home. The many memories from the special moments throughout those years will be in our hearts and in those dear to us forever."

Amparo Navarro Velasco, one of the three Navarro Sisters (along with Josefa and Soledad), classes of '65, '66, '68

Saints Peter and Paul Church in San Francisco. To the left is the Salesian priests' rectory and the house to the right is the convent. The school is built within the framework of the church.

The school is still operating today. The population is largely Asian, since most of the Italian families have moved to other sections of the city. However, all the parents are happy to have their children frequent the school. The education is one that develops the young students' potential and prepares them for a multicultural, globalized society.

The Candidates of Texas, meanwhile, had also begun a preparatory school at Houston Street in Laredo, which later moved to the famous "pink house" on Del Mar Boulevard. From there, candidates left for Aptos or New Jersey to continue their formative years. While Texas at this time was still part of the Mexican Province, the need for Sisters who were accredited as educators in the schools of Texas and who spoke English fluently prompted this decision.

On the feast of the Immaculate Conception, December 8, 1960, Mother Antoinette Pollini departed the Province for her eternal home in heaven. All the Sisters, young and old, as well as the Aspirants, Postulants, and, especially, the Novices among whom Mother Antoinette had spent her final years, spoke of her holiness, her love of Mary, and her kindness to all.

She herself said, "I would rather spend time in Purgatory for having spent my time helping my Sisters and seeing them smile than make any Sister weep. Life is difficult enough, and it is our sacred duty to make it easier for each one of our Sisters."

Mother Antoinette occupies a special place in the history of the Province, and her name is forever blessed among the Sisters. Most Sisters remember her with the Rosary always in her hands, a smile on her lips, no matter where she was headed.

Mario's Steak House

In 1961, Three Maple Lodge, known in Newton, New Jersey, as Mario's Steak House, put a "For Sale" sign on its property. The house was run down, but the spacious property with woodland and pond was situated about a half-mile from the newly-constructed Sacred Heart Novitiate.

Mother Theresa Casaro, the new Provincial, saw God's hand in the "For Sale" sign and deemed it an opportunity to buy the property. The Province considered the place suitable for a camp to accommodate young people each summer. She brought the matter to the Provincial Council who discussed the possibility of using the site for some youth work. A cabin was built near the old lodge, and Camp Auxilium was born. Here, in the bright sunshine and open space, young people from six to 14 years of age would have a place during the summer in healthy activity far from the moral and physical dangers of the city streets.

Sr. Rosalie Di Peri, first director of Camp Auxilium, rides a pony as campers assist her in 1963.

Sr. Rosalie Di Peri became the first camp director. With the help of her sister, Sr. Domenica Di Peri, Sr. Theodora Carabin, and friends from both Roseto, Pennsylvania, and Port Chester, New York, she readied the Camp for about 40 girls who came in June 1961 as the first campers. They stayed for eight weeks that summer. The camp was given the name "Auxilium," the Latin word for "Helper" to recall the motherly presence of Our Lady, the Help of Christians.

Much remained to be done, not only in the cabin itself, but also in the lodge that served as a residence for the Sisters and to the wilderness that surrounded the camp site on three sides. However, the joy of living in an atmosphere

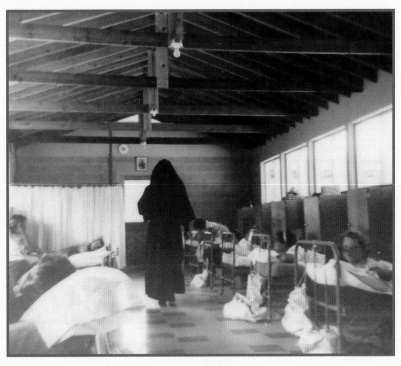

Campers sleeping in their cabins at Camp Auxilium as a dedicated Sister keeps watch over them in 1963.

of prayer and safety in true harmony with nature and the Salesian family spirit provided that permanent seal for this youth work. The same girls met at Camp Auxilium for successive summers, while improvements and new cabins were constructed.

While construction of the pool was under way, all work came to a sudden but temporary halt when the skeleton of a prehistoric mastodon was found during the excavation process! This created front-page news, and the entire area was blocked off until the archeologists were able to examine the area to ascertain whether all parts of the skeleton had been found. Once the excavation was completed, the Sisters donated the skeleton to the local museum.

Work on the pool continued, but it took longer than anticipated because of the "find." Arrangements were made to bring the campers to Swartswood Lake four miles away. So while the scientists combed the area for more treasures, the campers cooled off in the clear waters of the lake.

Each summer brought larger numbers of girls who spent all or part of their vacation at Camp Auxilium, either as resident or day campers. Constructed in 1965, a large recreation room became a sheltered play area on rainy days. Still today, along the front wall is a small chapel with folding doors to enclose the Tabernacle, altar, and kneelers. By retracting the doors, the spacious hall is transformed into a large chapel where the Eucharistic celebration could be a part of daily camp life.

In Lagaceville, Canada, girls arrive for the Saturday Oratory. Standing in the back are Sr. Alphonsine Roy, Sr. Diane Godin, Sr. Clemence Baudin, Sr. Estelle Johnson, and Sr. Suzanne Motte.

Camp counselors get ready to return to Swartswood Lake in their "Green Hornet" (as they called their stationwagon), with Sr. Rosalie Di Peri acting as chaperone.

Salesian Sisters fled Castro's Cuba in 1961 to live and work in the United States.

Another group of travelers, quite unexpected but certainly welcomed, arrived at the spacious Novitiate just a few days after the public celebration of the Feast of Saint Mary Mazzarello. Between May 24 and June 24, 1961, 84 Salesian Sisters, victims of anti-religious laws in Castro's Cuba, found a temporary home in Newton. With the exiled Sisters came 44 young women who took up residence at Mary Help of Christians Academy in North Haledon.

How did they get there? A real angel stepped in — Angel Oliva and his brother, Martin, of Tampa, Florida. Martin's wife, Alice, knew one of the secretaries in Washington, D.C., and traded oranges for quick processing of visa waivers. The Olivas paid for the Sisters' passage to the United States and sent them by bus to New Jersey. They knew the Sisters would be needed here and in other parts of the world – and they were!

All the houses in the Province joined forces to provide money, food, clothing, bedding, and other necessities for the refugees, while Mother Casaro, the Sisters, and the Novices did all in their power to ease the newcomers' sorrow and suffering. The Sisters found lodging in both the Novitiate and at Camp Auxilium in cabins that had housed the girls for the summer.

In July, their Provincial reassigned some of the Sisters to various Provinces, while others moved to North Haledon for English lessons. Sr. Theresa Franco, Sr. Elba Armas, Sr. Esther Cruz, Sr. Raffaella Penton, Sr. Gloria Machado, and Sr. Antonia Cvetko remained in the U.S. Province.

The first students arrived from Cuba in 1961 to study at Mary Help of Christians Academy in New Jersey.

Louisiana

Louisiana. The name is rich with centuries of historical associations: the scented brilliance of tropical flora; the varied accents of mingled languages; the proud memories of influential and varied cultures. Something of the diversified productivity of the Pelican State has characterized the presence of the Salesian Sisters in this southern state on the Mississippi.

The Sisters arrived in Baton Rouge in 1961 after years of prayer and repeated requests from the local diocese. Monsignor Louis Marineaux had pleaded with the Provincial to send Sisters to staff Our Lady of Mercy School long before its completion in 1954. Under the administration of Mrs. Clifford Blanchard, the school began with a staff of dedicated lay teachers.

When the media published the story of the Salesian Sisters fleeing to the States in the wake of Castro's takeover in Cuba, Monsignor flew to New Jersey to personally present his need. He told the Provincial that he would accept the Sisters from Cuba to begin the mission. His persistence won, and four Sisters, Sr. Teresa Franco, Sr. Elba Armas, Sr. Raffaella Penton, and Sr. Gloria Machado took up residence and began the mission, willing to learn the English language and American customs.

After this first year, the Province sent other personnel. With Sr. Filomena Conte as the administrator for the school and more than 650 students and 24 lay teachers in four buildings, the apostolate began in earnest. When Monsignor Andrew Frey was appointed pastor at Our Lady of Mercy, the spiritual life of the parish and school became even more intense. Improvements and growth occurred rapidly.

The Sisters became an integral part of the parish and, little by little, the "Preventive System" of Don Bosco and Mother Mazzarello took root. This system, an integral part of the Salesian charism around the world, sees education as a "matter of the heart." Children must not only be loved but

Cooking class at Mary Help of Christians Academy.

A Canadian newspaper welcomes the Salesian Sisters to Saint Claire Parish in Montréal in 1964.

must know that they are loved. The system, based on reason, religion, and loving kindness, seeks to prevent bad habits, instill good behavior and values, and build strong character.

Soon, catechetical instruction to public school students was incorporated into the program. This educational mission continued after 1987 when the division of the Province automatically relegated the staffing of Our Lady of Mercy School to the Western Province.

Canada

By September 1961, another dimension developed as the Oratory at Lavillette in New Brunswick, Canada, took shape. The Sisters began to commute to this little hamlet, and the work of the Oratory began.

To his very death, Father Patrick Doucet thought of his people, and among his last recommendations was the desire that a chapel be constructed at Lavillette. At his funeral, Bishop Camille Le Blanc presided, and the people asked the Bishop for a mission church for their area. Their hope was realized when, on June 25, 1962, the new mission church was dedicated to God in honor of Saint Dominic Savio. The Church became the focal point for worship and all other activities. In the dedication of the church, Bishop Camille LeBlanc expressed his sentiments that "the new mission church was erected to honor the presence of the Salesian Sisters who, with so much zeal and love, are dedicated to the young people of the district." Today, the church has been replaced with a new Church of Saint Dominic Savio.

The rapid expansion of the number of professed Sisters who returned to Pointe Verte, young and filled with the desire to promote Jesus and the mission of Don Bosco among their people, gave another boost to the work in Canada. Exchange of benefits and experiences helped spread the Kingdom. The Sisters kept in close communication and readily shared the dream among themselves and the youth of Canada.

Father Jean Émile Fournier arrived at Bertrand in 1954. The parish had been without a pastor, so there was much to be done. Father quickly set about the many tasks. He was a native of Pointe Verte and had seen the work of the Sisters. He asked for their collaboration in his parish, which was so much in need of revitalization. He was particularly interested in their work in the school and in youth ministry. He had already made the necessary repairs to the school, the rectory, and the church.

On June 27, 1961, Sr. Frances Miculin and Sr. Mary Palatini arrived at the parish of Saint Joachim in Bertrand to discuss the new field of labor. The negotiations were positive and the new community began in the parish on September 2, 1961. Sr. Frances Vegetabile, Sr. Raymonde Dery, Sr. Theresa Lagacé, and Sr. Monique Twyman were ready and willing to begin the mission. They were surprised to find two beautiful stained glass windows in the parish church representing Saint John Bosco and Saint Mary Mazzarello! They had preceded their daughters to Bertrand.

Besides the stained glass windows, another surprise awaited the Sisters in the church itself. After some observation, Sr. Frances asked, "Is this really a statue of Mary Help of Christians?" Father answered, "Yes, it truly is. She has been here a long time waiting for you."

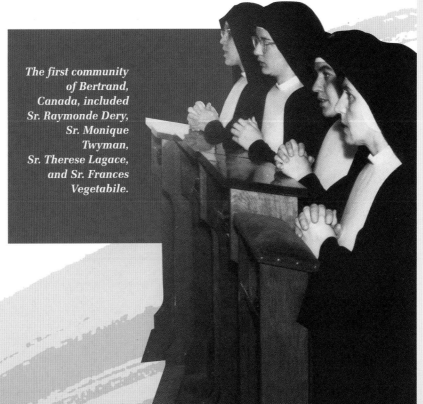

The first community of Bertrand, Canada, included Sr. Raymonde Dery, Sr. Monique Twyman, Sr. Therese Lagace, and Sr. Frances Vegetabile.

"Angelic" dancers perform in Lagaceville, Canada.

It was certainly part of the dream that no one had foreseen. Mary was already there ready to welcome the new community and take it under her protection. The opening of the Oratory on that first Sunday saw 72 young people who came to see and explore. The thought of the 72 disciples of Jesus instantly came to mind. The group was subdivided into three smaller groups, each with the magical and dear Salesian number: 24 (May 24 is the Feast of Mary Help of Christians).

On January 31, 1962, the Feast of Saint John Bosco was solemnly observed. All invited were asked to pray one Hail Mary with the same love with which Saint John Bosco had said the first one at Valdocco. Promptly and eagerly, the people responded. Nine girls went for an outing to Pointe Verte to meet the other Sisters and to interact with the Aspirants. After prayer, reflection, and discernment, six of these girls asked to remain for a time with the Sisters and Aspirants. Parents were reluctant, but eventually all six girls made the decision to come and see what the Lord wanted from them.

Sr. Rena Cormier was one of the girls who came on that day and gradually responded to the call of the Lord. After her religious profession, she spent time among the Sisters in New Jersey so that her formation could continue. Once her formation was complete, she returned to Canada and fulfilled her mission by helping in the formation and education of young children. Her availability, cheerfulness, and pleasant disposition have made her a positive presence in the communities of Sisters.

The number of young people who frequented the Oratory increased, and the Sisters set the upbeat rhythm of parish work, teaching, and liturgical animation. The communication among the communities at Lagáceville and Pointe Verte was strong and mutually enriching. The interactions between the young and the Sisters added wholesome and loving experiences to everyone's lives.

September 14, 1963 marked the 10th anniversary of a dream come true. Ten years earlier, four Sisters had arrived at Pointe Verte, the way four Sisters had arrived in New York harbor in 1908. Don Bosco's mission in Canada had developed beyond expectations. The Eucharistic celebration and the presence of the Provincial, Mother Theresa Casaro, were public thanks to God for the Salesian Sisters' presence in Canada, specifically in New Brunswick.

The daily paper, *L'Evangeline,* had a double page spread of the event, and congratulations poured in from many places and persons. The Gospel message was indeed the focal point of all the good done by the community of Sisters. The good news then radiated to wherever a Sister was present.

New Parishes, New Schools

Since many of the original parishioners of Saint Michael's in Paterson, New Jersey, had since moved to the suburbs, Msgr. Carlo Cianci constructed a chapel on West Broadway in 1962. Bishop Navagh advanced it to parish status as Saint Gerard's in 1965 with responsibility for parts of Paterson and Haledon. The same year, the Salesian Sisters commuted daily to Saint Gerard's from North Haledon in order to begin the elementary school.

In 1968, the parish bought a small house to serve as a convent so that the Sisters could continue the school and begin after-school care and catechetical instruction for the children. The number of students increased as the population shifted from the city streets to the suburbs.

The Sisters continued to serve Saint Gerard Parish and School until the year 2000, when the Sisters withdrew and the school was staffed entirely by lay teachers with a Filippini Sister as the principal.

Time for school in Roseto, Pennylvania!

Meanwhile, out West, the Provincial, Mother Ida Grasso, met with Cardinal McIntrye of Los Angeles. The winds of change had blown very strongly in the Archdiocese, especially among the Immaculate Heart Sisters who staffed many of its schools. The Cardinal asked Mother Ida to consider the needs of the schools in his jurisdiction and asked for help. Mother Ida listened with an open heart and promised to send the Sisters to staff Saint Mary School in Palmdale the following September. While in California, Mother Ida visited the Aspirants in Aptos and the Sisters in Watsonville.

The Salesian priests in Montréal, Canada, had repeatedly asked for the help of the Sisters in their mission in this metropolis. The Sisters finally arrived at the parish of Saint Claire on August 29, 1963. The Province had bought a small house on the other side of the street of the public school, a few blocks from the parish church. The Pastor received them in the parish church amid the singing of the "Te Deum" and declared that he was "the happiest man on earth."

Three of the Sisters who had the requisite academic degrees sought and obtained teaching positions in the public school of the area (unlike in the U.S., religious Sisters are allowed to work in public schools in Canada). They were hired for the first, third, and sixth grades. Sr. Lucie Meroni had come from Italy to share the dream of the new community in Montreal. Sr. Candide Asselin, Sr. Amelia Callegarin, Sr. Raymonde Dery, Sr. Claudette Fraser, Sr. Rose Marie Lagace, and Sr. Jeannine Trepanier arrived from different parts of the Province to complete the personnel serving this new mission.

Don Bosco's dream using the feminine creativity of Mary Mazzarello and the first Sisters had begun in Montréal. The cutting of the ribbon at 9 a.m. opened the doors of the Sisters' house to a swarm of young people who felt at home with the Sisters. Saint Claire Church opened its doors on Sunday. Then the young people crowded the church basement for the Oratory – a day of fun, games, prayer, and enthusiastic reception of the Word of God and of the Sisters.

Sr. Mary Louise Aguirre with a Confirmation class in Reading, Pennsylvania.

Aspirants in California taking advantage of a tree overturned by the previous night's windstorm in March, 1962.

Dedications and Blessings

In 1966, a bolt of lighting electrified the Province for a second time. Mother Lydia Carini, Provincial for only 18 months, was appointed to the General Council in Italy! Most Sisters thought the news was a mistake. Mother Lydia herself knew nothing of the appointment. Due to postal delays, she had only been informed that a new Provincial had been named, with no reference to herself. She calmly ended a visit to the Sisters in Canada, where the puzzling news had reached her, and she returned to Paterson. Eventually, when all the facts had been clarified, the Sisters who had just begun to rally from the loss of Mother Theresa, were once again asked to have faith in God's plan.

The altar dedicated to Mary Help of Christians at the Basilica of the National Shrine of the Immaculate Conception in Washington, D.C.

Before leaving for her new appointment, Mother Lydia participated in the blessing of the chapel dedicated to Mary Help of Christians at America's largest Catholic church, the Basilica of the National Shrine of the Immaculate Conception in Washington, D.C. Salesian Sisters, Priests, Brothers, Novices, Postulants, friends, students past and present – all converged on the nation's capital in April 1966. The magnificent altar of Mary Help of Christians, adorned with sculptures of Don Bosco, Mary Mazzarello, Dominic Savio, and Laura Vicuña, was surrounded by thousands of visitors.

The year 1966, a year dedicated to fidelity to Don Bosco, could not have had a more magnificent crescendo than this stupendous gesture of Marian love and devotion. Bishop Louis Morrow, on a visit from India, consecrated the altar of the new chapel of Mary Help of Christians. The homilist, Auxiliary Bishop Timothy Manning of Los Angeles, led in the honor given to Mary through word and song. The Year of Fidelity to Don Bosco unfolded in diverse ways in the communities, but always with a tangible surge of love and devotion for the Salesian founder.

The Louisiana communities of Baton Rouge and Metairie included Sr. Isabel Garza, Sr. Beatrice Valot, Sr. Leonia Pascucci, Sr. Ruth Stecker, Sr. Margaret Rose Buonaiuto, Sr. Mary Louise Aguirre, Father Sam Isgro (S.D.B. Provincial of the East), and his assistant.

Mother Theresa Casaro and Mother Mistress Adelina Gastaldo (seated)
with the 1962 Novices in Sacred Heart Novitiate.

Bishop Morrow stayed in America long enough to bless and dedicate Sacred Heart Hall in North Haledon on June 13, 1966. The three-story building housed a gymnasium complete with stage, bleachers, bookstore, and classrooms on the upper level; gym lockers, rest rooms, cafeteria, and kitchen on the second level; and a lower section with individual student lockers, rest rooms, and music rooms. The crowd cheered this new addition as a true step forward in the continuous development of the education given at Mary Help of Christians Academy.

Mother Lydia departed the Province, and it fell on her successor, Sr. Ida Grasso, to enlarge the dream and embolden the dreamers. She strode forward and carried the Province with her! Petite in stature, but great in heart and mind, she became Provincial at a difficult time both in the Church and in the evolution of consecrated religious life. She completed her year as Principal of Corpus Christi School in Port Chester, New York, and then took up her new assignment with courage and love.

One of the first red-letter days was the visit of Mother Ersilia Canta and Mother Letizia Galletti, both from the General Council in Italy. They came to the Province on November 24, 1966 to hold a series of meetings with the Sisters representing each community of the Province. These encounters took place in North Haledon and were followed by meetings in other regions. Their purpose was to clarify the directives given by Vatican II to religious Sisters and to prepare for the extraordinary Special General Chapter that would include the revision of the Sisters' Constitutions and Regulations.

The directives for renewal and updating religious life in the Church gave an impetus for studying and rethinking the Constitutions and Regulations according to the charism of Saint John Bosco and Saint Mary Mazzarello. Each Provincial had to answer a questionnaire, and every Provincial Council and community council had to answer another one. The documents of Vatican II, especially *Perfectae Caritatis,* mandated that each Sister take an active

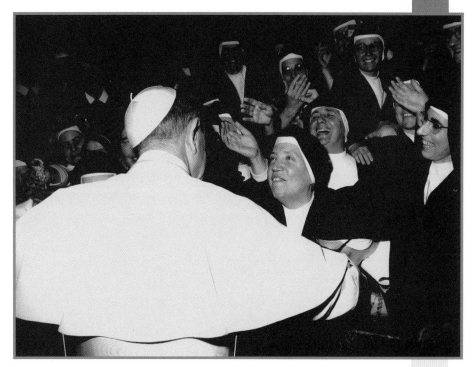

At an audience with Pope Paul VI in Vatican City, Sr. Mary Palatini, Sr. Michelle Bertrand, and Sr. Rose Oliveri greet the Holy Father.

part. Therefore, each individual Sister in the Province was given questionnaires to answer personally, seal her answers in an envelope, and send it to the committee preparing for the Special General Chapter. Time for reflecting on the questions was scheduled in the East, Canada, Florida, Los Angeles, and San Francisco so that each Sister was personally represented and gave her personal input. It was indeed a first for the Institute.

A second red-letter day occurred when, after months of preparation, planning, and substitution, every Superior presented her ticket at New York's John F. Kennedy Airport, destination Italy! Stops in Rome and Turin preceded their arrival in Mornese, the land of Don Bosco and Mary Mazzarello. Thrilled beyond belief, they could only repeat, "Am I dreaming?!"

The month-long trip proved to be a harbinger of spiritual renewal for all the Superiors of the U.S. Province. In Rome, an audience with Pope Paul VI proved to be one of the highlights. There Mother Ida spoke for the group. "Holy Father, we are the Daughters of Mary Help of Christians, the Salesian Sisters of Saint John Bosco from the United States. We live far, yes, but we are always close to the Vicar of Christ," she said.

California

The Sisters arrived in Palmdale, California, on August 25, 1968, to staff Saint Mary Elementary School. The pastor was Father Michael J. Moran, and the Sisters were Sr. Marie Dunn, the Superior, Sr. Assunta Sanchez, Sr. Irene Zaccagnino, and Sr. Dolores Bailey. A small furnished house with just enough room for the four Sisters became their home.

The Sisters soon learned that California's high desert weather was something to be reckoned with! Temperatures of 110 degrees were all too common from May to October; biting, sub-zero cold marked many a winter day. High velocity winds were as common as the sight of tumbleweeds

rolling around the streets. Initially the Sisters had the painstaking task of re-organizing the school into a smoothly-running educational institute based on Salesian principles.

That same year, the Sisters took over the administration of Saint Gertrude School in Bell Gardens, near Bellflower in southern California, at the request of Cardinal McIntyre. Bell Gardens was a place of poverty and promise. The Sisters were needed for education and religious instruction for many of the Hispanics who were migrating not only from Mexico but also from Cuba and other Central and South American countries. There was also a large number of very poor Caucasian children, who wore every combination of old uniforms available — children whose parents and grandparents had come to California after the devastating "dust bowl" in Oklahoma (recall John

Sisters using the library of the Sacred Heart Novitiate in New Jersey. Seated at the table are Sr. Theodora Carabin, Sr. Mary Schuchert, and Sr. Gisella Bonfiglio.

Steinbeck's *The Grapes of Wrath*) during the Depression and had settled near Bell Gardens.

Sr. Mary Helen Tafoya and Sr. Mary Mullaly commuted daily from Bellflower to Saint Gertrude. When the school opened, it had only four classrooms but eight grades, with two grades to a room. Sr. Mary Mullaly recalls teaching 28 second graders and 22 first graders in the same classroom that first year. One of the problems was that none of the first graders had had kindergarten experience, so she really had to lay down the foundations of their education.

The Sisters also helped in the catechetical instruction of the public school children. While the school had comparatively lower numbers due to the small number of classrooms, it was made up by the many hundreds of children in the religious education program. For many years thereafter, the Sisters were also able to direct the religious education program.

Eventually, the parish was able to give the Sisters a house of their own. On September 7, 1971, at the Eucharistic celebration, the parents and students thanked the Sisters for their willingness to staff a school that was principally for the poor. The parents had gathered many household objects and gave the Sisters a "shower" so that they would feel welcome and needed.

Once again the Sisters experienced the truth of Don Bosco's words: "Trust in Jesus and Mary, and you will know what miracles are."

The first graduating class of Saint Dominic Savio School in Bellflower, California, in 1961, joined by Sr. Lydia Carini (left), Father Dave Zunino, Pastor, and (right) Sr. Wilma Sanchez and Sr. Lucy Balistieri.

8 FILLING IN THE GAPS

The 1970's

*Sr. Adele Alvarez leads students
in song at Saint Genevieve School
in Panorama City, California.*

*"Saint Ann's Parish in Metairie, Louisiana,
welcomed Sr. Leonia Pascucci and Sr. Mary Louise Aguirre
in 1976. Bishop Philip Hannan of New Orleans
had asked for help in keeping the schools open
in his diocese. Sr. Leonia is remembered saying,
'When we arrived in Metairie,
there was nothing but sky and sand!'
Father Charles Duke, Pastor, welcomed them
and assured them of the cooperation of the parishioners."*

Virginia and Wisconsin

In the '70s, the call to arms was self-definition. To be a radical meant raising the stakes. Many claimed themselves to be above the law, including a President of the United States. Private worlds turned public, and deadly regional realities shadowed global power politics. The floppy disc and the microprocessor eased computing and made it portable. The "King," Elvis, was dead.

Should women vote... smoke... drink... sweat... wear pants... go to college... go to war... go to the moon... be equal? The godmothers, Bella Abzug and Betty Friedan, marched in 1977 for women's rights. At Kent State, four students were massacred as they demonstrated for peace.

The Vietnam Conflict was officially over. *Roe vs. Wade* became law. The world has not been the same since.

The Salesian Sisters, women themselves and working for the education of young people, especially girls, could ignore neither the movement nor the issues. They discussed, studied, prepared, and moved their educational vision in consonance with the findings of the Church and society. They became more determined to give the best of themselves for the future of youth. They imbibed the words of Don Bosco, "Education is a matter of the heart!"

Saint Mary of the Lake in Westport, Wisconsin, was yet another area that called for the help of the Sisters. Pictured here are the faculty from 1977-1978, including Sr. Clare Kennelly, Sr. Frances Gumino, Sr. Arlene Rubino, and Sr. Margaret Hinojosa.

The winds of change were still stirring in the Church in the U.S. and became more and more aggressive during the 70's. The religious of the U.S., especially Sisters, abandoned the education of youth in many parishes because they felt that the decrees of Vatican II encouraged new missions for them.

Pastors turned to the Salesian Sisters for help. A Franciscan priest, Father Salvator Ciullo, asked Mother Ida Grasso for Sisters for his mission in Woodstock, in the southern part of Virginia. Father asked for three Sisters who could teach religious education classes to the boys of the nearby Military Academy as well as to the small number of Catholics in the area. At first, Mother Ida told Father that they were unable to satisfy his request. Undaunted, Father Sal reiterated his request, and prayed until, on January 31, 1970, the Feast of Saint John Bosco, Sr. Letizia Sampo, Sr. Yamile Saieh, and Sr. Theodore Carabin settled into the house provided for them.

The mission, though largely surrounded by Protestants, flourished. The development of the mission, especially the attendance at the Sunday liturgy, soon surpassed the available space, and a new church was built and dedicated to Saint John Bosco. The mission lasted until the parishioners themselves were able to continue without the Sisters.

The Superintendent of Schools in the Diocese of Wisconsin approached Mother Ida for Sisters to staff Catholic schools there. Since the Provincial said that it was impossible, Bishop Cletus O'Donnell approached Mother Ida explaining the needs for his request. It was granted, and in Dane, Wisconsin, Saint Michael School was opened for first through sixth grades, and catechetical instruction was given to the older students who frequented public schools. Sr. Fernanda Rossi, Sr. Patricia King, and Sr. Jean Erickson pioneered this venture. It was the first experience in the central plains and in the rural farming areas for the Sisters. It took creativity and a tremendous love for souls by these pioneers in the new mission.

The Salesian Sisters continue to be blessed with vocations. Here, Superior General, Sr. Antonia Colombo, embraces Sr. Theresa Lee after taking her final vows as a Salesian Sister.

Mother Ida realized the isolation of the community and responded to a request for another foundation in the same general region. After much thought and consultation with the Sisters themselves, Saint Mary of the Lake in Westport, Wisconsin, opened. The school was a developing one, and the Sisters were well-received. Sr. Mary Palatini, Sr. Elaine Reeves, and Sr. Jean Erickson brought the mission forward. However, the severe winters, the minimal number of children, the isolation of the Sisters, and the lack of any opportunity to interact with the young people outside of school hours prompted the Provincial to leave the mission to the laity who lived and worked in the parishes. Nonetheless, the experience was an enrichment for all concerned, and some teachers and students never forgot the Sisters of Saint John Bosco. In fact, some correspondence still mentions how much the Sisters are missed.

Helping the Elderly Sisters

Once again, the Sisters dared to dream and turn it into reality. Saint Joseph's in North Haledon was no longer sufficient for the elderly and infirm Sisters; the Provincial and her staff stretched the limits of the Ward Street house. The initial formation house in Haledon needed better facilities to satisfy the fire department of the town. Added to this was the fact that Paterson had routed an entrance to Highway 80 right through the convent property!

A solution took shape in the Provincial Council. The plan focused on the property of Villa Don Bosco, adjacent to North Haledon. A central chapel, flanked by a community for the elderly Sisters on one side and one for the initial formation program on the other, seemed to answer the need. The chapel became the heart of the house, with the kitchen and dining services behind it. The Provincial rooms and offices took a portion of the upper floor immediately above the chapel. The chapel and kitchen services were shared between the two communities.

It took a while to solidify the dream and to ensure that the initial formation community and the elder Sisters were given priority. The new building was constructed and opened in 1972, the 100th anniversary of the foundation of the Institute that was being celebrated worldwide.

The extraordinary visit of the Mother General of the worldwide Institute, Mother Maria Ausilia Corallo, on February 1 of the centennial year 1972 was an

Mother Ida Grasso signing the parchment that will be inserted into the cornerstone at Saint Joseph Provincial Center in 1972, the centennial year of the founding of the Institute of the Daughters of Mary Help of Christians.

unexpected but welcome gift. The members of the Provincial Council and some of the Superiors of the nearby houses met her at the airport. Her arrival in North Haledon was exuberant and festive. Junior Professed, Aspirants, and Postulants as well as all the Sisters who could come were present to welcome "Mother General's Microphone," as she called herself!

Throughout the Province, Mother created a sense of renewed peace and joy, sharing her insight with extraordinary simplicity and directness while delicately showing her appreciation for each Sister's contribution. Mother Ausilia was still with the Province on April 22, 1972 when more than 1,500 people joined to celebrate the centennial of the Institute at Saint John's Cathedral in Paterson. The imposing structure was left without so much as standing room on that memorable day. Not even torrential rain could dampen the joy and enthusiasm during the Eucharistic celebration offered in gratitude to God for a hundred years of service in the Church.

The event inaugurated the regional festivities that extended the celebration of the Institute's centennial throughout the year. Later that same summer, Mother Lydia Carini, who was in the States attending conferences for

Saint Joseph Provincial Center in Haledon, New Jersey, built in 1972, which replaced Villa Don Bosco.

Major Superiors, represented the Mother General at the concluding jubilee event: the blessing and laying of the cornerstone for the new Saint Joseph Provincial House.

Soon after, Mother Ida took up residence in the new multi-purpose edifice that housed the Provincial offices, the rooms for the elderly, sick and retired Sisters, and the living quarters for the candidates of the initial formation program. Although each community functioned in separate wings of the two-story structure, they met daily in the central chapel where voices young and old mingled in fervent prayer.

Mother Ida Grasso's term of office as Provincial was extended from six to nine years due to a number of difficulties that the Catholic Church and consecrated religious life faced as a result of the implementation of Vatican II. The communities of the Sisters were present in 21 dioceses spread throughout the country, and 18 of the Bishops had asked that there be no major changes in the administration of the Sisters in the country. Religious life in the post-Vatican II climate was in turmoil and demanded energy, vision, and courage that were rooted in great confidence in God.

More Schools

The Lord called the Sisters through Cardinal John Krol in 1972 to serve the Church in Philadelphia, Pennslyvania, by staffing Mater Dolorosa Parish. Father Albert Palombo welcomed Sr. Leonia Pascucci, Superior, and Sr. Joanne Passarelli on July 19 to the "City of Brotherly Love." Soon, Sr. Amalia Gatti, Sr. Loretta De Domenicis, and Sr. Clare Kennelly came to complete the community. This community, under the patronage of Our Lady, was another example of Mary's special help and guidance for her daughters.

Besides the more than 400 members of the school, the Sisters assumed responsibility for the religious education program, the associations, and the choir. Participation in the Eucharistic Congress of 1976, active responsibility for the preparation of Pope John Paul II's visit in 1979, and, during his stay, the students' singing on radio and television were red-letter days for these inner-city boys and girls, opportunities for growth and the broadening of their horizons.

Sadly, the Sisters had to leave Mater Dolorosa after 19 years in 1991 due to lack of personnel.

The house in Ipswich, Massachusetts, remained an isolated community until 1973, when a second New England house was opened in nearby Boston. When Julie Billiart High School in the North End lost its religious faculty in 1973, students and parents alike were determined to keep the school open, regardless of cost. They prayed, wrote letters, petitioned the Archbishop, and brainstormed all possible alternatives. Christopher Columbus High School for boys, staffed by the Franciscans and separated from Julie Billiart by thin swinging doors, could not lose its sister school; the teenage girls of the area could not lose their only hope for Catholic education.

Against all odds and in the face of fierce difficulties, Mother Ida, at the request of Bishop Medeiro, sent five Sisters to Boston in August 1973. The Superior and new Principal was Sr. Louise Passero, accompanied by Sr. Julia Mazorati, Sr. Amparo Uribe, Sr. Monique Huart, and Sr. Leslie Satter. For eight years, the Salesian Sisters and spectacular team of lay faculty labored to maintain and develop the work. Business education and college preparatory courses filled school hours, religious education classes and recreational meetings filled the afternoons and evenings. Retreat teamwork with the brother Salesians in Ipswich claimed numerous weekends.

In 1973, the house of Saint Thérèse in Succasunna, New Jersey, was opened at the request of Bishop Lawrence Casey and the Superintendent of Catholic Schools. It had been staffed previously by the Dominican Sisters of Newburgh, New York, who left due to lack of personnel. Succasunna is a lovely town, nestled in the Morris County Hills. It was dubbed "the icebox of New Jersey," because the temperature is ten degrees lower than anywhere else in the state. The Sisters moved into Saint Thérèse on August 6, 1973, with Sr. Judith Suprys as Superior and Principal, and the community consisted of Sr. Mary Sedita, Sr. Rosemary Cordes, and Sr. Catherine Hurley.

The month before the opening of school was a busy one, but the very first "Good Night" message Sr. Judith shared in Succasunna set the serene and diligent work atmosphere: "Saint Thérèse will be another Mornese; the house of the love of God, and hence, a house of peace." The Sisters fully engaged themselves with the responsibility for the school, as well as the 900 public school students who came for religious instruction. On June 30, 1988, after fifteen years, the Sisters left beautiful Succasunna and the good people and families they loved and admired due to lack of personnel.

Students from Julie Billart School in Boston, Massachusetts loved the Salesian Sisters so much that they still hold reunions. Sr. Antoniette Cabrera, who ran the business program for six years, is pictured with some of her very successful past pupils.

The community from Saint Thérèse School in Succasunna, New Jersey, included Sr. Liz Ryan, Sr. Leonia Pascucci, Sr. Jerome Parinello, and Sr. Susan Bagli.

Mary Help of Christians, Laredo, Texas

"I attended Mary Help of Christians School from 1963-1973, from Pre-K through 8th grade. Aside from my family raising me in the faith, I received all my Catholic training during those years. I remember joining the choir and staying with the Sisters until my dad could pick me up. There was such a cheerful spirit among them! I envied them!

"At age 10, I asked to join them. The wise Superior, Sr. Consuelo Spezia, did not discourage me because I was too young. She suggested I say a decade of the Rosary each day to Our Lady, so that Mary would keep that desire in my heart. It worked! Two years later, I joined the Salesian Sisters as an Aspirant, and continued a more intense journey in my relationship with Jesus and Mary."

Sr. Ana Palacios, FMA

Mexico Arrives

On May 24, 1973, more good news was announced to the Sisters. The houses of Texas – which had been part of the Mexican Province – were being transferred to the U.S. Province. The reason? It was to facilitate the school situations for the faculty, students, and the accreditation of the schools. While there was general rejoicing at this new disposition of Divine Providence, there was also the inevitable pain of detachment for those Sisters who would decide to break their ties with Mexico. Those who chose to remain in Texas would transfer their obedience to Mother Ida Grasso.

The diminutive Provincial, with her exquisite, gentle heart, found every possible way to ease the transition for the Sisters who chose to transfer: Sr. Aida Chagin, Sr. Conception Sanchez, Sr. Maria de la Luz Reyes, Sr. Mary Louise de la

Vega, Sr. Maria Becceril, Sr. Teresita Delgado, Sr. Aida Flores, Sr. Ofelia Lozano, Sr. Olga Munoz, Sr. Guadalupe de la Garza, Sr. Elvira Velazques, Sr. Trinidad Reyes, Sr. Victoria Trejo, Sr. Assunta Sanchez, Sr. Trinidad Avalos, Sr. Sara Garcia, Sr. Mary Ann Villagomez, Sr. Olga Villalon, Sr. Anita Marinez, Sr. Guadalupe Medina, Sr. Roble Cavazos, Sr. Adela Lozano, Sr. Emma Stefanoni, Sr. Irene Tapia, Sr. Isabel Garza, Sr. Josephine Ochoa, Sr. Julia Anguiano, Sr. Sylvia Castillo, Sr. Angelina Gomez, Sr. Carmen Peña, Sr. Carmen Nieto, Sr. Hope Rodriguez, Sr. Mercedes Romo, Sr. Jane Jasso, Sr. Josephine Lopez, and Sr. Josephine Sanchez. They joined their Sisters who had already preceded them as missionaries to the increasing Hispanic community in the U.S.: Sr. Stella Ruiz, Sr. Jane Sanchez, Sr. Emma Mendoza, Sr. Mary Louise Aguirre, Sr. Teresa Murillo, Sr. Amelia Barbosa, Sr. Carmen Morales, Sr. Antoinette Cabrera, Sr. Mary Louise Mazzocco, and Sr. Mary Arciga.

The elderly and much loved Sr. Margarita Moreno serenely asked Mother Ida if she could join the Sisters already in retirement in Haledon for her short time remaining on this earth. Sr. Esperanza Cantu had recently gone to her eternal reward and Sr. Consuela Spezia soon entered the hospital where she died on January 13, 1974. The premature death of these promising leaders in the Texan educational mission was a loss on earth but a gain of heavenly intercessors.

Sr. Socorro Ortega was one of the first U.S. vocations from Texas.

And More Schools

The pastor of Saint Mary Parish in Paterson, Father Joseph Gallo, asked for Sisters. In doing the research for Saint Mary's, he told Mother Ida that the parish had been founded as Mary Help of Christians, so how could she refuse his request? His prayer to Mary was answered. The new administration of Saint Mary School began on July 16, 1974. It was a joyful coincidence as it was the 66th anniversary of the arrival of the first Sisters to America.

The community settled into its living quarters. The pastor, overcome with joy, celebrated the opening Mass. Among those present were Mother Ida Grasso, Provincial, Sr. Josephine Carini, Vicar, Sr. Rita Fantin, Superior, and the Sisters of the new community, Sr. Carmela Cesario, Sr. Pierette Carpentier, Sr. Angela DeCapua, and Sr. Carmen Botello. A number of Sisters came from the Provincialate and added their musical talents to the joy and solemnity of the occasion. During his homily, Father Gallo expressed his sincere gratitude to Mary Help of Christians for the graces received, and exhorted all to propagate devotion to our Heavenly Mother, especially by imitation of her virtues and by the recitation of the Rosary.

Besides immediately taking charge of the school, the Sisters organized classes for the reception of the Sacraments for the public school children, and on Saturday afternoons, the Oratory was opened for children in the parochial and public schools.

In September 1974, the Diocese of Paterson merged Saint Michael School, Saint John Cathedral School, Saint Agnes School, and Saint Boniface School into Bishop Navagh Regional School (later renamed Saint John Cathedral School). The Principal of this new school was to be chosen from applications sent to the Diocese from various religious congregations. As the Salesian Sisters were already staffing Saint John's, Sr. Margaret DiBari was selected as the first Principal. The Sisters' willingness to work with the Diocese in providing for the education of inner-city young people is a concrete example of living the charism of Don Bosco!

In 1974, the Convent of Our Lady of Grace was opened in Johnston, Rhode Island. The Rhode Island

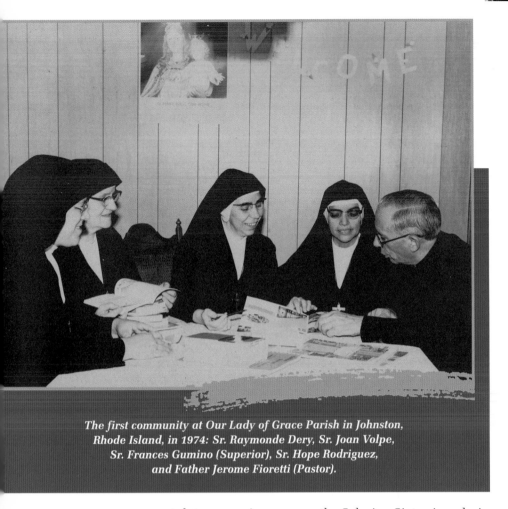

The first community at Our Lady of Grace Parish in Johnston, Rhode Island, in 1974: Sr. Raymonde Dery, Sr. Joan Volpe, Sr. Frances Gumino (Superior), Sr. Hope Rodriguez, and Father Jerome Fioretti (Pastor).

apostolate was unique among the Salesian Sisters' works in the U.S. The state allowed religious instruction in the public schools themselves. When the Sisters responded to the invitation of the pastor, Father Jerome Fioretti, to teach the children of the parish in the neighboring public school, it was a challenge and an adventure!

The Sisters found that life could be lived in different settings with varied schedules to accommodate the teaching of the faith to the young. Five days a week, using the facilities of the local public schools, the Superior, Sr. Frances Gumino, and Sr. Raymonde Dery, Sr. Hope Rodriguez, and Sr. Joan Volpe taught catechism to children aged five to 18.

In addition, they organized courses for adults, instructed parents of children in the sacramental programs, and prepared volunteer parishioners to become lay catechists. On Saturdays and holidays, the Sisters hosted a variety of activities for the youngsters who flocked to the Church basement. Until 1980, a summer camp run by the Sisters provided hours of wholesome fun and religious instruction for dozens of children.

Saint Genevieve School in Panorama City, California, was staffed by the Salesian Sisters in 1974 in response to the request of the pastor, Msgr. Thomas Kiefer, and in order to house the Candidates in formation until a new place could be opened for them; a previous formation house in Aptos was being replaced.

On August 15, 1974, the first Sisters arrived: Sr. Mary Helen Tafoya, Sr. Kathleen Conklin, and Sr. Elizabeth Russo. In a few short days, Sr. Maria Arroyo, Sr. Rose Zanella, and Sr. Beatrice Valot arrived with their Superior, Sr. Christine Hellen.

By 1974, it became evident that expansion in the city of Montréal, Canada, had to be undertaken in order to respond to the needs of the young people in the parish of Saint Dominic Savio. While the Sisters had done a remarkable service for the parish youth while commuting from Saint Claire, the Provincial listened to the Sisters who asked for a permanent presence in the parish itself. After the appropriate preparations, and the purchase of a house adjacent to the parish, the community moved into its residence on August 25, 1975.

Sr. Micheline Bertrand, Sr. Roberta Johnson, Sr. Raymonde Dery, and Sr. Alphonsine Basque joined Sr. Lucie Meroni in this new community. This mission was complicated for various reasons. English, Italian, and French were spoken in and out of school and the cultural setting represented a mixture of all three groups. The Sisters confidently set out to help children and parents of all backgrounds. Two Sisters opened the *garderie* (day nursery) so that parents would not worry about their children. Parishioners took care of lunch and maintenance.

The future Sr. Rena Cormier, second from the left, bottom row.

The parish hall was used for the kindergarten during the week. It was transformed during the weekend into a place for Eucharistic celebration and parish activities. The various celebrations began to take on a new dimension with the Sisters living in the parish. The music leader, Sr. Roberta Johnson, added solemnity to each religious celebration in Italian, English, or French.

The Lord was certainly pleased with the expansion, so much so that Sr. Candide Asselin asked to serve the Lord as a missionary in Africa. No one had foreseen this as part of the unfolding of the dream! Sr. Patricia Lacharite from Montréal followed in this missionary venture. The missionary vocation of these Sisters was nurtured in the fertile Canadian soil to the benefit of the youth in Africa.

On June 29, 1975, Sr. Marie Dunn, Sr. Florine Lagace, and Sr. Juanita Chavez went sent to Saint Peter Parish in Pleasantville, New Jersey, to respond to a request for help from the parish priests because the Franciscan Sisters who had been at the school were no longer there. The parish provided a convent for the Sisters next door to the church, rectory, and school. They instructed the children in religious education on Sundays, taught in the school, and took over the administration. Sr. Marie served as the Principal and a teacher, along with Sr. Florine and Sr. Juanita.

In Montréal, Canada, Sr. Claudette Parent opens the Oratory door to the young people as Sr. Alphonsine Basque and one of the helpers wait with the children to have their picture taken.

Besides this, the Sisters held different after-school activities to keep the children off the streets. Sr. Lucy Balistrieri and Sr. Shermane Delgado came to help Sr. Marie Dunn, replacing Sr. Florine and Sr. Juanita after three years of service. They were followed by Sr. Patricia Lacharite and Sr. Alice Fusco.

After six years, Sr. Ruth Stecker replaced Sr. Marie as Principal until 1984, when the Sisters left the mission at Saint Peter's. Lay people took over the administration and teaching of the school, continuing in the firmly-rooted Salesian spirit. Many of the parents and students were sorry to see the Sisters leave, nevertheless.

The development of Christ the King School serving the Tampa Bay, Florida, area had led the School Sisters of Notre Dame to double the classes for each grade. In June 1975, the School Sisters, who had been such successful educators in the Tampa Bay area, notified the pastor, Father Norman Balthazar, that they would no longer staff Christ the King. The pastor turned to Mother Ida. Could he have a principal and some Sisters for the parish school which served over a thousand students?

Mother Ida asked Sr. Mary Terzo to take on the responsibilities of Principal while Sr. Catherine Hurley began religious instruction for the older students. They commuted from Saint Joseph's each day to join the large lay faculty. Difficulties were not lacking, but prayer, sacrifice, and Salesian cheerfulness soon captured the hearts of all, and the first school year ended on a happy note.

On July 10, 1976, the first community of four Sisters moved into their own residence in Christ the King convent, thus establishing the third foundation in the Tampa Bay area. The Christ the King community included Sr. Mary as Principal and Superior, Sr. Frances Di Santo, Sr. Guadalupe Medina, and Sr. Marie Gannon. The official opening took place on July 16, the Feast of Our Lady, with a Eucharistic celebration at the convent by the pastor. In September, the school met the standards and received approval by the Florida Catholic Conference. In 1977, the school was accredited by the Southern Association of Colleges and Schools. These accomplishments encouraged the entire staff to maintain the high religious and academic standards for which they had worked so hard.

The Sisters continued their mission for another 24 years, and at the completion of the school year in 2005, left the development of the future of Christ the King School to others, who continue to carry out the Salesian mission of education. The Sisters and parishioners were grateful for the tremendous progress that had taken place and all the collaboration that had brought about a miracle of grace there.

Sr. Florine Lagace, Sr. Juanita Chavez, and Sr. Marie Dunn at the entrance of Saint Peter School in Pleasantville, New Jersey.

A Chapel in North Haledon

As the Salesian Sisters' community and student body in North Haledon continued to grow, they saw a need for a larger chapel. It was decided that the chapel was to be built where the Sowerbutt House and Sacred Heart Novitiate and chapel had stood for many years. Sr. Cecilia Besi was Provincial Economer and Secretary, and so oversaw the project. After the Sowerbutt House was demolished, they began to build the chapel in 1975, with Mr. Arthur Rigolo as the architect. Mr. Ell was the artist who designed the beautiful cross of the Resurrected Christ that hangs above the altar, as well as the Stations of the Cross, which hang from the ceiling to give the unique impression that one is walking with Jesus through the Stations. He also designed the different statues located within the chapel.

Sr. Rose McShane was famous for her musical talents, and upon the building of the chapel, she asked that an organ be placed inside. Mr. John Peragallo installed the organ, and he also promised that he would always service it. Today, his children continue their father's tradition and service the organ when the need arises.

The last special feature of the chapel is the small Madonna Chapel, as Sr. Josephine Carini called it, located in the back. Inside this small chapel, Sr. Josephine began to place many different pictures of the Blessed Mother. There are also stained glass windows which represent the Sacraments, another distinctive element. A little known fact is that the Sisters wished to "recycle" the old pews of Sacred Heart (later Don Bosco Hall) chapel, but couldn't find anyone who was willing to take on such a task. Finally, Sr. Lucy Balistrieri's brother-in-law, Michael Avolio, transformed the old pews into chapel storage shelves and cabinets, which are still there today.

Sr. Adeline Salvetti and Sr. Providence Favolaro shedding tears as they walk through the remains of the Sowerbutt House which served as the Sacred Heart Novitiate, Chapel, and Salesian College. It was torn down in preparation for Saint Joseph Chapel.

Sr. Frances Werwas (1870-1973)

"On August 4, 1972, I told her, 'Sr. Frances, tomorrow the Congregation will be one hundred years old. 18,636 of us will be celebrating throughout the world.' Putting her hands on her head, she exclaimed, '18,000! 18,000! How many? Are they all good?' I replied, 'We try to be.' Then, pointing first to her head and then to her heart, she continued, 'We must be good here and here. Jesus is the Papa and we are the children.' At 102 years of age, Sr. Frances realized and understood that there is room for improvement in living our religious commitment."

Sr. Ines Molano, FMA

On June 10, 1976, Father Samuel Isgro, Salesian Provincial, and the Salesian priests consecrated the altar. Relics of different Salesian saints were placed within the altar. After the blessing of the altar, the first Mass was held. Then on June 12, 1976, Bishop Lawrence B. Casey blessed the chapel with Mother Lydia Carini representing the Mother General.

Bathed in natural light, the Risen Christ hangs over the altar of the new Saint Joseph Chapel.

The Madonna Chapel, part of Saint Joseph Chapel, features stained-glass windows representing the Sacraments.

Sr. Rose McShane always said, "Saint Cecilia, offer our singing to God." She brought the Sisters and all who heard her the gift of the joy of music.

Corralitos

In August 1975, Mother Ida and Father August Bosio, who had preached the retreat to the Sisters, invited all those interested to visit the newly purchased site in Corralitos, California, which would replace the formation house in Aptos. Work had begun to transform the rough terrain into a haven for young people. Sr. Cecilia Besi, the Provincial Bursar, and Sr. Christine Hellen from Watsonville monitored the construction work undertaken by George W. Davis, the contractor.

The new site was a mere 15-minute drive from Aptos and was even closer to the FMA community in Watsonville as well as the Salesian parish of Mary Help of Christians, also in Watsonville. Its purchase was one of the last official responsibilities of Mother Ida; Mother Josephine Carini, who succeeded her, would see it to completion.

The official groundbreaking took place in November 1975. Father Harry Rasmussen, Provincial of the West, was invited to be the main speaker. Local dignitaries, Salesian Cooperators, benefactors, friends, and relatives of the Sisters were invited. Among the privileged ones to turn the first spade of earth were Sr. Anita Ferrari (the first California vocation), Sr. Mary Campi (the most senior Sister in California), Father Ernest Giovannini, Sr. Cecilia Besi (representing Mother Josephine Carini), Father Joe Watt (Pastor of Holy Eucharist Parish), and Father Rasmussen.

The construction crew lost no time getting to work. Steadily, three dual- winged dormitories were built on the upper terrace. Tennis, volleyball, and basketball courts as well as a baseball/soccer field were plotted out on the lower terrace. When the white brick buildings with the Spanish tile roofs were completed, the statue of Saint John Bosco which had so majestically overlooked the property of Aptos was brought to Corralitos and lowered onto the center of the quadrangle formed by the three sets of camp cabins. Phase I was complete. Phase II would include a cafeteria, kitchen and laundry; Phase III: a chapel.

Mother Josephine Carini, Provincial, offers the chalice to Bishop Harry Clinch during the blessing of the Mary Help of Christians Youth Center in Corralitos, California, in 1977.

Finally, many years later, a long-awaited residence for the Sisters was built. For all those years, they had used rooms off the various cabin wings as their sleeping quarters.

By summertime of 1976, the Sisters were able to make their retreat at Corralitos. Summer camp at Camp Auxilium continued that summer without interruption, even though the "kitchen" that summer was one of the tiny rooms at the end of a cabin, under the masterful hands of Sr. Mary Baroni. The Aptos Aspirants, who had been transferred to Panorama City after the closing of Mary Help of Christians Juniorate in Aptos, were again established in Corralitos. That fall, the new "Mary Help of Christians Youth Center" now included a kindergarten and pre-kindergarten as well as scheduled retreats for women and girls throughout the year. A Rosary group met weekly to pray and reflect, a group that continues to meet today.

Construction progressed, and when the California Sisters arrived for their 1977 retreat, Phase II was complete, and it was time for the blessing and dedication of the buildings. Bishop Harry Clinch of Monterey officiated at an outdoor Mass attended by all the Sisters of the various

Sr. Rosalie Di Peri, Principal of Saint Peter School in Laredo, Texas, hands out student awards.

Sr. Mary Mullaly, Principal of Blessed Sacrament School, addresses students around the Grotto of Our Lady.

California communities, many of their relatives, a large number of parents, students, benefactors, and even parish priests from the various parishes where the Sisters served.

As the Sisters prayed and discerned what else they could do to serve, God's will made itself clear. There was no Catholic school in the immediate vicinity. Soon the kindergarten parents and other members of the local community began to ask for a full scale elementary school. Phase III of construction had not yet even begun! Plans for a convent were postponed and a small school was designed for the spot where the convent would have been. By this time, Saint Joseph had strongly indicated that he wanted to have an important part in the work at Corralitos; many significant things were happening on days consecrated to him! So, when the permit to build the school hit unexpected snags, Saint Joseph was entrusted with finding a solution to the problem, and he came through with the needed grace. The County Supervisors granted the Salesian Sisters permission to build a school in Corralitos.

Exactly on March 19, 1979, the Feast of Saint Joseph, without any pre-planning on anybody's part, the new chapel was ready for use. Father Ernest Giovannini, SDB, celebrated the first Mass with the Salesian Sisters of Watsonville, and, later in the morning, Father Joe Watt, pastor of Holy Eucharist Catholic Community, celebrated the first Mass for the children of the school.

Mary Help of Christians stands at the entrance to the property and welcomes every visitor. May her blessings and miracles continue; may the sense of her nearness remain; and may Saint Joseph continue to give the Sisters his special attention!

More Schools

Saint Ann Parish in Metairie, Louisiana, welcomed Sr. Leonia Pascucci and Sr. Mary Louise Aguirre on July 19, 1976. Bishop Philip Hannan of New Orleans had asked for help in keeping the schools open in his diocese. Sr. Leonia is remembered saying, "When we arrived in Metairie, there was nothing but sky and sand!" Father Charles Duke, Pastor, welcomed them and assured them of the cooperation of the parishioners. The school opened on August 30, 1976, with 279 students from kindergarten through fourth grade.

In January 1979, the increased school enrollment prompted the pastor and parishioners to construct a new school building. The school population and the parents increased their support for the Sisters and never forgot the first Sisters who established the sound educational institution.

At the beginning of 1977, the Superintendent of Schools in San Antonio, Texas, Brother Charles Gerdt, S.M., asked for the Sisters to staff Saint James Parish, near Saint John Bosco School. The parish had been in operation since 1848, and the school since 1957, but the difficulties of running a school were steadily increasing. As a result, in September 1977, the Sisters went to Saint James School in San Antonio, forming a community in the parish that would improve educational opportunity for the children. The school had originally been staffed by the Marianist Sisters, but as the number of teaching Sisters declined, those Sisters had withdrawn.

As July 4, 1977 dawned, the three pioneers, Sr. Theresa Delgado as Principal, Sr. Josephine Sanchez, and Sr. Josephine Lopez were welcomed by the pastor, Father Enda McKenna, and the Saint James parishioners. Three weeks later, Sr. Adele Lozano joined the group. They were assured that there was a vast field of work before them. The community settled in a military barracks type convent on Nunes Street, across the street from the school that was, and still is, a military barracks.

In an effort to fulfill its apostolic mission, the community of Saint James dedicated its work to God and placed themselves under the protection of Mary Help of Christians, pledging to implement the Preventive System of Saint John Bosco. Teachers and students were a bit apprehensive on August 29, the opening day of school. Students feared their new teachers because the parents had told them that these new Sisters were very strict, would mete out punishments, and would make many changes in the school! Here, the task of the educators was to follow Don Bosco's advice: "It is not enough to love the children; they must know that they are loved." Therefore, they tried to win the hearts of their students before making changes of any kind.

As a result of their Salesian piety and sacrifice, the Sisters saw the enrollment increase and the spirituality of the parish gain in vitality as each school year unfolded. The children soon realized that the Sisters were interested in their activities, so in return they responded by applying themselves to their schoolwork. A real family spirit began to form, with Jesus and Mary as their guiding stars.

"Santa Claus," Sr. Ann Cassidy,
Sr. Martina Ponce, Sr. Nivia Campuzano,
Father Sam Isgro, S.D.B., and
Sr. Domenica Di Peri during Christmas
break in Marrero, Louisiana.

Father Joseph Autard, Salesian Cooperator and pastor of Saint Clement Parish in Hayward, in the Oakland Diocese in the East Bay area of California, had for years dreamed of having the Salesian Sisters in his parish school, which was, at the time, under lay administration and staffing. Knowing the current lay principal was planning to terminate her contract sometime within the year, Father Autard again requested the Salesian Sisters and received his wish this time. Sr. Cesira Pierotti, the Superior, with Sr. Sally Brown and Sr. Sharon Peck, were sent in July 1977 to bring a Salesian presence to Hayward.

On the opposite coast in Kenilworth, New Jersey, Saint Theresa School asked for Sisters, at least one as principal, in order to keep alive the school and the religious instruction in the area. Sr. Monique Huart already commuted from Elizabeth in order to prepare catechists through a flourishing religious education program. The pastor, Father Edward Hennessy, asked if the Sisters could also help in the administration of the school. The Dominican Sisters of Caldwell had left the school after the publication of the documents from Vatican II.

On July 16, 1978, the convent was officially opened with a Eucharistic celebration. Sr. Catherine Altamura, Principal, Sr. Donna Mae Epperson, Sr. Mary Ligregni, Sr. Felicia Simonetti, Sr. Elizabeth Schmidt, and Sr. Arlene Rubino were present. In the four weeks before school opened, there was much to be done. Everything in the school and convent had to be thoroughly cleaned and

Three cheers for Corpus Christi School in Port Chester, New York, with the help of Sr. Mary Anne Zito!

some modifications made. In just four weeks, desks were scraped, closets rearranged, supplies purchased, classrooms painted, and halls decorated. The school was ready for occupancy on September 6.

When the children entered the school, they stood, awestruck, at the transformation. The parents commented that their children had found a home in the classrooms. They felt surrounded by love and caring, learning devotion to Mary Help of Christians in an atmosphere of Salesian joy and grace. The means used to implement this spirit were optional daily Mass, preparation of special liturgies for feasts, the teaching of religion in every grade by the Sisters, and the "Good Morning" welcome given by the Principal.

Camp Auxilium Evolves

The county of Sussex, New Jersey, where the Newton Novitiate was situated, had experienced a tremendous growth in housing and, consequently, in number of children. Camp Auxilium was operating during the summers with resident campers who came largely from New York. The need for some activity for the local children surfaced.

The Provincial Council decided to experiment first with a Saturday Oratory to gauge the interest of the parents in the area. It was begun in the Novitiate and the Novices were the animators. The idea caught fire. Parents brought their children to the Novitiate each Saturday for an afternoon of fun, games, and religious instruction. The question surfaced, "Can we use Camp Auxilium all year around?"

God always has a positive answer, if people but listen. Camp Auxilium turned into a year-round educational institution in 1977. During this same time, the "old steak house" was replaced with new facilities, which would later serve a greater purpose than just camp.

Sr. Mary Rinaldi, in her position of Camp Directress for six years, listened carefully to the concerns of the parents from summer camp. She, inspired by Sr. Josephine Carini, began to ask parents if they would find it beneficial for the Sisters to remain at Auxilium year-round. Of course they would!

Sr. Mary Rinaldi serves up lunch to campers at Camp Don Bosco and Camp Auxilium in 1979.

Sr. Rose Zanella teaches religion to young campers.

to the parents' concerns. She became director of the Head Start program.

The Sisters taught 80 children at Camp Auxilium. The following year, Head Start found its own quarters, but the venture was such a success that, in two short years, Camp Auxilium was transformed into a year-round facility. The cabins were winterized, and adjustments were made to the facilities to meet the state standards. In 1979, Camp Auxilium Learning Center became a reality: it would be a camp during the summer months and an Early Learning Center the rest of the year.

The Sisters established a community to meet the needs of the young people from three to five years of age. Sr. Mary was joined by Sr. Mary Carone, Superior, Sr. Amelia Barboza, Sr. Angelina De Santo, Sr. Ercolina Perinciolo, and Sr. Grace Ruiz.

With God's hand guiding the works of the Sisters, word came that the Head Start program for pre-kindergarten children was looking for a temporary place for its students for the school year of 1978-1979. Sr. Mary found the answer

Pictured at the grotto of Our Lady in Newton, New Jersey, in the 1970's, are Sr. Frances Gumino, Sr. Elba Armas, Mother Ida Grasso, Sr. Josephine Carini, Sr. Adelina Gastaldo, Sr. Mildred Zanetti, and Sr. Regina Dunn.

The mission first undertaken by Sr. Mary Rinaldi with the community was a labor of love and sacrifice, and it continued under the leadership of Sr. Lou Ann Fantauzza and her staff. The Center became not only a showcase for the early education of children in a stimulating, Salesian environment, but it also helped working parents in the area. Camp Auxilium has also borne the fruit of vocations – Sr. Judith Suprys and Sr. Frances Da Grossa were once campers!

On the Westbank

On July 6, 1979, five Sisters arrived at a new educational mission in Marrero, Louisiana, a working-class suburb of New Orleans. Sr. Fernanda Rossi, Sr. Carmela Termine, Sr. Carmen Palacios, Sr. Janice Collins, and Sr. Martina Ponce were met at the airport by Fr. Charles Pagliughi, pastor of Immaculate Conception Parish, the Sisters' community of Metairie, and the Salesian Fathers from Marrero. The Sisters felt at home immediately, for the parishioners had placed a statue of Don Bosco on a table in the faculty room!

Soon, the rest of the community arrived: Sr. Domenica DiPeri, Sr. Louise Passero, Sr. Ann Cassidy, Sr. Donna Mae Epperson, Sr. Rita Bailey, and Sr. Leslie Satter.

The mission of this community included two schools: Immaculate Conception Elementary School with 900 students, and Immaculata High School, with 400 young women, as well as parish catechism classes.

Now the Salesian community on the Westbank was complete: Sisters, Priests, Brothers, and Cooperators spread the spirit of Don Bosco and Mary Mazzarello, bringing forth a harvest ripe in vocations! Connie Breaux, former teacher at Immaculate Conception Elementary School, and Deborah Walker, former student at Immaculata, joined the Salesian Sisters.

Having survived the devastation of Hurricanes Katrina and Rita (below), Sisters take a moment to enjoy the Café du Monde in New Orleans, Louisiana, on the 50th anniversary of Immaculata High School in 2006: Sr. Judith Suprys, Sr. Maria Colombo, Sr. Marisa De Rose, Sr. Ann Cassidy, and Sr. Rita Bailey.

9

FROM ONE PROVINCE, TWO

The 1980's

The Sisters of the Western Province of Mary Immaculate, represented here by Sr. Rosann Ruiz amid the golden poppies of California, are thankful for all that Sr. Cecilia Besi did to set the new Province along its way.

"The idea stunned most of the participants and, soon, objections were rising from all over the hall and a myriad of reasons were being presented why it could not be done. Unperturbed, Mother General received them all. We were asked to consider with all the Sisters, the vast geographical distances, the number of houses and Sisters, the difficulty of the visitations, and the cultural differences. Sometime after the visit of Mother General, the results of the study were in, and it was decided to form two Provinces."

Openings and Closings

For the "me" generation, the Eighties were a period of extremes. Supply-side economics promised growth and brought deficits. Fortunes were made. Markets crashed. The Berlin Wall came down! Communism in the Soviet Union and Eastern Europe withered away and collapsed. Violence became the typical media fare. Campuses seethed again, but this time the dispute went to the core of education: that which defines civilization.

Customs, family life, justice, peace, and the environment became issues without solutions. The education of youth became even more imperative, and the need to make choices became crucial for the Salesian Sisters. Difficult choices were made and living with the consequences was not always easy for the Sisters. Turbulence seemed always just below the surface. But everyone accepted the fact that adjustments had to be made.

Mother Theresa Sironi was appointed the 12th Provincial of the Salesian Sisters' Province of the United States and Canada in 1981. That same year "MM 81" was launched to commemorate the 100th anniversary of the death of Mother Mazzarello, with a new understanding of Saint Mary Mazzarello as a woman of prayer and faith. It also signaled a new direction in research and literature that delved into the Salesian charism. The anniversary and the Church's tremendous strides in religious life offered a new direction for the General Chapter which opened in Rome in September 1981 and closed in February 1982 with the renewed text of the *Constitutions,* the foundational documents of the Institute.

Canadian Sisters of the Province of Notre Dame du Cap with friends and collaborators.

Sr. Candide Asselin welcomes all to the new Laura Vicuña Center in Montréal, Canada.

In Canada in 1986, a new community at Rivière des Prairie opened. It was in a new section in Montréal that had expanded and had needed a stable presence of the Sisters. Previously some Sisters had come on Sundays from Saint Dominic Savio Parish to help animate the liturgies and to teach catechism. With the new residence, the Sisters opened a youth center for a full-time ministry. Years later, this center developed into the Provincial House for the new Province of Notre Dame Du Cap.

Also in Montréal, a new house for initial formation and for youth retreats was opened as an extension of the apostolate of the community at Saint Claire Parish.

Further south, in New Jersey, after many years of serving as an orphanage, a home to the Sisters, and then as the second Provincial House, the very difficult decision was made to tear down the White House in Haledon and rebuild it entirely. The foundation had been made of wooden beams which had weakened over the years. The plumbing and

Mary Help of Christians Academy

Odette Harris came from a poor Jamaican family living in Paterson, New Jersey. She attended Mary Help of Christians Academy on scholarship and graduated in 1987, went on to graduate from Dartmouth College, and was the first undergraduate to receive a Howard Hughes Medical Institute Grant. She is a graduate of Stanford University's School of Medicine with board certification in neurosurgery. She is also one of the first women to win the prestigious 2003 William P. Van Wagenen Fellowship, given by the American Association of Neurological Surgeons.

"My years at Mary Help were a pivotal time in my life," says Dr. Harris. "They have served as the foundation of my academic and spiritual life. I know the guidance and discipline I received helped me through college and medical school."

"Welcome to San Antonio, Mother Cecilia Besi!" proclaim Sr. Lupe Gomez, Sr. Cesira Pierotti, and Sr. Mary Becerril.

electrical wiring needed to be completely renewed, as well as much of the structure itself. The general layout of the house was not convenient for the Sisters anymore, either. The home could no longer accommodate all the Sisters. Privacy was lacking; each of the four individual bedrooms held up to five beds. The laundry room was in Don Bosco Hall rather than in the White House.

Overall, the White House was outdated. It would have been a costly endeavor to remodel the house. Thus it was decided that it would be more cost-effective to simply demolish and rebuild.

The groundbreaking for the new house occurred on May 12, 1986. Demolition began immediately, followed by the clearing, filling, leveling, and excavating of the land. By June 1986, foundations were laid and the new residence of the Sisters in North Haledon began being built. The White House was now a vivid memory in the hearts and minds of the Sisters.

The great day finally arrived on August 15, 1988, the Feast of the Assumption of Our Lady. The Sisters were given word that the construction was complete, and on August 19, 1988, they were able to take up residence in the new "White House."

"Gangway!" Sr. Teresa Xuan, Sr. Esther Lopez, and Sr. Gloria Mar lead the way to clearing the ground for the new Western Provincial Center in San Antonio, Texas.

Time to Divide

One of the major adaptations that had to be made in the 1980s was the division of the Mother Province into two Provinces. God had blessed the life and ministry of the Salesian Sisters, and it was time to give birth and to let go.

Mother Marinella Castagno, Mother General of the worldwide Institute, visited the Province from September 16-17, 1986. During this visit, she heard the concerns, the dreams, the hopes, and the needs of the Sisters regarding the re-dimensioning of the Province. After consultation, prayer, and sharing, the decision was made to form a second Province.

The idea stunned most of the participants and, soon, objections were rising from all over the hall and a myriad of reasons were being presented why it could not be done. Unperturbed, Mother General received them all. The Sisters were asked to consider with all the Sisters, the vast geographical distances, the number of houses and Sisters, the difficulty of the visitations, and the cultural differences. Sometime after the visit of Mother General, the results of the study were in, and it was decided to form two Provinces.

The announcement suprised many. However, all these factors called for a new way of living the Salesian charism in the United States.

In the spring of 1987, the work of the division began. By August 24, 1987, the Western Province of Mary Immaculate was formed. Sr. Cecilia Besi was appointed Provincial. She would reside in San Antonio, Texas, in a section of the convent of Saint John Bosco that would serve as temporary Provincial offices. The new Province would include the houses of Texas, Louisiana, and California (and, in the next decade, Arizona and Colorado). The Mother Province of Saint Philip the Apostle retained the communities of New Jersey, New Jersey, Florida, Pennsylvania, and Canada. Sr. Patricia King served as Provincial.

Later that very same year, Pope John Paul II visited three of the states in the Western Province. This was seen as a double blessing for the new Province.

Across the Sea

On August 6, 1988, a group of five Novices from Mary Immaculate Province and Saint Philip the Apostle Province left to make their Novitiate in Castelgondolfo, Italy. It was a historic moment for both Provinces, one that was filled with emotion. While it was painful for the Sisters to know that the Novices would be leaving the Province for two years, the benefits of the international experience at the heart of the Church and the Institute outweighed the pain. Sr. Suzanne Dauwalter and Sr. Ramona Beltre were the first two from the St. Philip the Apostle Province to benefit from this formative experience.

Camp Auxilium

"As I look back on my life, there are distinct memories that I cherish, and one being my times at Camp Auxilium. One of the highlights of camp life was winning Junior Miss Auxilium! I truly believe that my camp experiences as a young girl helped develop and build my spiritual foundation into the woman that I am today.

"When I received my Confirmation, I decided to choose JOY as my Confirmation name. I always received the JOY award at camp. I remember during one of our daily Rosaries, the Sisters said in order to have JOY in your life, you must have JESUS, OTHERS, and YOURSELF. I want to thank the Salesian Sisters for making me aware of what joy is, and I try to live life to the fullest every day."

Allison McCartney, Wharton, NJ

Bishop Frank Rodimer of Paterson, New Jersey, presents a picture of Pope John Paul II to Sr. Isabel Garza, new Principal of Pope John Paul II School in Clifton.

Sr. Catherine Hurley leads a dramatic retelling of the Last Supper for First Holy Communion children, Sacred Heart Novitiate, Newton, New Jersey.

At the same time, Sr. Maria Colombo was asked to begin a retreat house at the Sacred Heart Novitiate in Newton, New Jersey. This program would be a center of spirituality for any person or group looking for an environment conducive to prayer and reflection. Two years later, Sr. Carmen Peña and Sr. Catherine Hurley spearheaded the renovations needed to provide an improved facility for this new retreat program.

New Presences

In 1987, Bishop Frank Rodimer of Paterson asked Mother Teresa Sironi, Provincial, if the Sisters would help facilitate the closure of Saint Stephen School in Paterson. The Sisters of Nazareth were leaving the inner-city school and the Diocese felt it necessary to place the students in other viable schools. Sr. Frances Gumino and Sr. Emy DeFilippi agreed to ease the pain of the families and students at the school and help them find places in neighboring schools. Sr. Roble Cavazos, Sr. Mary Pellicione, and Sr. Louise Passero also brought their gifts for the service of the young during this difficult period. The school was officially closed in June 1990.

Beginning on July 16, 1987 Sr. Carmen Botello began to serve as Principal of Our Lady of Prompt Succor School in Westwego, Louisiana. By 1989, a canonical community was established with Sr. Carmen Botello, Sr. Juanita Chavez, Sr. Lourdes Trevino, and Sr. Theresa Xuan. The apostolic works included kindergarten through eighth

Sr. Domenica Di Peri, Sr. Leslie Satter, and Sr. Louise Passero are knee deep in Louisiana flood waters in 1980.

grade, before and after school care, catechism for public school students, and summer camp.

In 1988, the 100th anniversary of the death of Saint John Bosco mobilized the entire Salesian world in the United States for one grand celebration! Local communities of Sisters, Priests, and Brothers sponsored youth rallies, Eucharistic Celebrations, pilgrimages, and a host of other initiatives in their respective dioceses and archdioceses.

A national Don Bosco '88 committee was established in order to organize a huge youth rally at Madison Square Garden in New York City. And so it happened! Fr. Steve Schenck wrote a masterful musical entitled *Windows to the Word* in which Don Bosco came alive in the modern day. This experience was one that forever remained in the hearts and minds of all those blessed to be a part of it.

In September 1988, a group of Sisters attended the beatification ceremonies of Laura Vicuña at Colle Don Bosco in Becchi, Italy. Shortly thereafter, the construction of a new gym and youth center dedicated to Blessed Laura

Vicuña at Saint John Bosco School in San Antonio, Texas was under way.

By 1989, a house of formation was re-opened in Corralitos for the pre-novices. God and his Mother were blessing this Province with many and new vocations!

Also in 1989, Sr. Barbara Campbell was sent to Ascension of the Lord School in LaPlace, Louisiana, as the administrator. The school was located in a very poor area on the outskirts of the Archdiocese of New Orleans. Although she remained for only three years, the Salesian spirit caught on, and 19 years later, it is still evident! When Sr. Maria Colombo and Sr. Lise Parent of Immaculate Conception Parish were interviewed on WWL-TV in preparation for the centenary celebration, Sara Comiskey, the Communications Director for the Archdiocese of New Orleans, knew all about the Preventive System and its three-fold components of Reason, Religion, and Loving Kindness. When questioned as to how she could be so well versed in the Salesian spirit, she informed the Sisters that she was a past pupil of Ascension of the Lord!

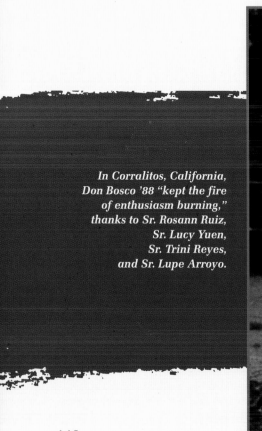

In Corralitos, California, Don Bosco '88 "kept the fire of enthusiasm burning," thanks to Sr. Rosann Ruiz, Sr. Lucy Yuen, Sr. Trini Reyes, and Sr. Lupe Arroyo.

The Partners Circle Board of Trustees, our outstanding friends and collaborators, gathered in Tampa, Florida, in 1992.

Development and Communications

A good organizer as well as a woman of vision, Sr. Patricia King, Provincial, took the first step in setting up a Development Office for the Eastern Province in order to support growth and to help meet the financial needs of the mission of the Sisters. The Development Office was established in 1989, and its first (and current) director was Sr. Mary Rinaldi.

Sr. Mary, over the years, has succeeded in making a significant difference in raising not only funds, but also outstanding friends and collaborators. One of the first successful undertakings of the Development Office was to form a Board of Trustees that gave invaluable help, direction, and focus to the new venture. The founding members of this board were: Sr. Mary Rinaldi, Director; Sr. Patricia King, A. M. "Bud" D'Alessandro, Barbara Hedgecock, Michael Massood, Lucy Nardella, Rosemarie D'Alessandro, Abelardo Sierra, Hon. Emiliano Salcines,

Dr. Vincent Bagli, Joseph J. McAleer, Sr., Jack Guggino, MD, and Sr. Carmen Peña. They created a mission statement and set distinct and reachable goals from the very beginning.

As educators, many of the Sisters had already been working in the area of critical analysis of the media. However, many Sisters found themselves left them feeling inadequate and unprepared for handling all of the issues emerging from the ever expanding media field.

Already back in the early 1960's Sr. Maria Pia Giudici had come from Italy and challenged the Sisters in the U.S. to look into the media that was flooding the American market, to enable students and parents to make critical evaluations. However, many Sisters felt that they themselves knew too little to help their students. Sr. Louise Passero was one of the Sisters who undertook the task of helping the communities establish some general evaluation principles. This was an "extra task" for her, over and above her usual responsibility, and mainly directed towards the Sisters and the young people in formation. With the explosion of the

Enjoying a "Getting to Know Us"
Province assembly are Sr. Rita Bailey,
Sr. Cecilia Henry, Sr. Charlotte Greer,
Sr. Theresa Jones, and Sr. Teresa Xuan.

media and technology in the U.S., Sr. Louise was often called upon for advice. She readily gave her services and became quite an expert in this critical field.

The Provincial, Sr. Patricia, proposed the founding of an Office of Communications that would assume responsibilities in this area and any others that would need some expertise for all those involved in the education of others. The proposal was accepted, and Sr. Louise Passero was officially appointed as full-time consultant for media and communications.

The division of the Province into separate Eastern and Western Provinces in 1987, and a Canadian Province in 1991, meant that Sr. Louise was responsible for all three Provinces as the media expert! In her new role, she also translated various documents for the Sisters, including *Da Mihi Animas,* the monthly publication of the Institute that is distributed worldwide.

Sr. Aida Flores prepares a feast for a
Salesian Sisters gathering at Camp Auxilium in Newton, New Jersey.

Let it snow! Not even bitter cold stops the smiles of the Salesian Sisters!

Students of Saint Michael School in Atlantic City, New Jersey, sing "Happy Birthday" to Frank Sinatra at the Golden Nugget Casino in 1982.

Sr. Virginia D'Alessandro welcomes Sr. Mary Rinaldi to Saint Joseph's in Tampa, Florida, in 1966.

10

WE ARE PARTNERS
The 1990's

"The Lord added the last event of the evening. The chapel's clear, high windows faced a woodland wonder. Suddenly, as prayer was in progress, Sr. Cecilia Besi stood and pointed to a deer peacefully grazing among the outside trees. Everyone realized that nature, too, came to celebrate the new home for the Sisters. Sr. Judith Suprys commented, as she observed the satisfaction of both the Sisters and families and friends, 'This is truly a house that love built.' A better summation could not be found."

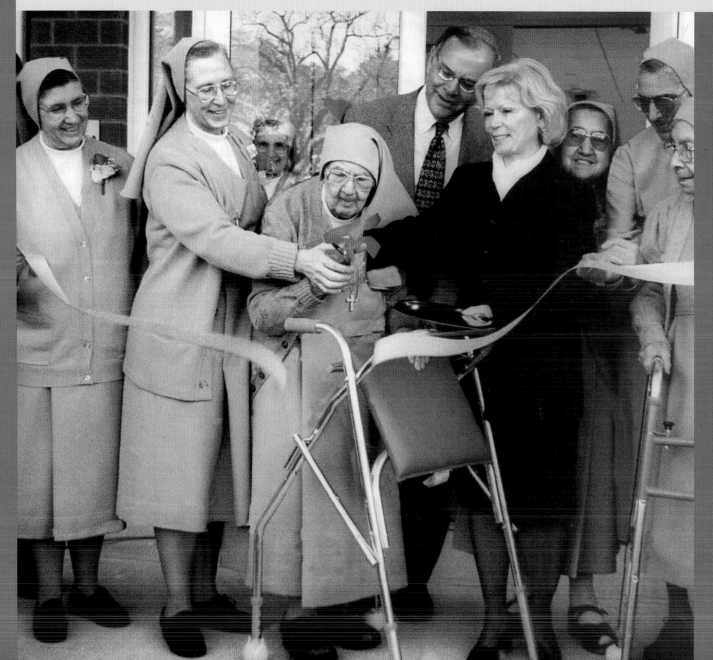

Sr. Mary Ligregni cuts the ribbon to open the new Saint Joseph's Provincial Center, aided by Sr. Theresa Kelly, Sr. Judith Suprys. Judge E.J. Salcines, Barbara Hedgecock, Sr. Philomena Martorana, Sr. Cecilia Besi, and Sr. Stella Ruiz.

This little chapel in Avondale, Arizona, is where children and adults gather for prayer and an Oratory, with Sr. Carmen Palacios, Sr. Adele Lozano, Sr. Guadalupe Gomez and Sr. Amparo Uribe.

A Province for Canada

The last decade of the century, in the last century of the millennium, has been shadowed by plague, civil war, and terror. Technological innovations globally connected the world. Atlanta hosted the Summer Olympics. The Oklahoma City bombing was only the beginning. The media had become omniscient and dictates what is newsworthy day by day.

A President was not only found wanting, but also brought dishonor to the Oval Office. It seemed that the moon landings and the invasion of other planets allowed us to neglect our own.

Once again, God's blessings called for another birth from the Mother Province. The Canadian Province of Notre Dame du Cap was formed. The Sisters again suffered the pains of separation, but faithfully knew that only when the seed dies can new life be born. And so it was!

On September 29, 1991, the houses of Canada were officially established as a pre-Province with the authorization to find the best way to serve the Church in that country. Always a woman of prayer and positive direction, the Provincial relied on God's help and on Mary Help of Christians. Sr. Eileen Joseph was named as the first Superior of the pre-Province in 1991.

Smaller yet again, but more than ready, the Sisters of Saint Philip the Apostle saw the signs of the times and the birth of a new Province as a call to action. Armed with the Word of God, a passion for the mission, and a love for young people, they regrouped, refocused, and recommitted themselves to living the Salesian motto, "*Vado io!*" "I'll go!"

Partners in Giving

In 1990, a year after the Development Office was formed, a bi-monthly newsletter was created to provide information, formation, and accountability to family and friends across the nation. It was named *Partners In Giving*. Dr. Joseph J. McAleer, Jr. has volunteered more than ten years as editor.

Sr. Mary Rinaldi still coordinates the efforts of all into a unified Partners in Giving service to youth; to new vocations to religious life; and in the care given to the elderly Sisters who have completed their ministry and are now in need of care, attention, and love.

Greater successes were yet to come! Soon, Sr. Mary and the Salesian Sisters Board of Trustees, following the advice of trustee, Mr. Joseph J. McAleer, Sr., founded the "Partners Circle" in 1991. These "Partners" are supportive of the Sisters' mission and offer financial support for emergency needs throughout the Province. They truly share the vision of the Salesian Sisters.

In 1991, a man named Fortune Bosco shared his idea of "adopting" a nun as a means of raising funds to support the Sisters' retirement needs. He explained how the people needed their prayers. After considering his idea, Sister Mary developed a program called "Adopt-A-Sister," which has been very successful in helping to support the retired Sisters.

ABC News' "20/20" Reporter Bob Brown interviewed Sr. Virginia D'Alessandro in 1999 for a story on the Adopt a Sister Program.

The program's focal point was to establish a "spiritual" friendship between donors and their "adopted" Sister. In gratitude, the Sister would become a prayer partner with the donor. Donations varied in size, each being just as meaningful. The beauty of the program is that the donation amounts are never disclosed, so regardless of donation size, the relationships formed were genuine because every person who donated received the same treatment – a beautiful Salesian prayer partner.

In 1995, the Adopt-A-Sister program hit local news and helped expand its success. But the big break came in

"Partners in Giving"

We're partners in giving, you and I,
for a dream that's shared can never die.
How blessed we are by God above
who hears our prayers and sends His love.
When freely given to meet a need,
love multiplies like harvest seed,
for the more we try to give away,
the more God blesses us each day!
We're partners in giving, you and I,
for a dream that's shared can never die.
– Clay Harrison

1999 when ABC News' *20/20* national television program picked up the story of the Adopt-A-Sister program and the need for a retirement home for the elderly Salesian Sisters. The *20/20* "miracle" was that, within 24 hours of the primetime broadcast, 10,000 people joined the program, and $1.4 million was raised for the Saint Joseph Provincial Center, a new home to house the elderly and infirm Sisters that would meet the needs of the Sisters and make nursing care available to them in a facility that met necessary regulations and standards. Thanks to *20/20*, when the ribbon-cutting took place in November 1999, the Sisters carried no debt.

The Development Office of the Salesian Sisters of the West was begun in the fall of 1997. The main purpose was to promote the work of the FMA among the young, especially the poorest, to spread devotion to Mary, Help of Christians, and to recruit funds for the elderly and infirmed Sisters. The first Development Director was Sr. Carmen Palacios.

New Horizons

In 1990, Saint Joseph School in Newton, New Jersey, was in need of a principal. Sr. LouAnn Fantauzza graciously accepted the responsibility and simultaneously served as the Principal of Saint Joseph's and Camp Auxilium Learning Center. Later, Sr. Betty Ann Martinez took over and successfully led the school through the Middle States Accreditation. The Sisters withdrew from Saint Joseph School in June 2001 but still maintain a cordial relationship.

On August 4, 1991, the Aspirants (candidates to the religious life) transferred their house of formation from Panorama City, California, where it had been for a number of years, to Corralitos (the Western house of formation had originally been in Aptos, but when the state took over the property to expand its community college, the Aspirantate had moved to Panorama City). The pastoral setting of Corralitos made it a very conducive location for the formation of the candidates.

In 1991, a second community was established in Toronto, Canada, and placed under the protection of Saint John Bosco. This community would provide the English-speaking Canadian Sisters an opportunity for ministry in their own country. Members of this community included Sr. Roberta Johnson, Superior, Sr. Estelle Johnson, and Sr. Patricia Melanson.

After years of dreaming and planning, the groundbreaking for the new Provincial Offices and Retirement Center of the West became reality in San Antonio, Texas. Sisters, priests, neighbors, and friends came together on August 24, 1991 to celebrate this special moment in the life of the new Province.

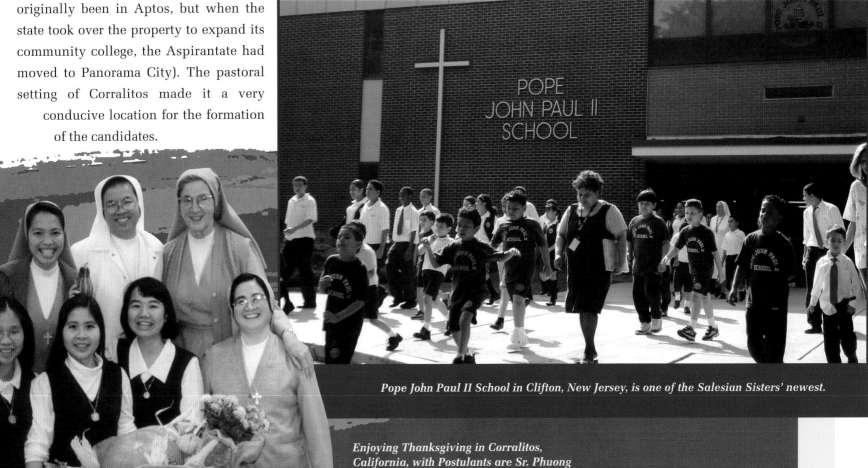

Pope John Paul II School in Clifton, New Jersey, is one of the Salesian Sisters' newest.

Enjoying Thanksgiving in Corralitos, California, with Postulants are Sr. Phuong Nguyen, Sr. Anna Bui, Sr. Cesira Pierotti, and Sr. Rosa Hoang.

By 1991, the deterioration of the building that housed Saint John Cathedral School in Paterson, New Jersey, was patently clear. Saint Joseph School, a few blocks away, had the same problem. The Diocese decided to merge the two schools. Confronting overwhelming difficulties and decisions that would deeply affect the children, Sr. Isabel Garza spearheaded the entire process.

By 1992, Pope John Paul II School, newly named and newly moved into the former Paul VI High School building in Clifton, opened. The success of this merger is a testimony to the dedication, perseverance, and love of Sr. Isabel for the children of Paterson.

Saint Anthony School in Hawthorne, New Jersey, would lose the Dominican Sisters in 1995. The pastor and the parishioners asked for a Salesian Sister to administer the school. Sr. Patricia Roche accepted the position and brought the Salesian spirit to yet another educational institution in New Jersey.

Missions Grow

In September 1992, the Sisters agreed to staff Saint Mary School in East Los Angeles, California. The Salesian priests and brothers were already staffing the parish, so the arrival of the Sisters made the family complete! Sr. Amparo Uribe and Sr. Olga Munoz were the first to bring the Salesian spirit to the students in the school. Sr. Teresita Delgado and Sr. Maria Arroyo later joined the Sisters in pastoral work that included caring for the physical needs of the poor in a program that came to be known as "*Pan de Vida*" (Bread of Life).

The Salesian priests and brothers assumed the administration of La Salle High School in Miami, Florida, in 1985. Originally named Immaculata-La Salle High School, it was born from the merger of Immaculata and La Salle High Schools. Its original ministry of serving the children of Cubans escaping the oppression in their homeland

Sr. Patricia Roche, Principal of Immaculata/La Salle High School in Miami, Florida, steps out with students.

The Pan de Vida program distributes food to the needy every Wednesday at Saint Mary Parish in East Los Angeles, California. One of the Sisters speaks to the group on Christian formation as well as on ways to better themselves and their families.

Hurricane Andrew

"Two weeks after Hurricane Andrew in 1992, my mother, my children, and I traveled to Miami to see Sr. Domenica Di Peri, Sr. Ruth Stecker, and Sr. Mary Terzo at La Salle High School. They showed us the once beautifully landscaped gardens, totally destroyed by fallen, centuries-old cypress trees. The weather bureau had reported 165-mile-per-hour winds, yet in the middle of the cypress grove, the small two-foot fiberglass statue of Our Lady was still on its pedestal untouched, unharmed, serenely gazing at the visitors. In an area close to the Bay, a giant oak had fallen inches away from the huge statue of the Sacred Heart, whose extended arms seemed to point to the destruction around the statue. I shall never forget what I saw and what I felt."

— *Maria Novas, kindergarten teacher at Villa Madonna School in Tampa, Florida.*

continues for second and third generations who have made America their home. Sr. Ruth Stecker, Sr. Dominica Di Peri, and Sr. Mary Terzo arrived in Miami to collaborate with their Salesian counterparts in 1992, along with Hurricane Andrew that would attempt to dislodge them all!

On August 24, 1992 Hurricane Andrew hit South Florida, resulting in 15 deaths, more than 250,000 temporary homeless, and $20 billion in damages. It was the most costly natural disaster to have occurred in the country up to that time. Hardly any part of South Florida was unaffected and recovery took years.

The devastation suffered by La Salle was extensive. Windows were blown out. Debris filled the campus. Even a cabin cruiser was relocated to the school parking lot! But true to the Salesian spirit, everyone joined forces to clean up and open the school as soon as possible.

Soon after her arrival in Miami, Sr. Mary Terzo found herself accepting a position as Associate Superintendent of Schools for the Archdiocese. In this position, she was able to spread the Salesian charism more widely.

In 1995, the administration of La Salle High School was transferred to the Salesian Sisters when the priests and brothers felt it was necessary to withdraw from this ministry. Today, the school has reverted to its original name and is known once more as Immaculata-La Salle High School.

The Salesian priests and brothers serving in Birmingham, Alabama, had long requested the presence of the Sisters. Women and young girls were in need of learning life-skills, the same needs as when Saint Mary Mazzarello began her work in Mornese.

Sr. Lucy Balistrieri tries not to blow away while setting up for a children's fair in Birmingham, Alabama.

On September 25, 1995, Sr. Lucy Balistrieri, Sr. Carmen Morales, Sr. Elizabeth Russo, and Sr. Inez Valentin journeyed to Birmingham. The Salesian fathers and brothers, and lay missionaries welcomed them warmly and enthusiastically. On September 27, 1995, Bishop David Foley and many friends of the Salesian family came to officially begin the mission with a prayer service.

This mission closely resembled the poverty that the first Sisters at Mornese experienced. Furniture and household necessities were lacking, but the work was ever present! The Sisters' mission with these poor and at-risk children included tutoring, skills training, and religious education. The mission continued until 2001 when the lay collaborators were able to continue the work themselves. Friendships remained and the good accomplished by the Sisters endures.

Reunited

Since 1993, the Salesian Sisters in the United States have been part of the World Youth Day celebrations that have taken place all over the world. Sr. Maryann Schaefer coordinated this experience for the 1993 World Youth Day, held in Denver, Colorado. More than 500 Salesian young people gathering in the Mile-High City. The atmosphere was charged with pride in being Catholic and with joy in being part of the experience. The Denver Police Department even reported that crime was down while World Youth Day attendance was up!

Following this first experience, Salesian youth from the U.S. have attended World Youth Days in Manila, Rome, Paris, Montréal, Cologne, and Sydney.

"I have been amongst millions of young people – young people who often are not spoken of in good terms by others!" Sr. Maryann recalled. "I've heard these World

In 1999, California Sisters from Bell Gardens and Bellflower gather: Sr. Refugio Gallardo, Sr. Victoria Graziani, Sr. Maria Becerril, visiting Councilor Sr. Teresa Curmi, Sr. Cesira Pierotti, Sr. Guadalupe Gomez, and Sr. Mary Link.

Sr. Elizabeth Russo admires a parent's cultural dress during a fair in Birmingham, Alabama.

Youth Days referred to as a 'Catholic Woodstock' – far from it! There is no violence; there is only worship. Coming home from World Youth Days finds me on a high, though physically tired. The young people talk about it for weeks, months, even years. 'We've seen the Pope!' 'We've met other young people from around the world!' 'This was a once-in-a-lifetime experience!'"

As Don Bosco would say it, Sr. Maryann was out with the youth, winning souls for God.

On March 23, 1999, a dialogue between Sr. Theresa Kelly, Provincial of the East, and Sr. Martina Ponce, Provincial of the West, began concerning the future of the Salesian Sisters' presence at Immaculate Conception Parish in Marrero, Louisiana. The Sisters of the West could no longer staff this ministry. Would the Mother Province be able to help?

The Province discerned, and Sr. Maria Colombo joined the Western Province for the 1999-2000 school year. Her role, along with Sr. Rosann Ruiz's, the current Principal, would be to transition the work to the Eastern Province. The 2000-2001 school year found a new community ready to continue the legacy of Saint John Bosco. Sr. Mary Terzo, Animator and Principal of both Immaculata High School and Immaculate Conception Elementary School; Sr. Domenica Di Peri, Assistant to the Principal; Sr. Florine Lagace, Elementary School Teacher; and Sr. Maria Colombo, High School Theology Teacher, formed the new community.

A strong desire on the part of the Salesian Sisters and Salesian Priests Provinces in North America to formalize their work resulted in the Salesian North American Conference (SNAC). This Conference brought together the six Provincial Councils of the United States and Canada. The resolution formed at the first meeting gave direction to youth pastoral ministry in the Provinces and also helped to unify collaboration between the FMAs and the SDBs.

At the Heart

As a means for on-going formation, each Sister in the United States was given the opportunity to participate in a pilgrimage to Salesian sites in Italy. These pilgrimages occurred during the summer months over a six-year period in the 1990s. Mornese, Turin, Becchi, and the Motherhouse in Rome were all part of the Sisters' itinerary. The groups were even able to visit Milan, Assisi, and Castelgondolfo, the summer residence of the Holy Father.

A particularly poignant moment in this pilgrimage was participation in a private Eucharistic celebration with Pope John Paul II. This experience deepened the Sisters' experience and their appreciation for all they had learned about Don Bosco and Mother Mazzarello.

As nations have become more and more interdependent, the Sisters in the United States broadened their horizons by participating in international meetings. Sisters have attended the Seminar on Prayer and the Congress for Salesian Cooperators, both held in Ireland. Other forums in which the Sisters currently participate include the Youth Congress in Chile, the Salesian School Convocation in Colombia, the CIEC meeting in Ecuador, and the Communications meeting in Costa Rica.

In 1998, the North American Conference (NAC), composed of the three FMA Provincial Councils, met with the inter-provincial conference of Mexico, Central America, and the Antilles (CIMAC). This first and historic meeting established communication and collaboration that would lead to future projects for the good of the young.

Tampa's Youth

As Villa Madonna School in Tampa, Florida, continued to grow, it became apparent to the Sisters that many of the neighborhood children were left to fend for themselves, and consequently they ended up in police custody or detention. Most of these children looked longingly over the fence to see the children of Villa Madonna at play or in school games on the spacious playground. The Sisters began a Saturday Club for these children as well as the students of the neighborhood schools.

This was not enough. Sr. Mary Rinaldi, herself a Florida native, with the Board of Trustees of the Salesian Sisters planned a renewal project that would benefit the youth of the Tampa district. An aggressive fundraising project began so that an abandoned gym, owned by the School Board of Tampa, could be acquired and used for the young.

Through Mr. Glenn Permuy, the President of Villa Madonna School's PTA and President of the Tampa Bay Boys and Girls Club, the Salesian Sisters established a partnership with the Boys and Girls Clubs of Tampa. In 1995, the Salesian Youth Center became a reality! The program was so successful in helping the young become better citizens, that in two years' time, the police attested that vandalism and violent crimes had almost disappeared from the northeast district of Tampa!

Expansion continued through the efforts of Sr. Mary Rinaldi, the Province Development Director; the

The Baldor Family joins Sr. Kim Keraitis in support of Villa Madonna School in Tampa, Florida: Liana Baldor, Stan Bunn, Javier and Cindy Baldor, and Carlos, Jr., and Maria Baldor.

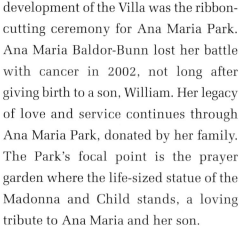

Board of Trustees; the Villa Madonna Development Council, Sr. Kim Keraitis, Principal of Villa; and the staff, parents, and friends of the Villa, especially Ann and Joe Garcia, the Baldor Family, the Middendorf Family, Ann and David Murphey, and Josie and Ray Campo.

A poignant moment in the development of the Villa was the ribbon-cutting ceremony for Ana Maria Park. Ana Maria Baldor-Bunn lost her battle with cancer in 2002, not long after giving birth to a son, William. Her legacy of love and service continues through Ana Maria Park, donated by her family. The Park's focal point is the prayer garden where the life-sized statue of the Madonna and Child stands, a loving tribute to Ana Maria and her son.

The centerpiece of Ana Maria Park at Villa Madonna School in Tampa, Florida, is this statue of Mary holding baby Jesus, a reminder of the choice Ana Maria Baldor-Bunn made to give life to her son.

Saint Joseph Provincial Center

Before Sr. Theresa Kelly's term as Provincial ended, she presided over the long-awaited groundbreaking for the new Saint Joseph Provincial Center and Retirement Home in Haledon, New Jersey, made possible by the outstanding fundraising efforts of the Development Office and the Partners Circle Board of Trustees. The groundbreaking took place in the parking lot of the Saint Joseph Provincialate on July 16, 1998, exactly 90 years after the arrival of the first four Sisters to their first home in Paterson. Construction was overseen by Sr. Cecilia Besi, Sr. Agatha Cosentino, and Mr. Joseph Pfeifer. This new structure would provide Provincial offices and a home for the retired and infirm Sisters.

One year later, on August 27, 1999, one could feel the excitement in the air. Something wonderful, something important was about to take place. The Sisters of the neighboring communities had been invited to escort the Sisters of Saint Joseph's to their new home. Sr. Cecilia Besi (in the absence of Sr. Judith Suprys, the new Provincial, who was in Italy), as animator of the community, reminded them that they were like the chosen people of old. They were called to leave known and familiar surroundings, cross the "Red Sea," and settle into the "Promised Land." She thanked all whose hard work and whose assistance in many ways had gone into the process.

The Sisters present drew a name of one of the elderly Sisters to be accompanied across to the new home. It was ready for occupancy. Only the Sisters and the Eucharistic Presence of Jesus were missing. Sr. Clare Kennelly and Sr. Teresita Teran carried the statue of Mary Help of Christians at the head of the procession of Sisters to their brand new home. So many persons gave their contribution in financial and personal help, and rejoicing could be felt in the air. Everyone joined in the Eucharistic celebration that took place, so that the permanent residency was given to Jesus Himself.

After the Eucharistic celebration, it was time "to check it all out." The Lord added the last event of the evening. The

Girls at the Salesian Youth Center learn about gardening, one of many activities on offer.

The Salesian Youth Center/Boys and Girls Club is a safe haven for inner-city kids in Tampa.

Aerial view of the new Saint Joseph Provincial Center in Haledon, New Jersey, opened in 1999.

chapel's clear, high windows faced a woodland wonder. As the prayer was in progress, Sr. Cecilia Besi suddenly stood and pointed to a deer peacefully grazing among the outside trees. Everyone realized that nature, too, had come to celebrate the new home for the Sisters. Everyone visited all the premises at their leisure. Sr. Judith commented, as she observed the satisfaction of both the Sisters and families and friends, "This is truly a house that love built." A better summation could not be found.

On November 6, 1999, the long-awaited blessing, dedication, and ribbon cutting ceremony took place, allowing guests to tour the facility. The first stop for many of the guests was the chapel, directly in the line of vision as

Sr. Mary Rinaldi, Director of Development, welcomes guests at the groundbreaking for new Saint Joseph Provincial Center on July 16, 1998, the 90th anniversary of the Salesian Sisters in the U.S.

soon as one entered the building. It is aptly called the Hagan Family Chapel, since Joseph Hagan, the last survivor of his family, had given a generous donation in honor of his family.

Joseph Hagan's one luxury was to watch the ten o'clock news every night on his old black and white TV. As God would have it, he turned on the news one day in 1995 to see a segment on the Adopt-A-Sister program, which was being discussed by Sr. Mary Rinaldi. Immediately he called the station, and proceeded to give to the Sisters. Sr. Mary decided that she wanted to visit Mr. Hagan, and from the visit a beautiful friendship developed between the two.

In 1998 as the Sisters were speaking of the need to rebuild Saint Joseph Center, Mr. Hagan told Sr. Mary he wanted to donate the chapel. He only visited the chapel once on May 13, 1999, when it was still under construction. Joseph Hagan and his family are remembered each time the Sisters step into this beautiful house of worship.

A Staff to Guide Them

On August 15, 1999, the feast of Mary's Assumption into Heaven, Sr. Theresa Kelly handed on a symbolic pilgrim's staff to Sr. Judith Suprys who accepted the role of Provincial in the Eastern Province.

The staff was especially meaningful because each FMA had signed this Scripture-rich symbol of leadership. A Bible, signifying the Word of God, and a candle, representing the journey of faith, led the Sisters of the Province into a new decade of life and ministry for and with the young.

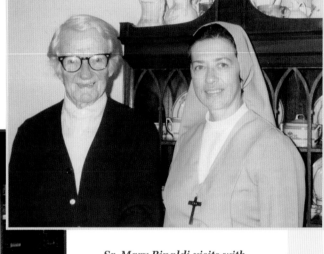

Sr. Mary Rinaldi visits with Mr. Joseph Hagan of Weehawkin, New Jersey, who gave $1 million for the chapel in the Saint Joseph Provincial Center.

Elderly Sisters, accompanied by younger peers, "cross the Red Sea" from their old home to the "Promised Land," the new Saint Joseph Provincial Center.

11 CHANGING THE WORLD
The New Millennium

"Slowly and painstakingly, committees were formed during the 2006-2007 school year allowing everyone the possibility of giving input for the new school in New Orleans. The first item on the agenda was the name and the logo of the school. Academy of Our Lady was selected because Mary was an important part of both campuses. The logo? The image of Mary Help of Christians stands before the fleur de lis, the symbol of Louisiana and its recovery in the battered South."

"We love Camp Auxilium" proclaim campers and Sisters in Watsonville, California.

Changes and Renewal

September 11 terrorist attacks stun America and put the world on alert. The space shuttle Columbia explodes. War in Afghanistan. War in Iraq. Hurricanes Wilma, Rita, Katrina. The violence of the last decade has escalated into the new decade. Cellphones. iPod. iPhones. Racial profiling. Homelessness. The great divide between the haves and the have-nots becomes more and more apparent as poverty is determined by accessibility to technology. The Catholic Church is plagued by scandal and buffeted by abuse.

As the Salesian Sisters of Saint John Bosco complete their first hundred years in the United States, youth is still their focus. They are well aware of the exciting possibilities and new dangers of the emerging twenty-first century for youth. So they step forward with the same love and determination for holiness that Don Bosco and Mother Mazzarello had inspired in Valdocco and Mornese. They, and the young people from generation to generation, form part of a vision seen by Mary Mazzarello years ago, and the voice of Mary that was heard to say, "I entrust them to you!"

What others consider "exceptional" is simply the charism that the Sisters live in creative fidelity to their Founders' dreams. On April 17, 2001, less than ten years after the merger of Saint John Cathedral School and Saint Joseph School into Pope John Paul II School in Clifton, New Jersey, the Principal of Pope John Paul II Elementary School, Sr. Theresa Kelly, received the prestigious Catherine T. McNamee, CSJ, Award presented by the National Catholic Educational Association. This award is given to a school for outstanding leadership in promoting a vision of Catholic education that welcomes and serves cultural and economic diversity.

Sr. Barbara Campbell and Sr. Josie Sanchez lead the Sisters in pilgrimage to Saint Theresa the Little Flower Basilica, the designated Jubilee 2000 church for the Archdiocese of San Antonio, Texas.

The telling of any history that touches the lives of any American is compelled to mention the terrorist attacks of September 11, 2001. The entire Salesian world rallied to the Salesian community in the United States with prayer, messages of concern, and financial help. The Salesian Sisters in the States provided for the emotional, spiritual, and financial needs of their young people and their families. Pope John Paul II, in his general audience on September 12, 2001, wrote a message to the people of America that hoped to heal everyone who was affected by this tragedy: "Let us implore God's comfort upon the injured, the families involved, all who are doing their utmost to rescue survivors and help those affected."

New Decade, New Presences

In August 2002, Sr. Mary Mullaly began her ministry as Director of Catholic Education of the Diocese of Colorado Springs, Colorado. She served as one of the Executive Directors of the Diocese, Superintendent of Catholic Schools, Director of Religious Education for the diocesan parishes, and supervised the Department of Youth Ministry.

Later, the Sisters' presence in Colorado Springs opened the way for evangelization in an area of religious poverty; Our Lady of the Snows community was established in 2003 with three Sisters. Sr. Patricia King was asked to serve as Animator of the community. Like missionaries of the Word, the Sisters traveled miles to the dispersed Christian communities of the outlying prairies while also offering their service in various religious education centers and local schools.

The weekend of October 5-6, 2002 was special as it marked the blessing of the renewed Mary Help of Christians Academy in North Haledon, New Jersey. In order to continue on its path of success into the 21st century, the Auxilium Building and Mazzarello Hall were in need of renovation and refurbishing. It was time for a $1.5 million

The new and improved "Mary Lee's Kitchen" at Mary Help of Christians Academy in North Haledon, New Jersey.

facelift for the Academy. Students from 1940 and 2001 had used the same exact facilities, without any upgrade in between the years.

The science and culinary departments of the Academy were completely upgraded, and new theology rooms were created. The halls and floors were also redone. It was the generous donation of Mary Lee and Fritz Duda, along with Beverly and Rodger Rohde, which spearheaded the "Challenge for Mary Help's Renovation," and, of course, the backing of the Partners Circle members and the many other "angels" who helped raise the funds.

Thanks to this upgrade, Sr. Susan Bagli began the Health Care Connections Program, a new initiative at Mary Help. This award-winning program provides hands-on experience to young women who are interested in the medical field. Through a partnership with the University of Dentistry and Medicine of New Jersey, the students are able to acquire college credit as high school students.

The new science rooms at Mary Help of Christians Academy feature up-to-date lab equipment.

In early 2002, Director of Advancement Christina McAleer, inspired by her late father-in-law, Joseph Sr., came up with the idea of forming a group of women who would care for Mary Help, the Salesian Sisters, and their works. The "Dames of Mary Help" is a volunteer service organization comprised of dedicated women who pledge their time, energy, professional expertise, and financial support through special events, fundraising, and public relations initiatives.

The group's first and current chairperson is Maggie Waitts, the President/CEO of Crown Roll Leaf, Inc., a leading manufacturer in Paterson. With her leadership and the help of all the Dames, the Salesian Sisters have been able to provide many young women with a solid, Catholic education at Mary Help.

Sr. Louise Passero at an international meeting in Quito, Ecuador.

Social Justice

The Western Province took a closer look at the issues of trafficking of children and women, child labor, domestic violence, and immigration. Sr. Phyllis Neves, Provincial of the West, invited specialists in this area to speak to the Sisters and to challenge them to respond. Some of the initiatives that resulted from this meeting include dissemination of information to the local communities, involvement in outreach programs, and collaboration with other agencies.

A foster care facility named Laura's House, a home for misplaced children in the Diocese of Phoenix, Arizona, was subsequently opened by the Salesian Sisters.

In the Eastern Province, Sr. Michelle Geiger was responding to these issues with her students. From 2001-2005, Sr. Michelle served on the Board of the Saint Vincent Pallotti Center. The Center's mission is to promote lay volunteer service that challenges the laity, clergy, and religious to work together in the mission of the Church. The Center takes its inspiration from Saint Vincent Pallotti (1795-1850) who believed passionately in the laity, in each person as an image of God and called by baptism to be an apostle. It was within this context that Sr. Michelle helped students engage in outreach to the poor and marginalized.

Social justice initiatives were coordinated between Mary Help of Christians Academy and Immaculata High School in Louisiana. Students from both schools worked with and for the poor in Washington, D.C. and Appalachia during one-week service experiences.

Middle School Students at Christ the King in Tampa and Immaculate Conception in Marrero wrote letters to their governors, Supreme Court Justices, President Bush, and local authorities regarding pending legislation on abortion, minimum wage, and stem-cell research. Hands-on activities, research, reflection, on-site visits to migrant worker facilities and state capitols, and Powerpoint presentations to State legislators enhanced the overall outreach and social justice efforts of these pre-teenagers.

While the United States was enjoying Christmas celebrations, a devastating earthquake and tsunami hit countries on the other side of the world. On December 26,

Happy Birthday, Sr. Irene Zaccagnino! Sr. Grace Ruiz and Sr. Carmela Termine join in the celebration.

A group of Salesian collaborators visit with Sr. Candice Asselin (right) in Africa.

2004, the Salesian Sisters living and working in Indonesia, India, Thailand, and Myanmar found themselves amongst the ruin left by these natural disasters. Although their houses and schools were not directly affected, and none of the Sisters had lost their lives, many of the students, past-pupils, and family members were victims of the disaster. The Sisters in the States, with the world-wide Institute, immediately coordinated relief efforts to send to their Sisters in need.

Volunteers International for Development of Education Services (VIDES) was officially established on December 31, 2005. VIDES provides opportunities for young adults to be God-bearers by promoting social justice, solidarity, and generosity in sharing and giving of themselves as they incorporate Christian spirituality into the rhythm of everyday living. Volunteers from the States have served in South Africa, Swaziland, Bolivia, Ecuador, Philippines, and Kenya. Sr. Denise Sickinger coordinates the program in the East and Sr. Gloria Mar in the West.

Working Together

East meets West again, and the winners were the Sisters of both Provinces. Love always finds a way when the bond of friendship is extended.

The 2005 appointment of Sr. Phyllis Neves, Provincial of the Western Province, as Provincial of the Eastern Province, brought a new appreciation and perspective of the Sisters' national presence and mission.

The 2005 hurricane season devastated the Salesian schools of the South, leaving Immaculate Conception School and Immaculata High School in Louisiana, along with La Salle High School in Florida, with facilities that were so damaged that school openings had to be suspended. While still recovering from Hurricane Katrina in August, Hurricane Rita struck in September, followed by Hurricane Wilma in October!

Mary Help of Christians Academy

"Before entering Mary Help of Christians Academy, there were many issues which I needed to work on. It was the patience and love of the Sisters that shaped me a great deal. From sports to my daily activities, they made it a point to be involved. They never hesitated to answer my questions, were never too busy to lend an ear to me, whether I called at 6 a.m. or 9 p.m.

"Upon graduation from the Academy, I still received e-mails, letters, and phone calls from my dear Sisters. Whenever I was venturing off, they seemed to contact me as if a direct call from God to get back on track.

"I love them dearly and feel blessed to have had a Salesian education. I can't imagine life without the Salesian charism."

— *Veronica Barrios, class of 2003*

Sr. Maria Colombo, Sr. Lise Parent, and Sr. Lucy Roces, in Marrero, Louisiana, at the time of Hurricane Katrina, evacuated with the thousands of others trying to escape danger. They found refuge in a hotel in Shreveport, Louisiana, five hours away from home. From their hotel room, they watched as Hurricane Katrina destroyed Southeast Louisiana. After Katrina passed, they began the journey back, staying in Baton Rouge with Mrs. Mertie Miller, mother of Sr. Suzanne Miller. The Sisters from Westwego, Louisiana had already arrived at the Miller residence. It was there that the Salesian community of Shaw was able to join the Sisters. They had evacuated after the Hurricane and found themselves sleeping in the car at rest stops. The Miller home gave respite to sixteen Salesian priests, brothers, and Sisters!

Finally, the people of Southeast Louisiana were told they could return to their homes on Labor Day. The Sisters

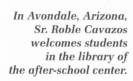

decided to try to get into Jefferson Parish the day prior. Armed with prayer and faith in the intercession of Mary Help of Christians, Sr. Maria Colombo and Sr. Lise Parent drove through the devastated back roads only to arrive at a checkpoint. The National Guard stationed at the checkpoint closed an eye and let the Sisters through!

Driving to the schools was a surreal experience. National Guards were stationed everywhere. The odor in the air was stale and uninviting. Electrical lines and trees blocked roads. Inspection of both schools brought to light the considerable damage that had taken place. Immaculate Conception had been hit by a tornado. Immaculata had been flooded and was full of mold. The Sisters left praying for a way to recover.

The way to recovery was already at hand. Sr. Mary Rinaldi and the Partners Circle began the "Hope for Katrina's Kids" campaign. Michael Guarnieri, the Partners Circle Chairman, announced that more than $176,000 had been raised! This fundraising event was aptly named

"Hope" for that is exactly what was given to those who had lost everything except their faith in God and the support of the Salesian community!

Meanwhile, in Miami, La Salle High School suffered severe damage from all three hurricanes. The roof of the library, the administration building, and the cafeteria was blown off, exposing the contents of the rooms to the elements. Sr. Pat Roche, Principal of La Salle, described how the students were eating lunch in a tent. However, in true Salesian fashion, she stated, "What a challenge faces us! But the Lord, in His mysterious way, will provide."

Although the school and the homes suffered damage, it was not as extensive as the damage done to Southeast Louisiana. Even in the midst of dealing with their own hurricane-related damages, La Salle sponsored a Walk-a-Thon Fund Raiser for their sister school in Louisiana. Themselves in tents and without electricity, they reached out to those whom they considered in more need.

In Avondale, Arizona, Sr. Roble Cavazos welcomes students in the library of the after-school center.

Another Time to Merge

Having barely recovered from Hurricane Katrina, the Archdiocese of New Orleans announced in April 2005 its decision to merge Immaculata High School with Archbishop Blenk High School, both on the Westbank of New Orleans. Parents and students alike responded with bitter resentment and anger. They protested with demonstrations, through the internet, and with letters. Sr. Maria Colombo was asked to administer the school that would be the result of the merger.

Sr. Celia Ramirez checks the forecast in her science lab.

As part of the preparation for the merger, Sr. Maria was asked to serve as Principal of Archbishop Blenk High School for the 2006-2007 school year. This way she would be able to meet the students and staff and gradually introduce the community to the Salesian philosophy of education. Sr. Antoinette Cedrone joined Sr. Maria in this endeavor and worked in the Guidance Department.

Sr. Marisa DeRose joined the community to facilitate the closure of Immaculata High School in the very year it celebrated its 50th anniversary. Sr. Lise Parent and Sr. Theresa Lee maintained the Salesian presence in Immaculate Conception Elementary School.

The local community's anger was, at times, directed to the leadership of the high schools. It felt much like what Saint Mary Mazzarello must have experienced when the school in Mornese, originally intended for boys, was given to the girls.

Slowly and painstakingly, committees were formed during the 2006-2007 school year allowing everyone the possibility of giving input for the new school. The first item on the agenda was the name and the logo of the school. Academy of Our Lady was selected because Mary was an important part of both campuses. The logo? The image of Mary Help of Christians stands before the fleur de lis, the symbol of Louisiana and its recovery in the battered South.

Adopt-a-Sister

"How could I not renew my spiritual adoption of Sr. Frances Gumino? Through my mother, the Lord put me in the path of Sr. Frances, and also Sr. Mary Palatini, Sr. Mary Ruiz, Sr. Nancy Zingale, Sr. Winifred Elly, Sr. Ida Ossi, and Sr. Julia Mazorati, who are now in Heaven.

"What a wonderful gift I have received in knowing Sr. Frances keeps me in her prayers and thoughts, and in return I do likewise. It is so soothing to hear from dear Sr. Frances. It certainly is a good feeling to know that there are our prayers 'pinch hitting' for the both of us."

Adopt-a-Sister participant, Tampa, FL

Although people feared that no one would come to the new school, and that it would fail, the Salesian spirit prevailed. Academy of Our Lady opened on the former Immaculata campus in August 2007 with 706 students! Archbishop Alfred Hughes celebrated the Inaugural Mass to which dignitaries from civil, state, and Church parishes attended. The current location of Academy of Our Lady is temporary; the Archdiocese is building a new facility in the vicinity. Then, the entire high school campus will be used by Immaculate Conception School for their middle school program.

FMA News

In May 2005, Sr. Lucy Roces was asked to serve at the Institute's center in Rome as the Webmaster for the international Institute. While her departure from the Province is a great loss, it does benefit the entire Salesian family. Her dedication to this work allows the mission of Don Bosco and Mother Mazzarello to spread throughout the world.

Sr. Carmela Termine's "*Vado io*" in response to the Mother General's request for missionary Sisters to serve at the International Novitiate in Rome was accepted. Her quiet, serene, and prayerful demeanor is an asset to the Novitiate community and serves the greater needs of the Institute.

Sr. Karen Dunn was sent to Italy for a year-long course in formation. Her participation in this course will help the Province develop a formation program that is tailored to the background and experience of those who feel called to Salesian life.

Sr. Denise Sickinger was appointed the FMA delegate for the Salesian Cooperators Council, which helps organize, assist, and guide the Cooperator Units of Saint Philip the Apostle Province. Although the Cooperators (lay people who choose to live the Salesian spirit) are self-governing, Sr. Denise provides spiritual guidance and serves as the link to the SDB and FMA branches of the Salesian Family.

When Bishop Arthur J. Serratelli of Paterson asked the Provincial, Sr. Phyllis Neves, if he could appoint Sr. Theresa Kelly as the Chairperson of the Diocesan Catechetical Commission, the answer, of course, was "Yes!"

Sisters from the three Provinces of the East, West, and Canada drop in for a surprise visit with former Provincial Sr. Josephine Carini during the Tri-Province Assembly, held in Newton, New Jersey, in 2003.

This Commission is responsible for developing policy to give unified leadership to various concerns reflected in catechetical ministry. Sr. Theresa is more than qualified and willing to serve in this regard.

On May 12, 2006, the Salesian Sisters of the Eastern and Western Provinces joined in the worldwide celebration marking the 125th anniversary of the death of Saint Mary Mazzarello. Today, there are more than 14,000 Salesian Sisters serving young people in 83 Provinces on every continent!

The summer of 2006 brought added grace to the Eastern Province. The Mother General, Mother Antonia Colombo, visited the United States. While here, she presided at the first profession of Sr. Mary Jackson and the perpetual profession of Sr. Theresa Lee.

From August 7-11, 2006, the Province of Saint Philip the Apostle had the joy of hosting the regional meeting as part of the General Chapter. Participating in the event were representatives from the two regional conferences: NAC (North America and Canada) and CIMAC (Central America and Mexican Conference). The 36 participants, including nine lay persons, represented nine Provinces and fourteen countries. The presence of Mother Antonia and four Sisters of the General Council increased awareness of the

Sr. Filomena Conti hugs a new friend in San Antonio.

Mother Antonia Colombo, Mother General of the Institute, arrived at Mary Immaculate Provincial House in San Antonio, Texas, in 2006 amid a joyful welcome of Sisters, young people, and lay collaborators.

tremendous work that is being achieved throughout the world.

Sr. Louise Passero, Communications consultant for the two Provinces of the United States, spent the month of August 2007 in South Africa and Zambia where she presented a week-long workshop in media and communications to the younger Sisters of the Province and to invited members of other congregations active in the area. She also gave workshops based on the Plan of Formation of the Congregation to the Sisters of the Province.

On February 25, 2007, the Salesian Sisters undertook the temporary administration of another elementary school, Sacred Heart in Dover, New Jersey. The principal of the

school had become ill and it was necessary for the pastor to find an interim principal. Sr. Domenica Di Peri happily took the role, accompanied by Sr. Esther Cruz. Both arrived in February, as the pastor described, "very light on accommodations but heavy on love and commitment."

From February 29 to March 9, 2007, a group of six Salesian Sisters and four Salesian young women participated in the United Nations 51st Commission on the Status of Women. The commission focused on the elimination of discrimination and violence against women and specifically, against young girls. Having participated in this Commission's work, the Salesian Sisters applied for formal status with the United Nations.

Enjoying a day by the sea in Clearwater, Florida, thanks to Sr. Agatha Cosentino's mom, Agatha (left), are Sr. Agatha, Sr. Kathy Keane, Sr. Mary Terzo, Sr. Lise Parent, Sr. Joanne Holloman, Sr. Gloria Machado, Sr. Theodora Carabin, Sr. Maryann Morabito, Sr. Kim Keraitis, Sr. Catherine Novo, Sr. Josephine Ochoa, and Sr. Theresa Jones.

New Beginnings

Twenty years from the time it had relocated to Italy, the Novitiate program returned to the United States in 2008. God has blessed both the Eastern and Western Provinces with an abundance of vocations, thus allowing the Novices to come "home."

At the Sacred Heart Center in Newton, New Jersey, the formation of the Novices will exist side by side with the ministry of the Sacred Heart Retreat Center for Sisters and lay people. Sr. Joanne Holloman, Director of Novices, and Sr. Margaret Wilhelm, Assistant, will guide the newest members of the Institute in faith, prayer, and Salesian spirituality. Sr. Nivia Arias, Sr. Eileen Tickner, and Sr. Mary Bertha Paquin will continue to bring the young to Christ and Christ to the young through retreats, seminars, and prayer experiences.

The Archdiocese of New York announced in March 2008 that six Catholic schools would close and that four would merge. Corpus Christi School in Port Chester, New York was mandated to merge with Holy Rosary School, also in Port Chester.

The announcement was unexpected and received with mixed emotions. Thankfully, the Salesian Priests and Brothers administered both churches so the educating communities were already members of the Salesian family. Sr. Agatha Cosentino, Principal of Corpus Christi School, spearheaded the process and has completed the merger in time for the 2008-2009 school year. Notwithstanding the magnitude of the task, the two schools did become one Salesian family with the invaluable support of the Salesian Sisters, priests, and brothers.

As one ministry suffers the pain of merger, another ministry awaits the Salesian Sisters in Pensacola, Florida. A parish with an elementary school that favors poor youth petitioned the Eastern Province for help. And help was granted. Sr. Isabel Garza, Sr. Betty Ann Martinez and Sr. Rufina Delgado are the missionaries who are bringing Don Bosco to the young at Saint John the Evangelist School. There, the Sisters will administer the school, coordinate the religious education program of the parish, provide tutoring, and do whatever else it takes to help the young!

Our vocations cup runneth over! Our 2008 group of Aspirants, Postulants, and Novices – one of our largest ever – gathers with the two U.S. Provincial Superiors, Sr. Phyllis Neves and Sr. Sandra Nieves.

The Dream Continues

One hundred years. Time that was has been celebrated. Time to come is glimpsed on the far horizons. It is a challenge to renew identity and purpose; it is a plunge into the unknown, a trusting in the future generations to keep the dream alive and vibrant. Persons have been celebrated; some called by name, others known to God alone and to Mary His Mother.

These hundred years have generated an ongoing celebration: a celebration of FMAs past whose faith transcended limits and restrictions and shaped dreams into realities for the sake of the young; the celebration of FMAs present whose courage guides the youth to stride into the future, trusting in God's "sweet Providence," channeling resources and opportunities into successes; a celebration of FMAs to come, inheritors of a vision to realize God's dream for youth of every time and age.

Another century begins. The dream continues with force and intensity, with Mary Help of Christians still at its center.

Even Salesian Sisters can hula-hoop, as Sr. Margaret Wilhelm and Sr. Helen Godin demonstrate!

"We declare the countdown to the Centenary Year open!" Cutting the big red ribbon in 2007 are (l-r) Sr. Danielle Gonzalez, Sr. Phyllis Neves, Provincial, Sr. Virginia D'Alessandro, and Sr. Mary Jackson.

Sr. Ramona Beltre, PK 3 teacher at Pope John Paul II Elementary School in Clifton, New Jersey, received the Hispanic Teacher of the Year Award for her innovative methods – including "Wheezy" the puppet!

Sr. Margaret Rose Buonaiuto makes Lenten crosses with her young students at Corpus Christi School in Port Chester, New York.

169

The primary mission of the Salesian Sisters to educate young people endures, as these happy faces attest at Villa Madonna School in Tampa, Florida.

A celebration of FMAs to come, builders of a vision that reaches into the past, shaped and fired in the crucible of the present, and launched towards the future, to realize God's dream for tomorrow's youth.

The inheritance of a century has finished and the results are positive. The FMAs lived the experience with "a new awareness of being women of prayer, women of faith, women of God." They discerned the problems and resources of the millennium. They are now ready to re-launch an educational mission for the ever changing, but ever present young people, especially those most in need and at risk.

The Daughter of Mary Help of Christians today still walks in truth, goodness, and love. She is present to the world of youth, still relevant to youth's promise and challenges. So long as the malleable, yet unchanging, world of youth remains, there will be a Daughter of Mary Help of Christians, a Salesian Sister of Saint John Bosco, an FMA.

A grand gathering of the Salesian Sisters of Mary Immaculate Province, led by Sr. Sandra Nieves, Provincial Superior.

Sr. Danielle Gonzalez instructs students at Mary Help of Christians Academy in North Haledon, New Jersey.

Technology is a key component of instruction at Salesian Schools. Here, Sr. Mary Jackson and Carlos Baldor, Jr. observe the excitement at Villa Madonna School in Tampa, Florida.

Our Centennial Celebration opens! Sr. Phyllis Neves cuts the cake with Nancy Corriere, Patricia Smith, Louise Roberge, and Nancy Romano – all past pupils!

12 OUR SALESIAN FAMILY ALBUM

Stephen Quesinberry cherishes the friendship with his Adopted Sister, Sr. Catherine Novo.

Our Wonderful Friends

How can we Salesian Sisters ever express our gratitude to all of our generous friends and family over the past 100 years? Your gifts of time, talent, and treasure have enabled us to continue our mission of service, especially to young people.

Many of you are "Adopters." Founded in 1991, the Adopt-a-Sister Program has earned international praise for its innovative method of fundraising to provide for the essential needs – including housing and health care – for the large number of elderly retired Salesian Sisters, religious women who have devoted their entire lives to the service of the poor, needy, and the young.

For an annual donation, an individual can join the program and "adopt" a Sister. In gratitude for the kindness and act of faith from the Adopter, the adopted Sister holds this person in daily prayer for the year, entering into a mutually beneficial correspondence and friendship.

Thanks to the support of countless friends in the Adopt a Sister Program across the nation, the Salesian Sisters have a proper Retirement Home, where they can live and be cared for in peace and without worry. Once educators themselves, the elderly Sisters have a new mission, praying for their many friends and family members in gratitude for the kind support.

On the next few pages are just a few of our dear friends who have supported us, as Adopters and as friends. We are sorry that we were unable to place everyone's photo as there was insufficient space to do so.

To all of the members of the Adopt a Sister Program and our many benefactors, we Salesian Sisters love you, thank you for your continued support, and hold you and your intentions in prayer. God bless you!

The "Dames of Mary Help" have dedicated their time, talent, and treasure to the support of Mary Help of Christians Academy.

The Partners Circle Board of Trustees spearheads the fundraising efforts of the Eastern Province, enabling the mission of the Salesian Sisters among young people to flourish.

1. Pearl Kalikow, Sr. Kim Keraitis, and Fr. James DeVita.

2. Fritz and Mary Lee Duda.

3. Tyson and Gail Lykes along with Sr. Mary Rinaldi.

4. Sr. Judith Suprys and Juanita Salcines.

5. Eve Barna accompanied by her Adopted Sisters, Sr. Frances Vegetabile and Sr. Frances Mitacchione.

6. Ken Sausville and Sr. Gisella Bonfiglio.

7. Sr. Gerard Barattino and Gail Miller.

8. Sr. Christine Hellen with Michael and Mary Losurdo.

1. *Sr. Rosalie Di Peri and Ed Mahoney.*
2. *Sr. Grace Ruiz with Sr. Virginia Dickey, and Joseph Hoffman.*
3. *Diane and Tony Ekonomou.*
4. *Sr. Claire Perino with Joseph P. Kelly.*
5. *John and Pat Connors and Joe and Terry Laudone.*
6. *Michael Guarnieri with Sr. Loretta DeDomenicis.*
7. *Sr. Claire Perino, Sr. Felicia Tanzella, Sr. Mary Carone,
Sr. Rosalie DiPeri, Sr. Mildred Zanetti and Sr. Mary Barone
visit with Sal Gagliano and Family at the Salesian
Sisters' "Retirement" Home, the Saint Joseph Provincial Center,
the "House That Love Built."*

175

1. *Sr. Mary Palladino and Beatrice Lightfoot.*

2. *Joe and Jo Ann Granatell, with Mr. and Mrs. Scavone.*

3. *Sr. Theresa Lee with members of the Hurricane Katrina Volunteer Service on duty in Marrero, Louisiana.*

4. *Sr. Colleen Clair enjoys fun summer days with the young people at Camp Auxilium in Newton, New Jersey.*

5. *Our "Tuesday Ladies," Irene Damiano, Sofia Stuart, Loretta Sanger and Margie Hnath, celebrate Christmas fun at our annual party!*

1. *The Corcoran Family visits with their Adopted Sister, Sr. Cecilia Besi.*

2. *Sr. Dora Adames and her former students from Villa Madonna School reunite in Tampa, Florida, in 2006.*

3. *Sr. Esther Cruz enjoys her reunion with the O'Halloran Family.*

4. *Sr. Frances Gumino is surrounded by her "fans" at the annual Salesian Sisters Christmas Party in North Haledon, New Jersey!*

5. *Riley Hogan with Sr. Carmen Peña and Sr. Gloria Machado.*

6. *Teriq Sheriff (at right), proud alumnus of Villa Madonna School in Tampa, Florida, celebrates with his family at the annual Partners Circle Gala.*

1. Sr. Theresa Samson with a student from St. Theresa School in Kenilworth, New Jersey.

2. Dr. and Mrs. Louis Gambetta and their sons, Joey and Matthew.

3. Sr. Karen Dunn, Sr. Suzanne Dauwalter, and Sr. Denise Sickinger – all New York Mets fans – meet Sr. Domenica DiPeri, a Yankees fan!

4. Salesian students celebrate their native homeland – Peru!

5. Young women from Mary Help of Christians Academy volunteer at the Salesian Sisters' annual Christmas Party.

6. Sr. Mary Jackson and summer campers enjoy a fun day together.

7. Tony and Phyllis Chernalis of the fabulous Market Basket in Franklin Lakes, New Jersey.

1. *Linda Crosby and Cynthia Blake of Villa Madonna School in Tampa, Florida.*

2. *Luis Garcia and Mariano Garcia.*

3. *Frank and Pat Middendorf.*

4. *Sr. Rose McShane and the Bill Leahy Family.*

5. *Malio Iavarone, Sr Mary Rinaldi, and George Steinbrenner of the New York Yankees!*

6. *Irena Medavoy, Edie Baskin, Sr. Mary Rinaldi, Cheryl Tiegs, and Jennifer Flavin Stallone.*

7. *Theresa Anderson with Mr. and Mrs. Fred Burdack.*

1. Mr. and Mrs. Anthony Rettino.

2. Ray and Josie Campo party with Caesar Rinaldi and Sr. Karen Dunn.

3. Philip Rinaldi, Gabriel Fernandez, and Judge E.J. Salcines.

4. New York Yankee legend Lou Piniella and Sr. Mary Rinaldi.

5. Joseph McAleer, Sr., with 20/20's Nola Safro with former Tampa Mayor Dick Greco.

6. Dr. Emilio Echevarria and Ernest "Cookie" Garcia.

7. Ann and David Murphey and Family.

8. Dr. Jack Guggino and Aida Jurado.

1. *Larry Stupski with the five students he sponsors at Mary Help of Christians Academy.*

2. *Rose La Malva, 102 years young, accompanied by her daughters and Sr. Margaret Wilhelm and Sr. Ida Ossi at Mary Help of Christians Academy.*

3. *Sisters and young people perform "Helping Hands Across the World."*

4. *Sr. Mary Louise Aguirre joins in the summertime fun with two campers from Mary Help of Christians Camp. Salesian camps provide thousands of inner-city kids a safe and healthy summer experience.*

5. *Sr. Isabel Garza leads a group of happy Saint Anthony students in Paterson, New Jersey.*

1. *Salesian camp counselors and children enjoying summer fun!*

2. *Sr. Theresa Kelly, the Easter Bunny, and a small friend enjoy their time at the annual Salesian Sisters Spring Party.*

3. *Sr. Virginia D'Alessandro and Sr. Jeanette Puglisi admire the hand-painted Salesian Sisters logo and the donor wall commemorating all those who took part in helping to build the Saint Joseph Provincial Center.*

4. *Mary Help of Christians Academy students enjoy the annual Spring Party benefiting their school!*

5. *Sr. Eileen Tickner with friends Rosemary Albrecht, Nancy Lopez, and Theresa Greif.*

1. Sr. Judith Suprys, Sr. Carmen Peña, Sr. Joanne Holloman, Sr. Loretta DiDomenicis, Sr. LouAnn Fantauzza, Sr. Helen Godin, Sr. Catherine Altamura, and Sr. Pat Roche get ready for delicious cake in honor of our Jubilarians!

2. Soffia, Thorunn, and Berge Wathne with their dear Adopted Sister, Sr. Christine Hellen.

3. Salesian Mother General Antonia Colombo (center) visits the United States and is accompanied by her Salesian Sisters and several high-school students.

1. *Camp Auxilium alumnae in Newton, New Jersey, reunite after 45 years!*

2. *Joe and Anne Garcia.*

3. *Sr. Lucy Roces along with John Cassara (second from right) and friends.*

4. *Peter Barsocchini.*

The United Nations

On June 6, 2008, we Salesian Sisters were accredited as a non-governmental organization by the Economic and Social Council of the United Nations. This prestigious recognition allows us to be present as an Institute in our own right at UN meetings, and the opportunity to be voices for the poorest and most abandoned young people on this great world stage.

As a global community, Christ's message of love challenges us to promote a more humane society. We pray always for peace within our society, peace between individuals and peoples – peace in our hearts, homes, and countries.

1. *A photo of the interior of the United Nations.*
2. *CBS Evening News anchor Katie Couric interviews a Salesian student at the United Nations.*
3. *Salesian Sisters and students who took part in the United Nations Council on the Status of Women.*

A Papal Visit

Tens of thousands of people flocked to New York City on April 19 and 20, 2008, for a chance to see and worship with Pope Benedict XVI – and Salesian Sisters, students, alumni, family, and friends were no exception!

Several Sisters were privileged to join the Holy Father for a special Mass at Saint Patrick's Cathedral. Others joined 57,000 people at Yankee Stadium for the Pope's farewell Mass.

Thank you, Holy Father, for your inspiration and holiness! And we are delighted you came to our neighborhood during the Centennial Year!

1. *The Popemobile and its special passenger!*
2. *Yankee Stadium fills with people awaiting the arrival of Pope Benedict.*
3. *Sr. Suzanne Dauwalter, Sr. Phyllis Neves, Provincial Superior, and Sr. Anna Ragogna joined clergy and religious for Mass with Pope Benedict inside Saint Patrick's Cathedral.*
4. *Sr. Maryann Schaefer, Sr. Betty Ann Martinez, Sr. Catherine Altamura, and Sr. Mary Rinaldi eagerly await the start of Mass.*

Provincial Superior Sr. Phyllis Neves cuts the ribbon to officially open the Salesian Sisters' Centennial exhibit at the Paterson Museum in New Jersey, joined by Sr. Frances Gumino, Fr. Joseph Orlandi, Pastor of St. Michael Parish, Mayor José "Joey" Torres, Sr. Domenica Di Peri, and Fr. William Keane, Vice Provincial of the Salesian Priests.

Our Centennial Celebration begins!

It all began in Paterson, New Jersey. In 1908, the first four Salesian Sisters in the U.S. were given their first home at Saint Michael Parish, headed by then Pastor Monsignor Felix Cianci. This missionary Order of religious women got to work – building a Catholic school program, teaching religious education, providing support to families and to children without parents.

Fast-forward 100 years. The Salesian Sisters' mission and works have grown from east to west and north to south across the United States. Their dedication to educating youth, especially the poor, is always filled with joy and hope. Armed with the principles of reason, religion, and loving kindness, the Sisters welcome all children regardless of race or creed.

Salesian Sisters, former teachers, and past pupils of Saint Anthony School in Easton, Pennsylvania, gather for a reunion!

On January 31, 2008, the Salesian schools of Louisiana celebrated the Feast of Saint John Bosco and opened the Centennial with an incredible spirit-filled Youth Rally of 2,000 students at the New Orleans Convention Center. A festive Mass and original works of art – live, dramatic student performances and videos commemorating 100 years in the U.S. - marked the day.

Five weeks later, on March 8, 2008, the Salesian Sisters in the New Jersey area celebrated the Centennial with special events in Paterson. The day included a visit to the Paterson Museum to view the Salesian Sisters' Historical Exhibit and Bishop Arthur J. Serratelli celebrated a special Mass at Saint Michael Church.

July 13, 2008 marked "FMA Day in Pennsylvania"! Planned by four dedicated Salesian alumni, over 100 friends and Sisters came together to celebrate the Salesian legacy in the Pennsylvania area and the many lives that continue to be touched in Easton, Philadelphia, Redding, and Roseto.

On February 28, 2009, the Salesian Sisters and friends in the Tampa, Florida area will celebrate the Sisters' great work there since the 1930s. A Mass and dinner reception will be held at Saint Joseph Church and Pavilion in Tampa.

The Grand Centennial Mass at Saint Patrick's Cathedral and the Gala will be celebrated in New York City on April 25, 2009. Many Salesian Sisters, alumni, friends, and benefactors are expected to attend and join the fundraiser aboard *World Yacht* later that evening. The Gala Yacht will sail the same waters as did the steamship *Montevideo* on which the first four Sisters came to New York Harbor in 1908.

Finally, on May 16, 2009 the Salesian Sisters' Centennial events will close with a family-fun finale for the tri-state area at the Sisters' North Haledon properties.

Since 1908, the dream of Saint John Bosco and Saint Mary Mazzarello grew and prospered in the United States! As the Salesian Sisters embark on their next century of caring for youth, we are all filled with hope as 26 young women are studying to be Salesian Sisters.

The future is bright... and the dream continues!

Salesian students celebrate the Salesian Sisters Centennial and the Feast of St. John Bosco at the Salesian Youth Rally with performances about the Sisters "Coming to America" and the local favorites of Louisiana, i.e. Café Du Monde

The Salesian Sisters from east and west Provinces join together to mark this most special day in Salesian history in Louisiana. (Left to right: back row – Sr. Thuy Virgine Nguyen, Sr. Theresa Lee, Sr. Debbie Walker, Sr. Maria Columbo, Sr. Lise Parent, and Sr. Mary Rinaldi; front row, Sr. Colleen Clair, Sr. Phyllis Neves, provincial superior and Sr. Michelle Geiger

Generations of Salesian Sisters who ministered in Pennsylvania are joined by postulants and clergy after a special Eucharistic Celebration in Easton.

The magnificent church of Saint Michael's in Paterson, New Jersey, was filled to the rafters on March 8, 2008, for the special Centennial Mass celebrated by Bishop Arthur Serratelli.

SALESIAN SISTERS OF SAINT JOHN BOSCO IN THE UNITED STATES AND CANADA 1908-2008

† indicates year of passing into Eternal Life

Adames, Sr. Dora
Agliardi, Sr. Antoinette (†1965)
Aguirre, Sr. Mary Louise (†2007)
Aichino, Sr. Amelia (†1963)
Aina, Sr. Josephine (†1987)
Altamura, Sr. Catherine
Alvarez, Sr. Adele (†2006)
Andorno, Sr. Angelina (†1953)
Anguiano, Sr. Julia
Arante, Sr. Suzzette
Arciga, Sr. Mary
Arias, Sr. Nivia
Armas, Sr. Elba (†2000)
Arroyo, Sr. Guadalupe
Asselin, Sr. Candide
Asselin, Sr. Réjeanne
Avallone, Sr. Italia (†1946)
Avigliano, Sr. Carmela (†1973)
Bagli, Sr. Susan
Bailey, Sr. Rita
Bailo, Sr. Mary (†1967)
Balistrieri, Sr. Lucy
Barattino, Sr. Gerard
Baroni, Sr. Mary
Basque, Sr. Alphonsine
Beboso, Sr. Corazon
Becerril, Sr. Maria
Beltramo, Sr. Antoinette (†1974)
Beltre, Sr. Ramona
Bensi, Sr. Santina (†1980)
Bertrand, Sr. Micheline

Besi, Sr. Cecilia
Bianco, Sr. Anna (†1967)
Bickford, Sr. Virginia
Bocanegra, Sr. Letizia
Bona, Sr. Florence (†1995)
Bonfiglio, Sr. Gisella (†2007)
Botello, Sr. Carmen
Brucato, Sr. Mary (†1992)
Bucci, Sr. Rose (†1983)
Buffoli, Sr. Emma (†1966)
Bui, Sr. Anna Goretti
Buonaiuto, Sr. Margaret Rose
Cabrera, Sr. Antoinette
Cahill, Sr. Linda Ann
Calcagno, Sr. Liboria (†1991)
Callegarin, Sr. Amelia
Camirand, Sr. Lucie (†1996)
Campari, Sr. Josephine (†1977)
Campbell, Sr. Barbara
Campi, Sr. Mary (†1985)
Cannizzaro, Sr. Mary (†1977)
Cantu, Sr. Esperanza (†1958)
Capozzi, Sr. Emanuella (†1997)
Capra, Sr. Anna (†1992)
Caprioli, Sr. Regina (†2004)
Carabin, Sr. Theodora (†2006)
Cardone, Sr. Josephine (†1994)
Carini, Mother Lydia
Carini, Sr. Josephine (†2006)
Carone, Sr. Mary (†2008)
Carpentier, Sr. Pierrette

Carrillo, Sr. Ignacia

Caruso, Sr. Eminia (†1982)

Casaro, Sr. Theresa (†1974)

Casertano, Sr. Antoinette (†1993)

Caspary, Sr. Mary Ann

Cassidy, Sr. Ann

Castillo, Sr. Silvia

Cavazos, Sr. Roble

Cedrone, Sr. Antoinette

Cesario, Sr. Carmela (†1978)

Chagin, Sr. Ida M

Chavez, Sr. Juanita

Chiaverano, Sr. Martina (†1990)

Cianci, Sr. Theresa (†1967)

Clair, Sr. Colleen

Colombo, Sr. Maria

Conte, Sr. Filomena (†2007)

Cordes, Sr. Rosemary

Cormier, Sr. Réna

Corrado, Sr. Michele (†1997)

Cosentino, Sr. Agatha

Cossette, Sr. Pauline

Costanzo, Sr. Frances (†1936)

Costanzo, Sr. Rosina (†1980)

Crotti, Sr. Rachel

Cruz, Sr. Esther

Curd, Sr. Kathleen

Curtis, Sr. Beatrice (†1973)

Cvetko, Sr. Antonia

Da Grossa, Sr. Frances

D'Alessandro, Sr. Virginia

Dauwalter, Sr. Suzanne

DeBerardinis, Sr. Tullia (†1957)

DeCapua, Sr. Angela

DeDomenicis, Sr. Loretta

DeFilippi, Sr. Emy

De La Garza, Sr. M. Guadalupe (†2003)

De La Vega, Sr. M. Louise

Delfino, Sr. Frances (†1967)

Delgado, Sr. Rufina

Delgado, Sr. Teresita

DeRose, Sr. Marisa

Déry, Sr. Raymonde

DiBiasi, Sr. Katherine (†1998)

Dicaire, Sr. Raymonde

DiCamillo, Sr. Mary (†1999)

Dickey, Sr. Virginia

DiGennaro, Sr. Emilia (†1966)

DiPeri, Sr. Domenica

DiPeri, Sr. Rosalie

Sr. Esther Cruz,
Sr. Virginia Dickey,
Sr. Nivia Campusano,
Sr. Theresa Lee,
Sr. Gisella Bonfiglio,
Sr. Clare Kennelly,
Sr. Stella Ruiz,
Sr. Judith Suprys, and
Sr. Agatha Consentino

DiSanto, Sr. Angelina (†1992)
DiSanto, Sr. Frances (†1989)
Do, Sr. Ngan
Do, Sr. Vuong
Dunn, Sr. Karen
Dunn, Sr. Marie (†2003)
Dunn, Sr. Regina (†1994)
Durocher, Sr. Anita
Elley, Sr. Winifred (†1979)
Erickson, Sr. Jean
Falco, Sr. Erminia (†1965)
Fantauzza, Sr. LouAnn
Fantin, Sr. Rita
Favaloro, Sr. Providence (†1995)
Ferrari, Sr. Anita (†2000)
Ferrari, Sr. Mary (†1995)
Filipas, Sr. Diana
Flores, Sr. Aida (†2005)
Florez, Sr. Fanny
Fontaine, Sr. Françoise
Fortis, Sr. Maria Gonzalez (†1937)
Franco, Sr. Theresa (†2002)
Fusco, Sr. Alice
Gaiottino, Sr. Theresa (†1968)
Galassi, Sr. Josephine (†1958)
Gallardo, Sr. Refugio
Gangi, Sr. Domenica (†1939)
Gannon, Sr. Marie
Garcia, Sr. Rosalba
Garcia, Sr. Sara
Garza, Sr. Isabel
Gastaldo, Sr. Adeline (†1974)
Gatti, Sr. Amalia (†1994)
Gatti, Sr. Helen (†1982)
Geiger, Sr. Michelle
Gentile, Sr. Gilda (†1972)
Germain, Sr. Claudette
Giaj-Levra, Sr. Vincent (†1974)
Gibson, Sr. Kathleen

Godin, Sr. Diane (†1993)
Godin, Sr. Helene
Gomez, Sr. Angelina
Gomez, Sr. Guadalupe
Gomez, Sr. Refugio
Gonzalez, Sr. Danielle
Graziani, Sr. Vittoria
Greenan, Sr. Mary
Greer, Sr. Charlotte
Grillone, Sr. Margaret (†1955)
Guarino, Sr. Mary (†1996)
Guilmette, Sr. Francine
Guitard, Sr. Lise
Gumino, Sr. Frances
Gutierrez, Sr. Teresa
Guzman Lopez, Sr. Marisol
Guzman, Sr. Angelita
Hellen, Sr. Christine
Henry, Sr. Cecilia
Henry, Sr. Sandra (†1987)
Hoang, Sr. Rosa
Holloman, Sr. Joanne
Hottot, Sr. Ann
Huart, Sr. Monique
Hurley, Sr. Catherine
Inciardi, Sr. Frances (†1979)
Ingrassia, Sr. Josephine (†1973)
Jackson, Sr. Mary
Jasso, Sr. Jane
Johnson, Sr. Estelle
Johnson, Sr. Roberta
Jones, Sr. Theresa
Joseph, Sr. Eileen
Joss, Sr. Pauline
Kassab, Sr. Emilia
Keane, Sr. Katherine
Kelly, Sr. Theresa
Kennelly, Sr. Clare
Keraitis, Sr. Kim

St. John Bosco, founder of
the Salesian Order

Khong, Sr. Thien Anh
King, Sr. Nora
King, Sr. Patricia
Labranche, Sr. Marie-Thérèse
Lacharité, Sr. Patricia
Lagacé, Sr. Florine
Laino, Sr. Rose (†1988)
Landoni, Sr. Anna (†1972)
Landry, Sr. Jeannine
Lanzio, Sr. Cecilia (†1984)
Le, Sr. Grace
Lee, Sr. Theresa
Li, Sr. Teresa
Ligregni, Sr. Mary (†2001)
Link, Sr. Mary
Lombardini, Sr. Elvira (†1974)
Lomeli, Sr. Celine
Lopez, Sr. Balbina
Lopez, Sr. Esther
Lopez, Sr. Ingrid (†1978)
Lopez, Sr. Josephine
Lozano, Sr. Adela
Lozano, Sr. Ofelia
Lujano, Sr. Maria Lourdes
Luong, Sr. Maria
Machado, Sr. Gloria
Mak, Sr. Rose
Mansoor, Sr. Elvira
Mar, Sr. Mary Gloria
Marasco, Sr. Mary (†1992)
Marengo, Sr. Olimpia (†1988)
Marinez, Sr. Anita
Martinetto, Sr. Pierina (†1991)
Martinez, Sr. Ana (†1998)
Martinez, Sr. Betty Ann
Martinez, Sr. Carmen
Martinoni, Sr. Giavannina, (†1966)
Martorana, Sr. Antoinette (†1941)
Martorana, Sr. Philomena (†2005)

Marturano, Sr. Rose (†1977)
Marzorati, Sr. Julia (†1993)
Maydagan, Sr. Trinidad (†2008)
Mazurek, Sr. Helen (†1976)
Mazzia, Sr. Antoinette (†1999)
Mazzocco, Sr. Mary Louise
McShane, Sr. Rose (†2005)
Medina, Sr. Guadalupe
Melanson, Sr. Patricia
Mendoza, Sr. Emma (†2001)
Miculin, Sr. Frances (†1999)
Miller, Sr. Suzanne
Milyo, Sr. Veronica (†2007)
Minelli, Sr. Louise (†2001)
Minutella, Sr. Domenica (†1992)
Minutella, Sr. Josephine (†1993)
Mitacchione, Sr. Frances (†2006)
Moiso, Sr. Erminia (†1950)
Molanok, Sr. Ines
Morales, Sr. Carmen
Moreno, Sr. Margarita (†1974)
Motte, Sr. Suzanne (†1992)
Mullaly, Sr. Mary
Muñoz, Sr. Olga
Murillo, Sr. Theresa
Muttis, Sr. Gemma (†1937)
Napoli, Sr. Cecilia (†1983)
Natal, Sr. Margaret
Neaves, Sr. Sandra
Nebbia, Sr. Josephine (†1968)
Neves, Sr. Phyllis
Nguyen, Sr. Phuong
Nguyen, Sr. Thuy Huong
Nguyen, Sr. Thuy Virgine
Nieto, Sr. Carmen
Novasconi, Mother Caroline (†1970)
Novo, Sr. Catherine
Novoa, Sr. Margaret (†1995)
Ochoa, Sr. Josephine

Orrick, Sr. Linda
Ortega, Sr. Socorro (†2002)
Ossi, Sr. Ida (†2004)
Ossi, Sr. Rena (†1996)
Ottaviano, Sr. Margherita (†1943)
Palacios, Sr. Ana
Palacios, Sr. Carmen
Palasota, Sr. Jeanette
Palatini, Sr. Mary (†1988)
Palladino, Sr. Mary
Paniga, Sr. Mary (†1988)
Paquin, Sr. Mary Bertha
Parent, Sr. Claudette
Parent, Sr. Lise
Parinello, Sr. Jerome (†1999)
Pascucci, Sr. Leonia (†1984)
Pash, Sr. Mary (†1953)
Pasquali, Sr. Eugenia (†1982)
Passerelli, Sr. Joanne (†1976)
Passero, Sr. Louise,
Pedrazzi, Sr. Josephine (†1989)
Pelliccione, Sr. Mary
Pena, Sr. Carmen
Penton, Sr. Raphael (†1973)
Perinciolo, Sr. Ercolina (†1989)
Perino, Sr. Claire
Pertile, Sr. Santina (†1946)
Petrotta, Sr. Rita
Pezzaglia, Sr. Magdalen (†1968)
Pham, Sr. Diep
Pham, Sr. Quyen
Piccirilli, Sr. Gaetana (†1992)
Pierotti, Sr. Cesira
Pinto, Sr. Lena
Pollini, Sr. Antoinette (†1960)
Pollini, Sr. Mary (†1972)
Ponce, Sr. Martina
Prandi, Sr. Brigida (†1930)
Principale, Sr. Frances (†1945)

Puglisi, Sr. Jeanette
Puppione, Sr. Angela (†1997)
Puppione, Sr. Mary (†1984)
Ragogna, Sr. Anna
Ragusa, Sr. Rosalie Ann (†1992)
Ramirez, Sr. Celia
Reeves, Sr. Elaine (†1996)
Reyes, Sr. Maria de la Luz
Reyes, Sr. Trinidad
Rinaldi, Sr. Mary
Riojas, Sr. Dolores
Riposi, Sr. Mary N. (†1964)
Roces, Sr. Lucy
Roche, Sr. Patricia
Rodriguez, Sr. Esperanza
Romo, Sr. Mercedes (†1985)
Rosi, Sr. Ottavia (†1937)
Rossi, Sr. Fernanda
Rousselle, Sr. Ethel
Roy, Sr. Alphonsine
Roy, Sr. Lilianne
Rubino, Sr. Arlene
Ruiz, Sr. Grace
Ruiz, Sr. Mary Estela (†2006)
Ruiz, Sr. Rosann
Rupert, Sr. Rita (†1945)
Rusciano, Sr. Mary (†1992)
Russo, Sr. Elizabeth
Ryan, Sr. Elizabeth
Saieh, Sr. Yamile
Salas, Sr. Cynthia
Salvetti, Sr. Adeline (†1988)
Sampo, Sr. Letizia, (†1981)
Samson, Sr. Theresa
Sanchez, Sr. Assunta
Sanchez, Sr. Concha (†1995)
Sanchez, Sr. Jane
Sanchez, Sr. Josephine
Sanchez, Sr. Wilma (†2001)

Sandino, Sr. Guadalupe
Schaefer, Sr. Maryann
Schuchert, Sr. Mary Sabina (†2007)
Sedita, Sr. Mary (†2002)
Segalini, Sr. Anna (†1994)
Segarini, Sr. Rose
Sferlazza, Sr. Antoinette (†2003)
Sferlazza, Sr. Gaetana, (†1980)
Sforza, Sr. Catherine (†1992)
Silenzio, Sr. Christina (†1982)
Simonetti, Sr. Felicia (†1999)
Simonetti, Sr. Mary N. (†1964)
Sironi, Sr. Theresa
Spezia, Sr. Consuelo (†1974)
Spizzirri, Sr. Raphael (†1971)
Spizzirri, Sr. Mary (†1992)
St. Pierre, Sr. Lucie (†2005)
Stazzi, Sr. Caroline (†1977)
Stecker, Sr. Ruth
Stefanoni, Sr. Emma
Suprys, Sr. Judith
Tafoya, Sr. Stella
Tamayo, Sr. Mary
Tanzella, Sr. Felicia
Tapia, Sr. Irene
Teran, Sr. Teresita
Termine, Sr. Carmela
Terzo, Sr. Mary
Tickner, Sr. Eileen
Torrisi, Sr. Rosina (†1993)
Tran, Sr. Lan Vy
Trejo, Sr. Victoria
Trevino, Sr. Lourdes
Uribe, Sr. Amparo
Valentin, Sr. Ines
Villanueva, Sr. Elizabeth
Valleise, Sr. Louise (†1955)
Valot, Sr. Beatrice
Van, Sr. Michelle

Vecchio, Sr. Marion (†2002)
Vegetabile, Sr. Frances (†2003)
Villagomez, Sr. Mary Ann
Villalon, Sr. Olga (†2001)
Volpe, Sr. Joan (†1977)
Walker, Sr. Deborah Ann
Werwas, Sr. Frances (†1973)
Wilhelm, Sr. Margaret
Winterscheidt, Sr. Mary
Winterscheidt, Sr. Patricia
Wong, Sr. Agnes (†2001)
Yacone, Sr. Jo Ann (†1993)
Younge, Sr. Edith (†1980)
Yuen, Sr. Lucia
Zaccagnino, Sr. Irene (†2006)
Zammit, Sr. Veneranda, (†1934)
Zanella, Sr. Rose
Zanetti, Sr. Mildred
Zangre, Sr. Mary (†1984)
Zingale, Sr. Nancy (†1982)
Zito, Sr. Antoinette (†1989)
Zito, Sr. Josephine (†1985)
Zito, Sr. Mary (†1980)
Zito, Sr. Mary Anne
Zorzi, Sr. Rose (†1999)

The community at Ward Street in the early 1930s: (front row) Sr. Mary Zito, Sr. Antoinette Sferlazza, Sr. Olympia Marengo, Sr. Domenica Gangi, and Sr. Lena Capozzi; (middle row) Sr. Emma Buffoli, Sr. Rose Bucci, Sr. Amelia Aichino, Sr. Gaetana Sferlazza, Sr. Mary Ferrari, Sr. Angela Puppione, Sr. Pierina Martinetto, Sr. Carmela Cesario; (back row) Sr. Mary Legrini, Sr. Caroline Novasconi, Sr. Mary Sedita, Sr. Giovannina Martinoni, Sr. Eugenia Pasquali, Sr. Veneranda Zammit, and Sr. Elvira Lombardini.

13 GIVING THANKS

Dedication Pages

Sr. Lydia Carini, at 95 years young, receives a loving gesture from Sr. Helene Godin at the Saint Joseph Provincial Center in Haledon, New Jersey.

I give thanks to God for you in every prayer that I utter.

~ Philippians 1:3–4

The Salesian Sisters thank and pray for their family and friends who, through these pages of dedication, made the **Centennial History Book** possible.

God bless one and all.

With Loving Gratitude to

**Sr. Veneranda Zammit, Sr. Antoinette Agliardi,
Sr. Frances Delfino, and Sr. Angelina Andorno**

whose commitment to Christ, love for the young, missionary spirit, and exemplary efforts
made St. Mary Mazzarello and St. John Bosco's vision a reality in the United States and Canada.

Dedicated by
Sr. Phyllis Neves, Provincial, and the Salesian Sisters of the U.S. and Canada

1908

In Honor of

Casimiro Hernandez Sr. and Casimiro Hernandez Jr.

Dedicated by

The Gonzmart Family, 4th, 5th, and 6th Generations
The Columbia Restaurant, founded in 1905, Ybor City, Florida

1909

In Loving Memory of

Jerry Rizzuto

Dad was a very giving person. After Mother passed he took care of us and we took care of him. He also took care of our Mother's parents. We lived with our parents and grandparents in two houses on one lot.

Dedicated by

Joanne and Geraldine Rizzuto

1909

In Honor of

Mary Pascucci

My big sister and best friend

Dedicated by

Celeste Tripi

1910

In Loving Memory of

Joseph A. Hagan

Dedicated by

The Salesian Sisters

1911

In Loving Memory of

Theresa Rizzuto

Everyone loved our Mother. She was very outgoing, made friends easily, and loved to sing and dance (at home). She never sat still and was always helping others. It was very hard to lose Mother. She was only 42.

Dedicated by
Joanne and Geraldine Rizzuto

1912

St. Anthony Parish is grateful for the work and dedication of the Salesian Sisters from 1912 to the present and for the ministry of Sr. Carmen Morales.

Dedicated by
Fr. Armand Quinto and St. Anthony Parish

1913

In Honor of

Sr. Gerard Barattino, FMA

on her 70th anniversary as a Salesian Sister

Dedicated by
Joan Oliver

1913

Congratulations to the Salesian Sisters for 100 years of service!

The Belloni Family
Josephine and Louis, and their children, Blanche, Josephine, Mary, Henry, Ann, Lucy, Joseph, Rose, and James

1913

In Honor of

Sr. Lydia Carini, FMA

"I left home on October 7, 1934, the feast of Our Lady, to become a Salesian Sister and I have never regretted this for a single day."

1914

In Loving Memory of Our Parents

Helen and Stanley Obiurka

Thank you for all your support and guidance.

Mom 1914–1976
Dad 1914–1996

Your loving children,
Maryann, Philip, and Paula

1915

In Loving Memory of

Lucy Nardella

An orphan returns to her roots.

Lucy with her first grade teacher, Sr. Angela Puppione

1916

To Our Loving Parents

Concetta and Leonardo Di Peri

With much love and grateful hearts, your children,
Sam, John, Rose, and Domenica "Mamie"

1917

In Honor of

Tom Larywon

who always put his cherished family first!

Dedicated with love

The Larywon children and grandchildren

1917

Sr. Wilma Sanchez, FMA

A loving and gentle spirit, Sr. Wilma
was the first Floridian to become
a Salesian Sister on August 5, 1938.

Dedicated by

Joseph and Anne Garcia

1918

In Honor of

The Spada Family

Dedicated by

Mark and Eleanor Spada

1918

In Loving Memory of My Parents

Suzanne and Peter Hnath

Mom, you have been my guardian angel since
I was 10, and Dad, you were my strength my whole life.

Dedicated by

Your daughter, Marge Hnath

1919

In Gratitude to

The Salesian Sisters

for their loving care

Dedicated by

Celeste Pascucci Tripi

1919

In Honor of

Rev. Monsignor Carlo Cianci, PA

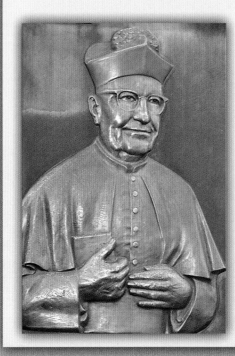

He served as pastor of St. Michael Church, Paterson, New Jersey, from 1919 to 1968.

Dedicated by

Vincenza Cianci and
Rose Cianci-Gasparrini

1920

In Honor of

Tomaso and Addolorata DiCamillo

Dedicated by

The DiCamillo Family
2nd, 3rd, and 4th
Generations

DiCamillo Bakery
Founded in 1920
Niagara Falls, New York

1921

In grateful memory of the Salesian Sisters whose work in Northern California will be fondly remembered for the next hundred years.

1922

In Honor of

Anne Larywon

who always put her cherished family first!

Dedicated with love

The Larywon children and grandchildren

1922

On September 6, 1922, **James and Margaret** sealed their love in the sacrament of marriage at St. Michael Church, Canyon City, Colorado.

That same day they boarded a train to Los Angeles. For such loving parents and for making us native Californians, their children are eternally grateful.

Dedicated by

Bishop Joseph Sartoris, Lomita, California

1923

In Honor of

Sr. Nancy Zingale, FMA

who began her religious formation with the Salesian Sisters of St. John Bosco on June 1, 1923

Dedicated by

Her godchild Ida Gulino

1924

Immaculate Conception School

Marrero, Louisiana

Dedicated by

The Faculty, Staff, and Students

1924

Sr. Josephine Carini, FMA
A true friend and inspiration

With gratitude
Janis M. Frisch, Ph.D.

1925

Sr. Nancy Zingale, FMA
made her first vows on August 30, 1925.

Dedicated by
Her cousin Anthony Gulino

1925

To the Salesian Sisters
Faithful signs and bearers of God's love for youth

Dedicated by
The Salesian Priests, Brothers, and Cooperators
of Mary Help of Christians Center, Tampa, Florida

1925

Anne K. Lebron

Dedicated by
Richard Lebron

1925

Eileen Hendron McNally

Dedicated by
Betty Turner

1925

In Memory of

Thomas Carola

Dedicated by your loving children,
Betsy, Tom, Maggie, and Jim

1926

This certifies that
Ephrem Ormezzano
*and **Lea O. Battiato***
have dedicated the year 1926
in honor of the marriage
of their parents.

1927

In Loving Memory of Our Dear Parents

Lucien and Denise Parent

who always lived with simplicty and integrity

We knew
we were loved!

Love, your children,
Pierre, Sr. Lise, Guy,
and Lucie

1928

Joseph and Jennie Lazzaro
In honor of their 50th wedding anniversary

With love,
Mary Rotholz

1929

In Memory of
Cathleen Carola

Dedicated by your loving children,
Betsy, Tom, Maggie, and Jim

1929

Ann Hendron Schlegel

Dedicated by
Betty Turner

1929

In Loving Memory of
Joseph J. McAleer Sr.

A remarkable father to his four sons and a generous father figure to the Salesian Sisters he loved so much

Dedicated by
David and Christina McAleer

1930

St. Joseph School
Tampa, Florida

Dedicated by
The Faculty, Staff, Students, and Families

1930

In Loving Memory of
Hope Marie McAleer

An exceptional woman and mother who inspired hope in everyone fortunate enough to meet her

Dedicated by
David and Christina McAleer

1931

Angela and Vincenzo Crociata

To all the Salesians, past, present, and future, who continue to shape our youth with the wisdom and spirit of St. John Bosco, in the traditions of our faith

Dedicated by
Angela Girolama Crociata Rodin

1932

Sr. Anna Ragogna, FMA
My earthly angel

Dedicated by
Maggie Waitts

1932

In Honor of Our Parents

Natividad and Romeo Aniceto

Dedicated by

Manny, Aris, Ruthie, and Homer

1933

In Memory of

Sr. Julia Mazorati, FMA

Student, principal, teacher, guidance counselor, and pillar of Mary Help of Christians Academy

Dedicated by

Her grateful alumnae

1934

In the year 1934, Don Bosco was canonized a saint. We pay tribute to the Salesian Sisters, who throughout the United States have striven to be saints and formers of saints with his spirit.

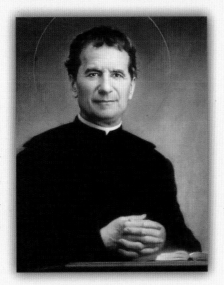

The Salesian Brothers and Priests of the Eastern U.S. Province

1934

To Our Parents

Pauline and Charles Giamonco

Dedicated by

Jerry and JoAnn Giamonco

Brownstone Agency Inc.

From left: Sr. Lucy Roces, Sr. Antoinette Cedrone, Rose Marie Amato, John Cassara, Sr. Rosalie Di Peri, Sr. Mary Ann Caspary, Sr. Domenica Di Peri, Sr. Ruth Stecker, Sr. Anita Durocher, and Sr. Mildred Zanetti

Dedicated by
John Cassara and the Brownstone Agency Inc.

1934

In Memory of
Robert Waitts

Dedicated by
Your loving wife, Maggie

1935

We give thanks for 100 years of loving to learn and learning to love!

Sr. Julia Garcia, Sr. Margarita Moreno, Sr. Anita Marinez, Sr. Mercedes Romo

From
Mary Help of Christians School, Laredo, Texas
St. John Bosco and St. James School, San Antonio, Texas

1936

The Salesian Sisters open the home
for the children at Villa Madonna School.

Dedicated by
The Villa Madonna School Family

1936

Mrs. Alicia Gonzalez Neve

My love and
eternal gratitude
for her guidance
during my life

Dedicated by
Alice R. Oliva

1937

In honor of the joyful
Sr. Mary Rinaldi and all the Salesian Sisters

In memory of another joyful lady
Alyda Jansen Calamita
May 11, 1937–April 27, 2000

Dedicated by
Her husband, Frank

1937

To Our Parents
Susan and Mario Nocera

Dedicated by
JoAnn and Jerry Giamonco

1938

In memory of **Rev. Gennaro J. Leone, CM**,
former pastor, for his tireless dedication
to Catholic education, and in honor of the
Salesian Sisters for their contributions
to Our Lady of Mt. Carmel School

Dedicated by
The Parish of Our Lady of Mt. Carmel
Roseto, Pennsylvania

1938

In gratitude for
the ministry of the Salesian Sisters
at Immaculate Heart of Mary School
from 1915 to 1938

and in memory of
Sr. Veronica Milyo, FMA,
the fruit of their labor

Dedicated by
The Salesians of Don Bosco
Preparatory High School
Ramsey, New Jersey

1938

In appreciation of the Salesian Sisters
and in loving memory of our parents,

Ludovico and Josephine Fantauzza

Dedicated by
Charles, Phyllis,
Antoinette, and
Sr. Lou Ann

1939

Sr. Adelina Gastaldo, FMA

Great niece of Sr. Petronilla Mazzarello,
who was the best friend of St. Mary Mazzarello

Novices became Salesian Sisters over 29 years
through her leadership, example, and prayer.

1940

In Loving Memory of

Margaret and James Pressimone

The Salesian Sisters
were a special part
of their lives.

Dedicated by
their daughter,
Katherine Zaretski

1940

Sr. Mary Palatini, FMA

The first principal at
Mary Help of Christians Academy

Dedicated by
Sr. Rosalie Di Peri and the Alumnae
of Mary Help of Christians Academy

1940

On January 25, 1940, they began their lives together.

In memory of my loving parents, Ralph and Wilma Rickman

Dedicated by
Beverly Rickman Parcasio

1940

Nancy and Augustus M. Rinaldi

who lovingly endured hard work
and sacrifice for their children

With everlasting gratitude,
Philip, Ernesta, Sr. Mary, Louis,
Eugenia, Caesar, and Josephine

1941

In Gratitude to
Bill and Pat McLaughlin
Charter Members of the Partners Circle

1941

A Loving Tribute to Our Parents
Stefan and Soffia Wathne

Dedicated by
Thorunn, Berge, Soffia, and Stefan

1942

Alice and Robert Salter

You've dedicated your lives to giving of yourselves in so many selfless ways to your family, your friends, and to your loved ones. God has brought us all together and we are eternally grateful for His blessings and kindness.

Dedicated by
Pat and John Connors

1942

Tom and Mary Rico

Angels in heaven, forever in my heart

Dedicated by
Pat Rico

1943

Sr. Helen Mazurek, FMA

A Sister who loved the people of Tampa.
She formed us to be leaders!

Dedicated by
Dr. Emilio Echevarria and Joseph Garcia, Esq.

1944

Mary Help of Christians Academy

Inspiring Dreams...Building Futures

Dedicated by
The MHCA PTG and Student Council, in honor of
all those who have made the Academy what it is today

1945

In Memory of

Ramon and Josephine Campo

Dedicated by their children,
Daniel and Diana

1945

Four Generations of Angels
committed to "The Villa"

Angel Oliva Sr. (deceased), Angel Oliva Jr. (Class of '45),
Angel Oliva III, and Angel Oliva IV

1946

In Loving Memory of Our Dear Parents

Frank and Pearl Sickinger

Dedicated by
Frankie and Sr. Denise Sickinger, FMA

1947

In Memory of

James and Elinore Collins

Dad and Mom,

Thanks for the gifts
of life and love!

Gratefully,

Janice, Stephen,
John, Joyce, and Brian

1948

In Loving Memory of

Sam and Ann Di Peri

Dedicated with love by
Patti Kearns and Bart Di Peri

1948

To all the Salesian Sisters in the U.S.,
past, present and future.
Thank you for your loving service to us.

Dedicated by
The Cosentino Family
Nick and Agatha, and daughters, Laura and Sr. Agatha,
both alumnae of Mary Help of Christians Academy,
North Haledon, New Jersey

1949

In Memory of My Mother

Elizabeth Heldak

and in gratitude to the Salesian Sisters at
Sacred Heart Center in Newton, New Jersey,
whose friendship we will eternally cherish

Dedicated by
Betty Heldak

1950

In gratitude to the Salesian Sisters of St. John Bosco.
May God bless you with more vocations in this
Centennial year and grant you all health,
happiness, and holiness of life.

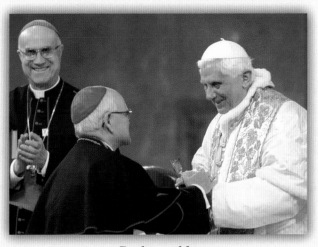

Dedicated by
The Most Rev. Alfred C. Hughes, STD

1950

In Honor of

Janet Laudone

You were more than a sister-in-law and aunt to us, you were a friend. We miss our talks, your laughter, and your curious nature.

Dedicated by

Terry, Joe, and Michael

1950

Congratulations on your Centennial year! Your presence in Southern California has made a difference in the lives of so many young people.

Pupils, Past Pupils, and Friends of the Salesian Sisters

1951

Chris and Minnie Trujillo

My loving parents

Dedicated by

Donna Trujillo-Mungaray

1951

Salesian Sisters' outing to the Rinaldi home in San Antonio, Florida

1952

*Congratulations and best wishes
for another successful 100 years!*

Dr. Vincent and Dorothy Bagli
and Family

1953

The Manny Alvarez Family

To our dear family,

With love on our
55th wedding anniversary.

Mom and Dad

1953

We Celebrate

Rose Mary and Joseph Clair

whose love radiated
on one another, their
16 children, and
62 grandchildren!

May God continue
to bless the Clair family.

1953

Born in Briançon, France,
Sr. Suzanne Motte was
one of the first four
Daughters of Mary Help
of Christians to begin
the Salesian Sisters'
work in Canada. She
was an excellent educator,
and a woman of profound
faith and incredible zeal.
Many were touched by
her great Marian devotion.

Dedicated by
The Salesian Sisters of the Pre-Province
Notre Dame du Cap, Canada

1953

Thank you, dear Salesians,
for your dedicated service to
Mary Help of Christians Church
in New York City. We miss you!

Dedicated by
The Bonica Family

1953

The students of Mary Help of
Christians School, New York
City, thank the Salesian Sisters
for all their love and caring,
and for instilling in us
the love of Mary Help
of Christians.

Dedicated by
Sofia Stuart, Class of 1953

1954

In Loving Memory of
Donald M. De Rose
Jun 15, 1954 – Jan 30, 2007

Always in our hearts!

Dedicated by
The De Rose Family

1955

In Honor of
Robert L. Obenberger

A loving and caring
husband who has always
been there for anyone
who needed help, and
in honor of the Salesian
Sisters for all the prayers
they have offered to God
for our family and friends

Dedicated by
Mary J. Obenberger

1955

Dedicated to

Charlie and Alma Curcio

We honor the Salesian Sisters.

Through their prayer, love and selfless giving they have touched our family deeply in so many ways.

Thank you!

The Piotrowski Family

1956

May Mary Help of Christians watch over my loving daughter Anna Maria, her husband, Anthony, and their children, Lauren, Christopher, and Alana.

Dedicated by
Teresa Gutto

1957

Joe and Anne Garcia

In gratitude for your vision, leadership, and true love for Tampa's children, especially at the Salesian Youth Center Boys and Girls Club

Dedicated by
The Salesian Youth Center Board of Trustees

1957

Hope and Joseph McAleer

Dedicated by
The McAleer Family

1957

May Mary Help of Christians
watch over my loving son Michael and
his children, Kristen and Michael.

Dedicated by
Teresa Gutto

1958

IMMACULATA LA-SALLE
Celebrating 50 Years of Family
1958 – 2008

1958

May Mary Help of Christians
watch over my loving son Anthony, his wife,
Nancy, and their children, Angelica and Julia.

Dedicated by
Teresa Gutto

1959

The Best 50 Years of Our Lives
"Thanks Be to God"

Producers Charles A. Lechner Jr. and Pauline J. DiPrima
Best Actress Denise T. Lechner-Fischer
Best Actor Charles A. Lechner III
Best Supporting Actress Francesca N. Lechner
Best Supporting Actors Carlo A. Lechner and
Matthew J. Fischer

1959

To all the Salesian Sisters who
have served at Corpus Christi School since 1959

Dedicated by
The Priests and Parishioners of Corpus Christi Church
Port Chester, New York

1959

A Tribute to Our Parents
Araceli and Silvestre Villarin

In honor of their
50th Wedding Anniversary
April 4, 2009

Love,
Jett, Patit, Karla, Maia
Jondi, Pau, and Carlo

1960

To the Salesian Sisters
who pioneered the work
of St. John Bosco
and St. Mary Mazzarello
in North America and
to the scores of Sisters
who followed in their
footsteps with utter
devotion and dedication,
we extend our indelible
admiration and gratitude.

The Altamura Family renders tribute to
Sr. Catherine Altamura, FMA

1960

Sr. Jeanette Puglisi, FMA

Dedicated by
Richard Caruso

1960

In Loving Memory of Our Parents

Vincent and Lillian Dauwalter

Dedicated by
Sr. Suzanne, Kevin, and Stephen

1960

Angel and Estela Oliva

Dedicated by
Angel Jr. and John Oliva

1961

With heartfelt gratitude for embracing us and giving us a home away from home

With love,
The Cuban Girls: Amparo, Elsa, Josefa, Lourdes, Martha, Nancy, Natalia, Rosario, Soledad, Teresita, and Sr. Teresa

1961

We have been blessed to have our "adopted" Sisters, as part of our family.

Sr. Catherine Altamura
Sr. Lucy Balistrieri
Sr. Letizia Bocanegra
Sr. Gisella Bonfiglio
Sr. Lydia Carini
Sr. Mary Carone
Sr. Theresa Franco
Sr. Danielle Gonzalez
Sr. Frances Gumino
Sr. Monique Huart
Sr. Veronica Milyo
Sr. Frances Mitacchione
Sr. Carmen Morales

Sr. Mary Louise Mazzocco
Sr. Claire Perino
Sr. Mary Rinaldi
Sr. Liz Ryan
Sr. Frances Vegetabile

With love,
Eve and Peter Barna, Lisa, Tom and Brooke,
Elizabeth Wagner, Peter, Anthony Barna and Kim Oxford

1961

The Year of Our Marriage

What a Wonderful World!

Beverly and Rodger Rohde

1961

In Memory of

Sr. Trini Maydagan, FMA

With love and tears
we bid you farewell
on April 11, 2008.

Dedicated by
All your students
at Mary Help of
Christians Academy

1962

Bertha Levonas

Dedicated by
Joseph Levonas

1962

In Memory of

Ruth Middendorf

Our thanks to the Salesian Sisters

Dedicated by
Pat and Frank Middendorf

1962

May Mary Help of Christians watch over my loving daughter Phyllis, her husband Gerard, and their children, Gregory and Thomas.

Dedicated by
Teresa Gutto

1962

Michael and Grace Guarnieri

In gratitude to the most wonderful parents in the world for giving me life… and to God for giving them to me

Your son,
Mike

1963

A Tribute to Our Loving Parents

James and Fannie Notte
Stephen and Grace Scillieri

On the occasion of our 45th wedding anniversary

Dedicated by
Antoinette and Joseph Scillieri

1963

In Memory of

Sr. Josephine Carini, FMA

Her dedication made her a great teacher to children and adults, a mentor to those in need, and a friend to all.

She influenced so many of us and her life will continue to touch generations to come.

Today, we pay tribute to the memory of our friend, teacher, and source of inspiration.

Adrianna Lodeserto, Barbara Ralph, Frances Ferraro, Giovanna Vollaro, Jaye Hedrick, Judy Olander, Lucille Mauro, Maria D'Ippolito, Marianna Benn, Mary Baccaro, Mary Pat Pierangeli, Pat Gilland, and Sue Fiorilla

1964

Mark and Karen Zaretski

In remembrance of the first day of the 1964 school year at St. Anthony School, Paterson, New Jersey

Dedicated by
Katherine Zaretski

1964

In thanksgiving and deep gratitude to the Salesian Sisters, especially Sr. Josephine Carini and Sr. Ida Grasso, for being such a wonderful influence in my life and in the lives of countless others.

Dedicated by
Judy Olander

1965

Sr. Louise Minelli, FMA

A gentle Sister who loved and cared for the little ones at St. Joseph School in Tampa, Florida

Dedicated by
Dr. Emilio Echevarria and Family

1966

In Honor of
Past and Present Provincials
of the Salesian Sisters

Seated, from left: Sr. Lydia Carini, Sr. Josephine Carini, and Sr. Ida Grasso; standing, from left: Sr. Judith Suprys, Sr. Patricia King, Sr. Lise Guitard, Sr. Phyllis Neves, Sr. Theresa Sironi, Sr. Theresa Kelly, and Sr. Cecilia Besi

1967

Mr. and Mrs. Richard D. Grady

Life is beautiful when we're together!

1967

Our family has been blessed by being a part of the Salesian family since 1975. We are so thankful for the guidance and memories the Sisters have provided us many times over the years. We will be forever grateful to God for this.

Dedicated by
The Wagner Family
Bobby, Cynthia, Tricia, Cyndi, and Bobbi Ann

1968

In Gratitude to
Bob and Laura Reiter

*Friends of the Salesian Sisters
from Atlanta, Georgia*

1969

A Tribute to
Sr. Rena Ossi, FMA
My 8th grade teacher

Dedicated by
James Gambino

1969

Faith and Lawrence Menard

For all your love, sacrifice, hard work, and
inspiration, Mom; and to Dad, who continues to
watch and bless us from above in heaven.
I am eternally grateful for you both.

Love, your daughter, Christina

1970

In Honor of the Birth Year of
Sr. Colleen Clair, FMA

Dedicated with great love by
Wayne and Brigid Obetz

1971

In Memory of
Fr. Peter M. Rinaldi, SDB

Dedicated by
Linda and Peter Christiansen

1971

Alphonse Alagia

In loving memory of our
grandfather who braved
an ocean crossing at age
16 to pursue the American
dream, who served his new
country in World War I,
and whose quiet dignity
and devotion to work and
family leave us full of
love and admiration for
this wonderful man.

Dedicated by
The McAleer Family

1972

Ann Lowry Murphey
A woman of great faith and action

Dedicated by
Msgr. Lawrence Higgins

1972

In Loving Memory of
Ana Maria Baldor-Bunn

Ana Maria, you had the heart of a lion and the soul of an angel.

We love you and will cherish you all the days of our lives.

Love,
Stan and
William H. Bunn

1973

In Honor of a Dear Aunt
Sr. Candida Aspesi, FMA

who exemplifies the Salesian spirit of caring for the young and the poor. She served the Salesian Sisters worldwide as Councilor for Administration (1996–2008), discharging the manifold duties of *Economa Generale* with humility, dedication, and compassion.

Dedicated by
The Rigolio Family

1973

In Memory of
**Sr. Michele Corrado, FMA and
Dr. Anthony Galizio**

Dedicated by
The Corrado Family

Éditions du Signe

It is an honor to produce the Salesian Sisters' Centennial history book
which commemorates the Salesian Sisters' presence in the United States and Canada.

We wish to thank the Salesian Family for the confidence placed in us for so many years.

   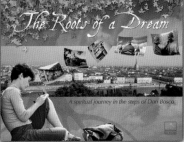 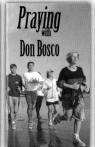  

Dedicated by
The Staff of Éditions du Signe

1974

Our Special Year

Dedicated by
Aleta and Rich Taylor

1975

In Loving Memory of
Sr. Rose McShane, FMA

Dedicated by
Dawn Alexander Makowski

1975

**Mannoia and Vitriola
Families**

Dedicated by
Frances and Michael Mannoia

1975

*In honor of and in gratitude to all
the **Salesian Sisters** who taught at
Corpus Christi School, Port Chester,
New York, from 1986 to 2001,
especially †Sr. Frances Vegetabile,
Sr. Lise Parent, Sr. Susan Bagli,
and Sr. Catherine Altamura*

Dedicated by
The Scala Family
Anthony, Mary Ellen, Anthony,
Victoria, Alicia, and Christopher

1975

Oresta M. Ferrito, MHCA 1979
Science Teacher at MHCA, 1979–1989

Dedicated by
Graduates of St. Michael School
Paterson, New Jersey
Florence Casbarro Ferrito, Class of 1937
Emmanuel L. Ferrito, Class of 1965
Michael G. Ferrito, Class of 1965

1976

Edmund J. Greco Sr.
A great husband, father, and grandfather

Love always from,
Anna, Eddie Jr., George, Caroline, Eddie III, Richie,
Annalise, Adriana, Juliana, Liliana, and Christopher III

1977

In Honor of
Liliana and Christopher Budesa
The best children anyone could ever have!

Love always from your mother,
Caroline Greco-Budesa

1978

In honor of the Salesian Sisters' arrival at
St. Theresa School, Kenilworth, New Jersey

Thirty years of love and
dedication to STS children!

Gratefully,
The Home School Association of St. Theresa's

1978

In Gratitude and Love to

Sr. Antoinette Cabrera, FMA

My "sister" and spiritual inspiration

Dedicated by

Patti Gauthier, 1978 graduate of Julie Billiart Central
High School, Boston, Massachussettes

1979

In thanksgiving to the Salesian Sisters
for over 25 years of service to the families and
children of Immaculate Conception School
and Immaculata High School

2004 Jubilee Honorees
*From left: Sr. Rita Bailey, Sr. Martina Ponce, Sr. Domenica Di Peri,
Sr. Carmela Termine, Sr. Louise Passero, and Sr. Janice Collins*

Dedicated by

Immaculate Conception Parish, Marrero, Louisiana

1980

In Loving Memory of

My Mom

Since the day of my First Communion, you took me every morning, rain or shine, to receive Jesus in the Eucharist. You told me that Jesus would help me in everything. You were right, Mom. It was indeed the greatest gift you gave me. Pray for me from heaven that I might be faithful and loving like you were.

Dedicated by

Sr. Phyllis Neves, FMA

1981

In Memory of

Michael Middendorf

Our thanks to the Salesian Sisters

Dedicated by

Pat and Frank Middendorf

234

1982

Sr. Nancy Zingale, FMA

departed this life on January 1, 1982,
after 57 years as a Salesian Sister.

Dedicated by

Her cousin Nancy Gulino

1983

In Loving Memory of

Sr. Leonia Pascucci, FMA

Our sister and best friend

Dedicated by

Celeste Pascucci Tripi and Mary Pascucci

1984

Edward William Bednarz
and
Son, Edward William Bednarz Jr.

Dedicated by

Bernice Bednarz

1985

*The Massood Family
congratulates the Salesian Sisters!*

Dedicated by

Elias, Michael Jr., Edward, Mary,
Bernadette, Michael, and Norma Massood

1986

Donate and Adam Amatuzzi
Loving parents and devoted role models

Dedicated by
Dr. Joseph R. and Rose Amatuzzi

1986

Lucy Alagia

In loving memory of our grandmother, a lady of singular devotion to work and family. Her fortitude kept family and home intact through the Great Depression, and her sense of fun and strong Catholic faith endeared her everlastingly to her grandchildren.

Dedicated by
The McAleer Family

1986

Isola Olivieri

Olivieri and Menloni Families

Dedicated by
Adelaide and Joseph Olivieri

1987

To Our Precious and Beloved Mother

Hope McAleer

No words could do justice to her beautiful spirit, indomitable faith, and devotion to family. In the perfectly chosen words of her eulogist, "where there was Hope there was life, and where there was life there was Hope." Ever present in our hearts, with love and affection undiminished.

Dedicated by
The McAleer Family

1987

The Archdiocese of Miami thanks
the Salesian Sisters who have served at
La Salle High School for over 15 years.

God bless you!

Archbishop John C. Favalora
Bishop Felipe J. Estevez
Bishop John G. Noonan
and the people of the
Archdiocese of Miami

*His Holiness John Paul II
during his visit to Miami,
Florida, in 1987*

1987

Trusting in Mary's help
With gratitude we remember our heritage
With joy we celebrate the present moment
With hope we look to the future

PROVINCE OF
MARY IMMACULATE

Western Province of the Salesian Sisters

1987

In Memory of

Sr. Josephine Carini, FMA

We love you dearly.

She listened with her heart
We shared laughter and tears
She smiled with pride.
She said, "I am here for
you, now and forever.
I am your friend."

Dedicated by

Elsa and Dana Carin Martinez

1988

In Memory of

Anna "G.G." Granatell

Our loving grandmother and great grandmother.
You are always in our thoughts.

Dedicated by

Joe and JoAnn Granatell and Family

1988

Debi Debiak and George Holland

1989

In Gratitude to

Fortune Bosco

for inspiring our highly successful
Adopt-a-Sister Program

Dedicated by
The Salesian Sisters

1990

Leo F. Voytko

Dedicated by
Mary T. Voytko

1990

In Loving Memory of

**Ken Sausville and
Sr. Gisella Bonfiglio, FMA**

Dedicated by
James Sausville

The Beatification of

Blessed Philip Rinaldi

Dedicated by

His great grandnephew Philip Rinaldi
and his wife, Barbara

In Gratitude to

The Founding Members of the Salesian Sisters Partners Circle

Mike Massood, Sr. Mary Rinaldi, Joseph J. McAleer Sr., Lucy Nardella, A.M. "Bud" and Rosemarie D'Alessandro

In Honor of

Sr. Eileen Joseph, FMA and Sr. Domenica Di Peri, FMA

Dedicated by

James Gambino

In Honor of

The Salesian Sisters in Canada

Dedicated by

The Salesian Priests and Brothers of Canada

1992

*May God's blessings descend
in abundance on Sr. Colleen Clair
and all the Salesian Sisters!*

Dedicated by
Fr. Benedict P. Militello

1992

*In Loving Memory
of the Deceased Members of*

The Federici and Gutto Families

Dedicated by
Teresa Gutto

1992

**Lauret Roberge
and the
Roberge Family**

Dedicated by
Louise Roberge

1993

Fr. Peter M. Rinaldi, SDB

Our dear and cherished friend, who opened to us a deeper love and appreciation of Christ through the Holy Shroud, and who inspired us by his perfect embodiment of Christian living. In his holiness and fatherly care for our souls, he was truly the image of Don Bosco.

With gratitude and affection,
The Martedi Family

1993

In Loving Memory of

A.M. "Bud" D'Alessandro

Congratulations to the Salesian Sisters!

Dedicated by

Rosemarie D'Alessandro and Family

1993

In Memory of

Fr. Peter M. Rinaldi, SDB

Dedicated by

Beruta and James Dell'Orto

1993

In Loving Tribute to

Theodore Zoppo

A man of humility, kindness, and charity whose personal life reflected the same dedication to family, God, and religion as the Salesian Sisters into whose care he entrusted us. Until we meet again.

Dedicated by

His son-in-law and daughter, James E. and Rita Zoppo Vietmeier

---

1994

In Loving Memory of

Mr. and Mrs. Wm. Chernalis

Our heartfelt thanks to all the Salesian Sisters at Mary Help of Christians Academy

1995

Congratulations to the Salesian Sisters for 100 years of service to the young in the United States!

Dedicated by
The Salesian Family in
Westwego, Louisiana (1987)
Avondale, Arizona (1995)
Colorado Springs, Colorado (2003)

1995

Sr. Kim Keraitis, FMA
Simply the best!

To Sr. Kim, for your special leadership at the Salesian Youth Center Boys & Girls Club and Villa Madonna School. Your servant leadership style inspired everyone to go the extra mile. You are a remarkable person whom I admire, love, and respect more than words can express.

On behalf of the Permuy Family and the families of all the children whose lives you have positively changed and in some situations saved, thank you!

1995

St. Anthony Parish Community
in Hawthorne, New Jersey, and the
Salesian Sisters who have served
our school since 1995

share a jubilee together,
joyfully living Christ's mission
for a century and beyond.

1996

In Gratitude to
Dr. Joseph J. McAleer Jr.

Partners in Giving editor, Partners Circle trustee, "adopter," and true friend to the Salesian Sisters

Thank you, Dr. Joe!

1997

Reanna Marie Theresa Medore

Dearest Reanna,

You were the light in our lives! Your smile never failed to light up a room and you always kept us laughing! You have been in heaven for more than ten years, but we still see the twinkle in your eyes as if it were only yesterday.

Love,
Mom, Dad, Joleen, and Victor

1997

A Loving Tribute to Our Parents

Their love and dedication to their family lives on in us, their children.

Alfred, Andrew, Jim, Daniel,
Paul, David, Therese, Lucia, and Joan Fontanella

1998

Salvatore Seminerio

A devoted husband and loving father
Graduate of St. Michael School

Dedicated by

His wife, Carmela, and children, Tommy,
Annmarie, Richard, and Brenda, and grandchildren

1999

Sr. Margaret Wilhelm, FMA

Exceptional woman of faith!

We honor Sr. Margaret for her devoted leadership and dedication to Mary Help of Christians Academy. She is an extraordinary person whom we admire and respect. We love our special Salesian Sister and hope that she always has time for ice cream!

On behalf of the staff at MHCA, thank you for being a committed servant to the young people.

Lillian Brunetti, Marie Chirico, Alexandros Dimitriadis, Beth Evans, Richard Futrell, Irene Gold, Gary Gratto, Marie Hess, Carol Krushinsky, Elizabeth Manzella, Patti Megalos, Liz O'Connor, Ann O'Meara, Marie Reenstra, Vincent Rivieccio, Maryann Riordan, Carmen Saidi, Betty Sanchez, Joseph Spinelli, and Dominic N. Stimola

1999

In Loving Memory of

Nancy Rabito

To my beautiful mother,

I miss you and love you always. Not a day goes by that I don't think of you.

Your loving daughter,
Marie

Nana, thanks for your strong example of faith!

Your grandchildren,
Sr. Fran, Sam, Darrin, and Maria DaGrossa

2000

In Loving Memory
of the Deceased Members of

The Massood Family

Louis and Mary Massood
Helen (Hayek) Massood
Rose Ward
Albert Massood
Jeannete Massood
Biagio Verone

May they rest in peace.

Dedicated by
Mike and Norma Massood

2001

Josie Campo and her Salesian Youth Center children

2001

Joseph J. McAleer Sr.

Our magnificent father, a true self-made man who was unassuming in his many successes. A man of boundless generosity and a true friend to the Salesian Sisters as founder of the Partners Circle. A man of stature and bearing, but always grounded in his faith, never more so than when confronted with terminal illness. A champion of life—respected, loved, and missed by his family.

Dedicated by
The McAleer Family

2002

Groundbreaking of Ana Maria Park

Tampa, Florida

Dedicated by

The Partners Circle Trustees

2002

To my dear friend and angel in heaven, Sr. Theresa Franco

Dedicated by

Teresa Gutto

2002

In Loving Memory of

Mary Catherine "Nanny" Florio

Our loving grandmother and great grandmother. Everyone misses you so much. You are always with us in our prayers and we know God is letting you watch over us.

Dedicated by

JoAnn and Joe Granatell and Family

2003

A Tribute to

Joe Pfeifer

who supervised the construction of St. Joseph Retirement Center

Dedicated by

The Partners Circle Executive Committee and the Salesian Sisters

Henry F. Roman

Dedicated by

Maryann Roman

Mary Help of Christians, watch over
our loving children and grandchildren.

Dedicated by

Beverly and Rodger Rohde

Sr. Kim Keraitis, FMA and Villa Madonna School

Dedicated by

The Baldor Family
in memory of Ana Maria Baldor-Bunn

The Salesian Spirit Lives On!

In grateful appreciation to the Salesian Sisters
for 29 years of dedicated service to
Christ the King Catholic School, Tampa, Florida

2005

Sr. Susan Bagli, FMA
In gratitude for 25 years and
counting of dedicated service

Dedicated by
Robert and MaryAnn Harkins and Family

2005

In Gratitude to
The Salesian Sisters
in the aftermath of Hurricane Katrina

Dedicated by
The Faculty, Staff, and Students of
Immaculate Conception School, Marrero, Louisiana

2006

N. Johannes I. Calamita
Born on May 28, 2006
Oxfordshire, England

Tips his hat to Sr. Virginia D'Alessandro
and all the Salesian Sisters

Dedicated by
His grandfather Frank Calamita

2006

In Honor of
Sr. Domenica Di Peri, FMA
My first grade teacher

Thank you for your lifelong devotion to God and
your students. May God bless our Salesian Family.

Dedicated by
Mary and Michael Sottile

Academy of Our Lady High School
Marrero, Louisiana

Through the Salesian spirit of reason, religion, and loving kindness, the Academy of Our Lady instills in young women the drive for lifelong learning, the skills to succeed in society, and the values to live as Catholic Christians.

Proud to be the newest member of the Salesian Sisters Family!

To My Parents
Mr. and Mrs. M. De Vita
On the 50th anniversary of my ordination

Dedicated by
Fr. James C. De Vita

Every year is a tribute to our mothers, Esperanza Garcia and Lily Muto, who have influenced our lives forever.

With love,
Mary and Luis Garcia,
our 6 children, and 13 grandchildren

Dedicated by
Rene and Sally Zarate

2007

In Memory of

My Loving Wife Nelle

Jim and Nelle Deignan
May 11, 1963

2007

*In gratitude to all the donors and volunteers
who have helped the Salesian Sisters, especially*

Eugene T. Phillips and
Prof. Vern Smith

Dedicated by

Sr. Mary Rinaldi and the Development Office Staff

2008

Congratulations to my "adopted" Sister

Sr. Frances Gumino, FMA

On the occasion of her 65th anniversary

Dedicated by

Teresa Gutto

2008

In celebration of our Golden Wedding Anniversary on June 29, 2008, and in remembrance of the first anniversary of our dear Sr. Veronica Milyo's passing on April 13, 2007

We make this dedication for all the blessings the good Lord has given us.

Dedicated by

John and Frances Lombardi and Family

May the angels in heaven
watch over my angels here on
earth, my nine loving grandchildren:
Lauren, Christopher, Alana, Kristen, Michael,
Angelica, Julia, Gregory, and Thomas.

Dedicated by
Teresa Gutto

In Honor of

Sr. Mary Rinaldi, FMA

for all her wonderful achievements

Dedicated by

Matt and Lee Sabatine
Sabatine Foundation

His Holiness
Pope Benedict XVI

graced the United States with his presence.

Dedicated by
Fritz and Mary Lee Duda

Partners Circle Members were treated to
an evening with Mother Antonia Colombo,
Superior General of the Salesian Sisters.

*Standing, from left: Christina McAleer, Rodger Rohde,
Mother Antonia Colombo, Mike Polizzi, and Bill McLaughlin
Seated: Twinkie Polizzi, Beverly Rohde, and Pat McLaughlin*

The Salesian Sisters of St. John Bosco

Today, a hundred years later, the Daughters of Mary Help of Christians in the

United States and Canada continue to minister to the youth, especially the poor and marginalized.

Their joy and enthusiasm to fulfill their mission will never waver.

The legacy lives on.

Dear Sally,

I sincerely feel very privileged to have known and lived with BOTH Sr. Amalia and Sr. Helen. They, so different from each other, but both JOYS in their own way! May God bless you and the family and may you all receive many graces from my TWO BELOVED SISTER Friends

Sr. Ruth, FMA

Dear Sally,

Many blessings from the Lord,

Sr. Esther Cruz

Dear Sally,

I love you and pray for you. May our Blessed Mother obtain an abundance of graces for you.

Love,
Sr. Gerard B.

Dear Sally

Thank you for your remembrance of us Salesian Sister. You are in our prayer. God bless you.

Sr. Carmela Termine

Dear Sally

God bless you kindness to us. Love & prayers by Mutshel

Dr. Rose Segarini, FMA

Dear Sally

Thank you for your generosity and great kindness. May God bless you abundantly. Sr. Amalia and Sr. Helen were very dear Sisters. With much love and prayers, Sr. Letizia B.

Dear Sally,

Love and Prayers

Sr. Emilia Kassab